GLOBAL GRACE CAFÉ

THE HISTORICAL SERIES OF THE REFORMED CHURCH IN AMERICA
NO. 109

GLOBAL GRACE CAFÉ
A Love Story about Battles Lost and Won to Keep Families Together in America's War on Immigrants

Elizabeth Colmant Estes

Did no others turn and give glory to God besides this foreigner?
—Luke 17:18

REFORMED CHURCH PRESS
Grand Rapids, Michigan

The Historical Series of the Reformed Church in America

The series was inaugurated in 1968 by the General Synod of the Reformed Church in America acting through the Commission on History to communicate the church's heritage and collective memory and to reflect on our identity and mission, encouraging historical scholarship which informs both church and academy.

There are over a hundred other stories in the Historical Series of the Reformed Church in America, from exciting tales of missionaries to engaging stories of people helping others and sharing the Good News of Jesus Christ to scholarly texts on the background of the denomination's four centuries. Check with your local bookseller or Amazon.com.

www.rca.org/series

General Editor
    James Hart Brumm, DMin
    New Brunswick Theological Seminary

Project Editor
    Maria Orr
    Reformed Church in America

Production Editor
    Russell L. Gasero
    Archivist Emeritus, Reformed Church in America

Cover design by Maria Orr: The mosaic by Genese Sodikoff on the front cover enwraps the outside of the Reformed Church of Highland Park and captures the community's prayers for peace.

General Editor Emeritus
    Donald J. Bruggink, PhD, DD
    Van Raalte Institute, Hope College

Commission on History
    Corstian Devos, MDiv, Churchville, PA
    Katlyn De Vries, MDiv, Western Theological Seminary
    Daniel Meeter, PhD, New Paltz, NY
    Steven Pierce, DMin, Grand Rapids, MI
    Doug Shepler, MDiv, New Brunswick, NJ
    David Zomer, MDiv, Kalamazoo, MI

In memory of Franco Juricic, M.Div,
who strengthened caring communities that save our world.
"In the same way, let your light shine before others,
so that they may see your good works and
give glory to your Father in heaven" (Matthew 5:15-16).

© 2023 Reformed Church Press/All rights reserved

ISBN: 978-1-950572-30-4

Library of Congress Control Number: 2023948112

Contents

	Foreword	
	Wesley Granberg-Michaelson	ix
	Introduction: Before You Begin	xvii
1	The Raid	1
2	A Recipe for Disaster	7
3	American Ambivalence	23
4	Seeking Safety in Church	27
5	Life after the Raid	35
6	Building a Responsive Community: The Background	41
7	Converting Hearts	45
8	Caught	55
9	Resistance is Futile	57
10	A Light in the Darkness	63
11	A Wing and a Prayer	71
12	A Broken Communion	77
13	Imprisoned on the Far Western Tip	81
14	Hope Stirs in the Dark	85
15	The Mystery of Easter	89
16	Loosened Chains	91
17	Hope Returns	95
18	An Extraordinary Agreement	99
19	Changing National Priorities	109
20	A Grim Discovery of Human Trafficking	117
21	Betrayed	127
22	The Longest Night	137
23	Relentless Pursuit and a Last-Ditch Sanctuary	145
24	Sanctuary Life	155
25	Slipping through the Cracks	165
26	A Superstorm to Remember	171
27	Victory in the Dark	181
28	Refugees on the Horizon	189
29	Interfaith RISE and a Café of Global Grace	195
30	The Nightmare Returns	203
31	The End of Humanitarian Discretion	213
32	Questions with No Answers	221
33	What about the Children?	227
34	A Global Community Celebrates Anyway	235
35	Some Who Are Vile and More Who Are Splendid	245

36	Aiding the Advocate	259
37	Remembering the One Who Holds Us Fast	271
38	Justice This Time	279
39	An Accidental Immigration Attorney	289
40	A Small Splash in a Very Big Pond	297
	Afterthoughts in 2023: Standing on Shifting Ground	307
	The Author Gives Thanks	317
	Index	321

Foreword

The power of the gospel is seen through stories. That's what makes the four Gospels in the New Testament so compelling—the stories of what happens, through the presence of Jesus, when the transforming love of God intersects with those in the hills of Galilee and the centers of power in Jerusalem. Who Jesus reaches, whom he includes, where he goes, how others respond, and what Jesus says—these all demonstrate what happens when God's incarnate love breaks into the world, in concrete places and lives. God's liberating, healing, inclusive, relentless love flows forth through Jesus in the work of radical transformation, confronting confounded, threatened, and hard-hearted religious and political rulers. When it seems as though their power will prevail, resurrected Life triumphs, and this redeeming love of God is victorious over all the powers of bondage, brokenness, destruction, and death. That becomes the story of those called and claimed by Christ.

The story continues in Acts, as the Spirit forms those claimed by this gospel into a radically new community, empowered to embody the ongoing presence of Jesus in the world. This body of Christ breaks boundaries, divisions, classes, as well as entrenched social prejudices and economic inequalities with the embodied experience of an inclusive love poured out through God's Spirit. Missional outreach drives the life of this faith community forward across the boundaries of race, culture, and religious exclusivism through the liberating power of God's Spirit, making real the ongoing presence of Christ in bread, wine, and the bonds of love. It's the story of what happens when a people are "called by God, and empowered by the Holy Spirit, to be the very presence of Jesus Christ in the world."[1]

That same story, demonstrating the power of the gospel, continues today. This book, *Global Grace Café*, tells one amazing, inspiring, and dramatic chapter of how this timeless story—our story—unfolded in a specific place and time. Today, in our secularized culture, people don't want to simply hear the gospel. They want to see it. And that's right. The Word, after all, became flesh. Our temptation is to reduce it just to words. That's why it is so fresh and so necessary to see the gospel embodied in particular people, specific situations, concrete social realities, and living communities of faith.

That's what Liz Estes does in this book. The story first centers on Harry and Yana Pangemanan, Indonesians who are ethnic Chinese Christians, and who fled persecution in their homeland, arriving eventually in central New Jersey. And it's the story of Seth Kaper-Dale, called to be a pastor in the Reformed Church in America with his spouse and co-pastor, Stephanie. Further, the story of the Reformed Church of Highland Park emerges as a specific expression of the body of Christ which is transformed by the power of the gospel, inviting and liberating many others. Reading almost like a good novel, this story enfolds the journeys of countless others and reveals the weight and reality of oppressive social forces disrupting and brutalizing the lives of thousands. Except this is no work of fiction. It is as real and true as the gospel itself.

Rabbi Jonathan Sacks has pointed out that the Hebrew scriptures contain one verse about loving one's neighbor as oneself, and thirty-seven direct commands to care for the strangers in their midst.[2] The New Testament continues in this call to radical hospitality, and Jesus even links it directly to the criteria for God's final judgment in Matthew

---

[1] Reformed Church in America, "Mission and Vision Statement Presented to the 1997 General Synod," in James Hart Brumm, ed., *An RCA Reader*, number 104 in *The Historical Series of the Reformed Church in America* (Grand Rapids, Mishigan: Reformed Church Press, 2022), 523.

[2] Jonathan Sacks, *Faith in the Future* (London, UK: Darton, Longman & Todd Ltd., 1995), 78.

25. Few biblical injunctions are clearer and as persistent. Yet church communities often cling to the comfort of those who are familiar, and are timid in their response to the refugee, the stranger, and the sojourner who appear in their towns, and even in their neighborhoods.

A different story happened in Highland Park. Gracious hospitality extended to one in need, who was a victim of systemic injustice, created space for the power of the gospel to emerge. The story that follows, documented by the author in painstaking and pain-revealing detail, continues for years. The personal becomes political as the complex and frequently de-humanizing machinery of an unjust and dysfunctional immigration system grinds its way forward, crushing lives. The hospitality, solidarity, and eventually the sanctuary of the Reformed Church of Highland Park embraces a widening community of families caught in the snares of this system. And the witness to God's justice and love becomes public and prophetic, echoed on airways, in lawyers' offices, at city halls, within federal agencies, at a governor's mansion, and through the halls of Congress.

Some lessons for all of us stand out.

First, mission is not a program. When Seth Kaper-Dale and the Highland Park church reached out in simple solidarity to those in the Indonesian Chinese Christian community, discovered in the church's environs, it was not part of a five-year strategic plan. It was not a project of a mission committee in the church. It was not a program devised by some consultant as part of a church growth plan. Rather, it was prompted by compassionate attention to the place and people where the church community was situated. And it was grounded by a commitment to participate in God's ongoing missional presence in the world.

A "missional church" is one which grounds its identity and life in its ongoing participation with God's mission in the world. Of course, the term "mission" needs to be decluttered from its colonial legacy of privileged superiority. But it brings into focus that the presence of Jesus Christ in the world is not centered within the cloistered confines of sanctuary walls. Rather it is discovered in the ongoing work of God's Spirit as brokenness is being healed, and lives are restored to the fullness desired by God. The missional church centers itself through discovering and participating in this active work of God in the world.

So, we must never say that that the church "has a mission." This is not one of several programs delegated to a committee or agency. Rather, the church is the fellowship of those who join in living the embodied love of Christ amid all the world's pain, injustice, and brokenness. This is how others see the presence of Jesus. To speak theologically, the congregation is intended to be the hermeneutic of the gospel.

The Reformed Church of Highland Park came to grasp this, not through some six-week course, but through doing it. Seth Kaper-Dale, as a co-pastor, was an inspiring, catalytic leader. But this emerging, unexpected, pervasive mission was embraced by the whole congregation. It shaped their understanding of what it meant to be the presence of Jesus Christ in the world. And it grew in ways never planned, never anticipated, but usually welcomed. One can't help but hear some echoes of Acts.

The key, I think, is readiness—a willingness to discover where God is calling, what God is doing, and how Christ's love is beckoning us. Congregations today need this spiritual preparedness more than strategic plans. The requirement is to nurture resilience, through gifts of the Spirit, rather than adopting mission "projects."

Second, the gospel is public as well as personal. The American church finds itself in a highly polarized and political and cultural context which has infected its capacity for public witness. Thus, acts of personal and private compassion are welcomed, but attempts to address the patterns of social injustice which create personalized suffering are resisted. Pastors are continually warned that in their preaching and their action they must not be "political." In part, that's because of the ugly examples of pastors from rigidly conservative, evangelical congregations that became unabashedly "political" in their support of Donald Trump and his brand of politics. Those in more moderate evangelical and mainline congregations don't want the poisonous politics of the nation introduced into their pulpits and witness, whether from "conservative" or "progressive" agendas.

But there's a problem. When parishioners leave a Sunday service and tell the pastor at the door not to bring politics into the sermon, the pastor's honest thoughts are likely to be, "Well, I guess I can't preach from the Gospels. Or the Old Testament prophets. Or several parts of the epistles." The original meaning of politics has to do with how public life ("polis") is ordered and arranged for the sake of the whole community. And from a biblical perspective, that is a continual theme, from creation onward, with the people of Israel, and then in the message and ministry of Jesus, into the life of the early church, and to the book of Revelation. The Reformed worldview has always understood this. Certainly, the gospel addresses us as individuals, inviting us into a redemptive personal relationship with Jesus Christ. Yet it never stops there. God is always at work through the revelation of Christ and the work of the Holy Spirit to create a just, whole, and peaceful reign for all that God has created. The world belongs to God.

In that deeper sense, then, the witness of Christian faith in our time will always have a "political" dimension if it is faithful to all that God desires and intends for the world. But it should never be partisan, never tied to a specific political ideology, and never be hostage to a secular political agenda. Further, its witness will be rooted in solidarity with those suffering from society's injustices, those pushed to the margins, those victimized by social and economic forces that degrade their God-given dignity. Thus public Christian witness shouldn't descend down from some secular ideology or political party platform. It should emerge up out of concrete solidarity with pain and injustice of suffering victims of a broken world.

That's the picture one sees in reading *Global Grace Café*. Families who were victimized by seemingly random and brutal injustices of an immigration system were personally embraced. Bonds which were formed compelled advocacy to those holding power. Widening solidarity exposed the depth of systemic injustices holding thousands voiceless and powerless, severing families, falsely assuming the worst of loyal citizens, and desecrating the inherent image of God in one seen only as the "other." So, the witness of the gospel became public and political, forcefully.

The skill by which Seth and his colleagues focused their public voice so it could be heard was masterful. But it was always a voice pleading the cause of the stranger, showing hospitality to the foreigner, and visiting those in immigration prisons. It was the voice of the gospel of God's grace and liberating love. The story in these pages demonstrates how true faithfulness to the personal message of the gospel shared in solidarity with those crying out for God's justice will lead to the public, "political" expression of the gospel. The witness of the church must embody all that God intends for this world, beginning in solidarity with the least of these, and holding those entrusted with power accountable. This story shows how that can be done.

Third, participation in God's mission can deepen a congregation's experience of living as a community, empowered by the Spirit. The Americanized church generally lives with a division between evangelism and social action. Further, outward social witness is often divorced from inward spiritual nurture. And efforts to build the vitality of fellowship in a congregation are usually segregated from engagement in external mission and activism. In ecclesiological terms, we separate *koinonia* from *diakonia*. But the church, in my view, is not intended to function in that way.

Recent decades have seen a search for effective models of congregational revitalization, recognizing the drift toward dormancy afflicting churches losing their vitality through aging and the desertion of younger members. Whether through models of small group ministry, the retooling of worship styles and music, strategies to build church health, or programs to discover and exercise the gifts of each member, there's a yearning for the right "fix" which will foster new congregational life, and with it, attract new members and dollars. Sometimes these efforts bear fruit.

Yet there's another approach, more biblically rooted, in my view, which is often overlooked: discovering how a congregation is called to participate in God's ongoing mission in the world as the natural means to foster vitality and deepen bonds of belonging. I often reflect on the gospel story where Jesus sends the seventy out in pairs to the villages and places in the region (Luke 10). When they come back, he gathers them, and they retreat to a "deserted place" to share what they had seen and experienced. Their *koinonia* is nurtured in the process, and reflection, from their participation in God's work in the world. The inner bonds of community and the outward call to discover where the kingdom is breaking in are linked together, as part of one whole. It's a foretaste, early in the Gospels, of how the body of Christ will eventually function.

The story of the *Global Grace Café* offers a reflection of this ecclesiological truth. Many of those who were initially the recipients of the church's active hospitality become agents of the congregation's ministry. Others, who had distanced themselves from any church, witnessed the power of the gospel in the congregation's missional outreach, and decided to join this expression of the body of Christ. This wasn't because they were given a welcome bouquet when visiting one Sunday morning, but because they were inspired by seeing what it looked like for a local church to strive to be the presence of Jesus Christ in the world in courageous, costly, and sacrificial ways.

At one point, Seth Kaper-Dale said, "We don't need to control everything in the body of Christ—that's where many churches fail." He called his approach, "creating intentional, compassionate community." This seems to happen continually in this story. Compassionate community springs forth through all the challenges and growing complexities of joining God's work in the world.

Like every story of the church, *Global Grace Café* is full of grace and pain. The congregation is far from perfect, its attempts at outreach go through trials and tribulations, and leadership is often stymied, caught in the inevitable tension between the pastoral and the prophetic. But the story is real. It is instructive, revealing, and hopeful. We see the power of the gospel at work. The Spirt of the Lord is upon these people as they strive, following the words that began Jesus's ministry, to set the captives free. Liz Estes has given a rich gift to the Reformed Church in America, and to the wider church ecumenical, through telling how our old story takes on this fresh, new expression in our place and time.

Wesley Granberg-Michaelson
July 19, 2023

Rev. Wesley Granberg-Michaelson was general secretary of the Reformed Church in America for seventeen years, from 1994 to 2011. Previously he was Director of Church and Society for the World Council of Churches, and he continues today in the leadership of the Global Christian Forum. He is the author of ten books, most recently, Without Oars: Casting Off into a Life of Pilgrimage.

Introduction: Before You Begin

In Readington, New Jersey, 2023

    The decades-long story in this book, about an undocumented family's struggle to stay together in Central New Jersey, dramatically revitalized a 150-year-old church that committed to help them. In 2001, its elderly congregation had dwindled to a few dozen members, and they were considering closing.

    Today, hundreds of new members, of numerous ethnicities and global origins, crowd into its pews. The church leads an affordable housing corporation that owns more than twenty-five properties in seven municipalities for veterans, women aging out of foster care, developmentally disabled adults, homeless youth, and chronically homeless individuals. More than 160 rental units serve refugees, asylum seekers, and re-entering citizens who may be unable to secure an apartment due to poor (or no) credit history and temporary unemployment.

    But this story is about far more than church revitalization.

    It is about a devastating, decades-long war that the United States continues to wage against immigrants, asylees, and refugees. Superhuman feats kept a single family intact.

It's a complicated story, filled with tremendous suffering and yet bursting with beauty. The Global Grace Café that lends its name to the title is a pay-what-you-can lunchtime cafeteria located in the church. Each day a refugee chef from a different country serves specialties from the home to which they cannot return.

I took part in this story as a church member. The faith, hope, and love I received from my immigrant friends led me to rethink everything I believed, both as a follower of Jesus and as an American citizen, starting with the simplest questions, such as, from the Gospel of Luke: Who is my neighbor? And from the U.S. Constitution: Who is a person?

To follow along, it may help to first wrap your head around two facts.

During the late nineteenth and early twentieth centuries, an immigrant seeking to enter the United States might have been required to provide the name and address of a distant relative who was already a resident; to prove that they were not indigent; and to show they came with a genuine promise of employment.

My impoverished Sicilian grandparents and great-grandparents told my mother about these kinds of challenges.

However, this tale was ignited by explosive events in the late 1990s. And by then, there was no reliable path to authorized residency for industrious but unskilled workers like my grandparents who did not have a U.S. citizen spouse or parent. Nor for unskilled Indonesian Christians of ethnic Chinese descent with bare-subsistence incomes, like my friends.

That's the first fact you need to know.

At the story's center is an Indonesian couple, Harry and Yana Pangemanan, who have lived in New Jersey for more than twenty-five years. Harry's children, aunt, uncle, cousin, and even sister are U.S. citizens. Those familial relationships, however, are irrelevant to Harry's ability to live here from the perspective of immigration law today.

The second fact is that in May 1998 all hell broke loose nine thousand miles from the Central New Jersey neighborhood of the church. That is when hundreds of ethnic Chinese women like Yana Pangemanan were assaulted, and some were even gang-raped, by mobs incited by the Indonesian military. Yana fled for her life while the Chinatown of Indonesia's capital city, Jakarta, burned.

Along with crowds of ethnic Chinese, Yana boarded a plane, leaving behind her son and parents in their island home of Papua. That first flight took her to the Netherlands. The next one landed Yana in the United States. She has not returned to Indonesia.

And it will help to know this, too: The government of the Netherlands ruled Indonesia as a colony and protected Christian churches there from 1816 until 1941, when Japan occupied Indonesia for four years. Today, Indonesia is the most populous Muslim-majority country in the world, with about 231 million adherents residing on the country's seventeen thousand islands. But for the past thirty years or more, the Christian churches of Indonesia have been subject to terror, burning, and bombings by Muslim extremists.

If you didn't know any of this, don't worry.

I didn't either, until this story turned my life upside down.

CHAPTER 1

The Raid

In Avenel, New Jersey, 2006

On a summery Tuesday night before Memorial Day in 2006, Yana Pangemanan came home exhausted from her late-night job. Her daughter, four-year-old Jocelyn, was up later than usual because she had just finished a nebulizer treatment to combat her asthma. Yana's husband Harry dragged Jocelyn's toddler bed close to theirs so they could watch over their daughter's breathing.

The family settled down around one.

Except Yana was four months pregnant.

Around 3:30, with the weight of the baby pressing on her bladder, Yana awoke to use the bathroom. She heard a commotion outside and peeked through her bedroom window. From her third-floor apartment, Yana saw the street below flooded with headlights.

She feared she had awoken to her worst nightmare: an immigration raid in her home while she slept. A thought shot through Yana's mind: maybe her family could escape through the back of their complex.

Crouching on the floor in her living room so that she wouldn't be seen from below, Yana strained to pull back the sliding glass doors that opened onto the balcony, and she crept onto the balcony's chilly cement.

Shouts echoed from the walls of the many buildings that enclosed the grassy open space in the middle of the complex. Across the way, to the right and left, Yana watched Indonesian men try to push air conditioners out of the windows of two separate apartments. The men were trying to escape by jumping to the ground. But what these frantic Indonesians couldn't see was that, on the lawn below them, agents bearing rifles and walkie-talkies had already handcuffed a dozen people.

Yana recognized men who were friends, neighbors, and fellow church members in the lineup of handcuffed men.

In the pre-dawn dimness, Yana followed a white, unmarked van as it cut across the complex's central lawn. At the top of a little hill, the doors of two other vans were pulled back, exposing rows of empty seats, waiting to be filled with people who Yana surmised would be detained.

When the white van stopped nearby, agents, uniformed and armed, disembarked and climbed up the fire escapes of two buildings.

Yana slipped back inside, pushed the sliding door shut, and snuck back to the bedroom. It was too late to flee.

She ran to Harry and shook him awake.[1]

What do you think, she asked her husband. Is that ICE outside?

Harry had slept peacefully until that moment in the early morning of Wednesday, May 24, when he was startled awake by his terrified wife followed by angry, deep-bass commands that boomed throughout his apartment complex's open-air hallways.[2]

"Open this door. Open up now!" Harry heard, along with the pounding of metal rifle stocks and riot batons on heavy metal front doors.

Harry shot up and ran to check his apartment's front door. Instinctively, he knew better than to open it. Instead, he peered through the peephole. In the hallway, Harry counted seven or eight armed federal agents facing the doors of other apartments.

Be quiet! Yana whispered when her husband returned to her. He was the one that agents were after.

---

[1] Yana Pangemanan provided her perspective on the story in 2021, answering questions posed by Jocelyn Pangemanan.
[2] This chapter mostly follows the story of the raid as Harry Pangemanan described it in interviews in February and March 2017.

Jocelyn was still asleep—a small miracle. Her parents were terrified their preschooler would wake up and make noise. They affectionately called Jocelyn their "crybaby." Yana left Harry to snuggle with their toddler in bed. Harry hugged Jocelyn and pulled the bed covers over them to muffle any noises.

Yana dragged a chair against the front door for added security. But that didn't stop the agents from banging on the door and demanding, *Open up!*

To Yana, their voices sounded like screaming.

"I did not open the door," Yana said later. "I didn't want to."

Under the covers of the couple's king-size bed, Harry and Yana paused for a moment together to beg their Creator to deliver them from this raid.

"Save us, Almighty God," they prayed. "Lord Jesus, protect Jocelyn, and save us. Please keep our family together. You are our hope and our salvation. We trust in you always."

Other than agents of the federal government, no Americans knew that families who lived beside Harry and Yana in the Woodbine Apartments of Avenel, NJ were caught in the sights of a nationwide dragnet.

A four-year-old government entity called Immigration and Customs Enforcement (ICE) had dubbed this enforcement campaign "Operation Return to Sender." Across the country, the "Operation Return to Sender" initiative erupted in hundreds of coordinated raids that began during the week ending on May 26, 2006.

As Julie L. Myers, assistant secretary for ICE, later explained, "Virtually every field office in the nation from ICE's Office of Investigations and ICE's Office of Detention and Removal Operations carried out the enforcement operation in conjunction with numerous state and local law enforcement agencies."[3]

Back in January of that year, agents had begun scrutinizing New Jersey for convenient targets for immigration raids that would guarantee to net dozens of people who could be deported at once.

They needed to look no further than the Woodbine Gardens Apartments. It was there that Harry and Yana, along with dozens of

---

[3] "ICE Apprehends More Than 2,100 Criminal Aliens, Gang Members, Fugitives and Other Immigration Violators in Nationwide Interior Enforcement Operation," Office of the Press Secretary for ICE Public Affairs in Houston, Texas, June 14, 2006, https://web.archive.org/web/20061010203846/http://www.dhs.gov/dhspublic/display?content=5689.

compliant "illegals," had pre-registered their addresses with the federal government's Department of Homeland Security.

This residential complex in Avenel—an unincorporated northern tip of the much larger Woodbridge Township—promised a high concentration of deportable people at their most vulnerable: sleeping in their beds beside their young children.

Avenel is not a particularly cohesive neighborhood. New Jersey's major highways—the New Jersey Turnpike, the Garden State Parkway, and Routes 1, 9, 27, and 35—all intersect there. It is the kind of place where no one needs to worry too much about upsetting the neighbors. Fifteen hundred men are incarcerated there in the East Jersey State Prison. (Formerly known as "Rahway State Prison," the prison had been renamed at the request of nearby homeowners in Rahway Township.) Another seven hundred people, convicted as sex offenders, are housed in Avenel's Adult Diagnostic and Treatment Center. Woodbridge Center Mall, a mecca for shoppers from Staten Island, New York, seeking tax-free clothing in New Jersey, is two minutes away from the Woodbine apartments.

By May 2006, as many as seventy Indonesian families had settled together in thrifty and convenient Woodbine Gardens Apartments, where rows of chunky, 1960s-style concrete columns mix with cinderblock walls, forming a kind of campus that encloses a large, grassy square. Most Indonesians had fled waves of violence and persecution focused on ethnic Chinese and Christian minorities, touched off by the Indonesian military in 1998. Most families included one or more members who were Indonesian citizens and had overstayed tourist visas.

In the Woodbine complex, balconies with wooden banisters overlooked the common lawn where Harry and Yana Pangemanan and their friends hosted barbecues and watched their children play. When someone needed to raise a great deal of money—for a medical expense or a family member's funeral back in Indonesia—residents would open pop-up tent canopies and invite people who attended nine Indonesian churches in the area over for an Indonesian food bazaar crammed with Chinese-Indonesian specialties such as pork and chicken satay with peanut sauce and steaming rice, glowing yellow with turmeric.

Woodbine families shared cooking, culture, and a common language. They helped one another with babysitting, illnesses, and finding jobs—except on Saturday and Sunday mornings. When it came to worship, each family followed divisions forged in the churches of the thousands of native islands of their homeland. Families worshiped in separate churches spread across different denominations. Each Saturday or Sunday, Seventh-day Adventists, Presbyterians, Roman Catholics, plain old Protestants, and Pentecostals drove twenty to forty minutes from Woodbine Apartments to worship in churches nestled into cozier hometowns with tree-lined main streets and names like Metuchen, South Plainfield, Franklin, and Highland Park.

At first, Harry and Yana worshiped with the Indonesian Protestant Church at four o'clock on Sunday afternoons in the sanctuary their congregation shared with the Reformed Church of Highland Park. In 2003, the Pangemanans began also worshiping at 10 a.m. with the congregation led by the Reverends Seth and Stephanie Kaper-Dale, who had been installed in 2001 as co-pastors of the American congregation in the mainline Reformed Church in America denomination.

By May 2006, Harry and Yana had officially become members of the Kaper-Dales' English-speaking congregation, and the two couples—Indonesian and American—had become friends and co-workers in the church. They shared a common faith and a commitment to shared parenting.

Pastors Seth and Stephanie shared a single full-time pastor position and tried to limit themselves to each working half-time to jointly raise their two daughters.

Harry and Yana also managed to share the parenting of their daughter Jocelyn, a U.S. citizen born in 2002. The Indonesian couple held down two full-time positions to meet their expenses, including financial support of more than a dozen family members in their home country.

Harry worked the first shift, 8 a.m. to 4:30 p.m., as the distribution manager of a warehouse in nearby Edison. Yana worked the second shift, 3 p.m. to 11 p.m., operating a machine that made analog thermometers.[4]

Most mornings, Jocelyn and her mother cooked together and cuddled in front of the TV, watching *The Wiggles* and singing along to songs like "Toot Toot, Chugga Chugga, Big Red Car." After lunch, Jocelyn liked to drive her own battery-operated red car to the Woodbine complex playground, even though, as Jocelyn's mom jokingly told me, her little girl who had been born three months premature was large for a four-year-old and barely fit inside.

---

[4] Interviews with Harry and Yana Pangemanan in February and March 2017.

When Yana left for work at two, she dropped her daughter at a neighbor's house that was full of Indonesian American children whose parents were also at work. Three hours later, Harry picked up Jocelyn, cooked dinner, sang more songs, and said goodnight prayers—all before Yana returned before midnight.

Weekends were family time. The Pangemanans never missed a Sunday at church, worshiping in English at ten o'clock each morning in Highland Park. At 4 p.m. on Sunday afternoons, they worshiped in the same sanctuary, this time in Indonesian.

In the early morning of May 24, after he and Yana prayed for deliverance from federal agents, Harry grabbed his cell phone and called the pastor of their American congregation.

"Where are you right now?" Pastor Seth wanted to know. Harry said they were in their apartment, under the bedclothes with Jocelyn, terrified that agents would bust their apartment door open.

"I'll be right over," Seth replied. He looked up the "tips" number for the local cable news team and left a message with Harry's address in Woodbine Gardens Apartments in Avenel. He hoped that reporters with TV cameras would catch the ICE agents in action.

Then Seth put on his clerical collar and drove from his home in Highland Park to Avenel as fast as he could.

CHAPTER 2

A Recipe for Disaster

In Indonesia and New Jersey, 1993 to 2006

It can take thirty-five minutes to reach Avenel from Highland Park, where Seth and Stephanie Kaper-Dale lived in the parsonage next door to the Reformed church.

By the time Seth arrived at Woodbine Gardens on May 24, 2006, the sun was rising. The lawn and the complex sat empty. As he surveyed the area, his footsteps echoed on the pavement. Considering the earlier chaos Harry had described over the phone, the silence felt eerie. Seth walked around wearing his clerical collar and greeted the local cable TV news crew as it arrived.

Hiding upstairs in their third-story apartment, the Pangemanan family watched cable TV news where they saw Seth talking to a reporter just below their apartment. But Harry and Yana did not dare walk down their building's concrete steps to visit with their pastor in their courtyard.

When ICE agents had banged on their door, Harry and Yana had not opened it. Later they learned that in every apartment where someone had opened a door, a parent had been detained.

Family members who remained, mostly women and children, ventured outside in their pajamas to speak with Pastor Seth and the reporters. Children wailed, crying for missing parents and neighbors.

Until 2003, most of the Indonesians at Woodbine lived under the radar of immigration authorities. Their immigration status, names, and addresses would have been unknown, and locating them would have been very difficult.

But if you were a man from a mostly Muslim country and your authorization to reside in the U.S. had run out, the immigration rules had changed abruptly for you as a direct result of the terrorist attacks on September 11, 2001.

On June 6, 2002, as part of the newly declared Global War on Terror, U.S. Attorney General John Ashcroft introduced a new enforcement strategy called the National Security Entry and Exit Registry System, shortened to NSEERS.

Capitalizing on the public trauma of September 11, 2001, Ashcroft transformed foreign-born community members into enemies worthy of suspicion, fear, and terror.

"In this new war, our enemy's platoons infiltrate our borders, quietly blending in with visiting tourists, students, and workers," Ashcroft said. "They move unnoticed through our cities, neighborhoods, and public spaces. They wear no uniforms. Their camouflage is not forest green, but rather it is the color of common street clothing. Their tactics rely on evading recognition at the border and escaping detection within the United States. Their terrorist mission is to defeat America, destroy our values and kill innocent people."[1]

The 9/11 hijackers were citizens of countries that were U.S. allies: one from Egypt, another from Lebanon, two from the United Arab Emirates, fifteen from Saudi Arabia. None came from Afghanistan or Iraq. All 9/11 hijackers entered legally on business, tourist, or student visas.[2] Nevertheless, the new act focused on people who were not criminals but whose immigration status had lapsed or who had entered illegally.

Though Ashcroft's wide-ranging rhetoric cast suspicion on all foreign-born residents, the act specifically required undocumented

---

[1] "Attorney General Prepared Remarks on the National Security Entry-Exit Registration System," Department of Justice, June 6, 2002, https://www.justice.gov/archive/ag/speeches/2002/060502agpreparedremarks.htm.

[2] Robert Farley, "9/11 Hijackers and Student Visas," FactCheck.org, Annenberg Public Policy Center, May 10, 2013, https://www.factcheck.org/2013/05/911-hijackers-and-student-visas/.

men—not women—between the ages of 18 and 65 from twenty-five Muslim-majority countries to register with the U.S. government. Many consider NSEERS to have been the dangerous and racist predecessor to the Trump administration's Muslim ban in 2017.[3] Penalties promised to be severe. While overstaying a visa was not a criminal offense, failure to register would be treated as a criminal offense and could justify immediate deportation.

Also, that year the Homeland Security Act of 2002 consolidated several border and revenue enforcement agencies, including the former Immigration and Naturalization Services (INS), into U.S. Immigration and Customs Enforcement. The goals of the 2002 act were not about providing a more perfect union nor weaving together diverse groups of people into the fiber of our nation so that all people can better work together for the common good. The primary mission was (a) to prevent terrorist attacks within the United States, (b) to reduce the vulnerability of the United States to terrorism, and (c) to minimize the damage and assist in the recovery from terrorist attacks that do occur within the United States.[4]

Colloquially known as ICE, U.S. Immigration and Customs Enforcement became the largest investigative and enforcement arm of the Department of Homeland Security and the second-largest contributor to the nation's Joint Terrorism Task Force.

ICE became that agency through which the Global War on Terror would be fought in American neighborhoods, schools, and hospitals.

In May 2006, the Reformed Church of Highland Park had just invited me to join their board of elders, a group of leaders who supervise the congregation together with the ministers. I had hoped to spend the first part of my three-year term quietly observing. But the Avenel raid challenged all of us. I quickly realized how little I knew about the post-9/11 immigration landscape.

Like many U.S. citizens, I believed I had a decent enough handle on immigration. After all, I was a second- and third-generation Sicilian American. Sunday dinners with extended family members included the stories that generations before mine told about how they had immigrated and navigated challenging rules at the turn of the last century.

---

[3] Kaveh Waddell, "America Already Had a Muslim Registry," *The Atlantic*, December 20, 2016, https://www.theatlantic.com/technology/archive/2016/12/america-already-had-a-muslim-registry/511214/.

[4] Homeland Security Act of 2002, Pub. L. 107-296, 116 STAT 2135 (2002), https://www.dhs.gov/sites/default/files/publications/hr_5005_enr.pdf.

But everything I thought I knew was no longer valid.

By the late 1990s, there was no reliable path to residency for industrious but unskilled workers, especially if they did not have a U.S. citizen spouse, child, or parent. Still, in 2023, aunts, uncles, cousins, and even siblings are simply unable to apply for residency or citizenship for their loved ones. Without an immediate family connection, the only other option (besides lotteries for citizens of a few well-favored countries) is employment-based immigration. Providing an employment-based visa required a serious commitment of time and money on the part of employers. Both family- and employer-based immigration was strictly limited.[5]

Most Indonesians in the faith communities of Central New Jersey entered with tourist visas and simply overstayed those visas, years before the terrorist attacks of 2001.

It wasn't hard to overstay. Antiquated immigration systems didn't always properly inform immigrants about visa expirations or the proper timelines for re-applying. Indonesians found jobs, joined churches, raised families, and bypassed immigration authorities—both knowingly and many times unknowingly.

In the economic boom of the Clinton era, a culture developed in which employers who needed to fill unpopular overnight shifts or low-paid but difficult positions welcomed responsible immigrants and then looked the other way when it came to verifying their immigration status.

Harry and Yana Pangemanan, like many other immigrants, obtained social security numbers during a time when they were not required to prove government authorization for their status. Not only did they pay taxes for decades, but like millions of undocumented immigrants they also paid money into Social Security and would probably never be able to access its benefits.

Immigrants got jobs. The U.S. economy got workers and taxes.

Harry and Yana didn't have the time or money to correct their status, so they took their chances. Along with many of their fellow Indonesians, some of whom had arrived years before them, they each had entered with a valid tourist visa and then overstayed—a civil

---

[5] For a helpful overview of how immigration works in the United States, see "How the United States Immigration System Works," American Immigration Council, September 14, 2021, https://www.americanimmigrationcouncil.org/research/how-united-states-immigration-system-works?gclid=Cj0KCQjw0PWRBhDKARIsAPKHFGioCNez4vcrAQePUB2OMFbhVkyH1f9KdIJVHdKogCJSZ1pnECWKyzQaAoU6EALw_wcB.

offense, not a criminal offense. In the back of their minds, they had an emergency plan: if an immigration case was filed against them, then they would hire an attorney who would plead their case in court.

"Many, many of our friends lived in the U.S. for decades while being undocumented," Yana explained when asked why she waited so long to apply for asylum. Compared to the dangers and intense persecution that ethnic Chinese Christians like Yana encountered in Indonesia, the risk was worth it.

Indonesians weren't proud of the fact that they were "out of status," but fixing their status meant hiring attorneys and engaging in an extreme gamble. If they weren't granted some form of residency, the court most likely would order them to be deported. For people who had serious reasons not to return to their home country, living quietly without status, under the radar, was the safest approach.[6]

The Global War on Terror changed the immigration rules for men who held expired visas from Muslim-majority countries. By 2003, Harry and Yana's Indonesian congregation had grown to nearly 100 people. Indonesian leaders asked Pastor Seth and a few elders of his congregation to attend a meeting where, for the very first time, the Americans learned about the attorney general's new NSEERS registration program.[7]

The Indonesians sought advice from their American partners in church ministry. After living under the immigration radar for many years, should Indonesian men now trust the U.S. government with the private contact information they had concealed for so long? They were terrified, because men who failed to report to ICE faced being treated as terrorist fugitives by the United States government. They feared punishment that would be far worse than a civil violation for overstaying a visa. And they feared separation from their families.

In an honest, open, and vulnerable discussion in the church dining room, Indonesian men revealed their fears about the U.S. government requirement to register and hoped American church leaders could advise them on the best course of action.

Speaking in Indonesian, with a smattering of English, Indonesian men expressed their love of the United States for providing them with

---

[6] Interviews with Yana Pangemanan, February and March 2017.
[7] Seth Kaper-Dale, *2013 Revitalization Book* (henceforth SKD), 34–35. Seth entrusted a fifty-six-page draft of a book on church revitalization to me and encouraged me, as he said at the time, to "use all of it" in the present book, *Global Grace Café*, to tell the story of how he, the Pangemanans, and the Reformed Church of Highland Park fought to keep undocumented Indonesians families together.

a haven where they could safely practice their religion. Many had fled violence against ethnic Chinese Christians in Indonesia, and they wanted to help America win the Global War on Terror. They wanted to comply with the government to combat terrorism while hoping for a path to citizenship.

"I had no idea most of their members were undocumented," Seth said later. "That is when I found out." Over ninety percent of the people in the room that night had entered the United States on a tourist visa and had overstayed. He learned, too, that six other brand-new Indonesian congregations in the area were also predominantly made up of people without legal permission to reside here.

Conversing with Indonesian leaders, Seth received a crash course on recent Indonesian history. He learned both that when Indonesia's Suharto regime collapsed in the late 1990s there was a violent backlash against anyone who was ethnic Chinese, and that this community in New Jersey was composed of mostly ethnic Chinese Indonesians.

Ethnic Chinese Christians had fled wherever they could get a visa, and many had been able to get tourist visas to the U.S. Because tourist visas to the U.S. can be notoriously hard to come by among poor populations, desperate Indonesians were surprised and did not understand why they were now able to get visas, but by the grace of God, they received visas!

It's worth noting here that with a sizeable number of ethnic Chinese Christian Indonesians in danger, the U.S. government had the option to offer them a formal refugee resettlement program. Such a program would have required significant funding, political willpower, and international statesmanship. In the absence of such a program, caring individuals in American embassies handed out six-month tourist visas to persecuted Indonesians. Thousands of tourist visas.

To prepare for meeting with the men from the Indonesian congregation, Seth called his contacts and found an immigration attorney who was willing to participate. However, NSEERS was so new that no one knew what to expect from the attorney general's program. Some attorneys hoped that registering would prove to be a step on the elusive path to citizenship.

"The congregation was asking for my advice," Seth remembered. "I and an attorney, and other pastors as well, advised the group to report to ICE."

Seth, immigration lawyers, and community leaders believed that the Indonesians had compelling asylum cases, and they hoped that this NSEERS program might end up being a blessing in disguise. In the face of the unknown, Seth and the other advisors fell back on naïve optimism.

"We believed that honesty was the best policy," Seth said.

One frigid morning in February 2003, Harry Pangemanan led dozens of Indonesian men who lined up outside the Newark ICE office starting at 2 a.m. Registration for NSEERS was scheduled to open that day, and Harry and his friends wished to show their eagerness to comply.

It was as if Seth and Harry were taking a page from the Gospel of Matthew, where Jesus says, "If anyone forces you to go one mile, go with them two miles" (Matthew 5:41, NIV).

Indonesian men took a major risk coming forward. They felt ashamed of their lack of immigration status, even though overstaying a tourist visa was a civil offense, comparable in severity to running a red light. They hoped to demonstrate their trust in God and in the country that had saved them from religious persecution. They hoped they would be shown mercy.

Because Yana, too, like many Chinese Christian Indonesians, had fled Indonesia during the anti-Christian and anti-ethnic Chinese pogrom that followed the demise of the Suharto regime in May 1998, Harry and Yana simultaneously filed for asylum.

"Asylum," "withholding of removal," and "continued presence," are three categories of authorization that enable non-citizens to reside in the U.S. These authorizations are managed by a federal organization called U.S. Citizenship and Immigration Services (USCIS), the pro-citizenship side of the Department of Homeland Security. After a hearing, judges in non-criminal federal immigration courts are empowered to grant a change in status to asylum, withholding of removal, or continued presence.

Once granted one of these statuses, immigrants receive work authorizations. Withholding of removal and continued presence provide a kind of stateless limbo with no pathway to citizenship. Those authorizations dissolve once a person leaves the United States. To hold onto them requires never returning home. Only the asylum grant enables immigrants to apply for permanent residency, colloquially called a green card, after one year. After the green card, the path to citizenship requires residency for five years.

Yana had entered the U.S. in May 1998 after a narrow escape while Jakarta's Chinatown burned, and gangs had publicly raped ethnic Chinese women like her. Harry's immigration story stretched back five years earlier than Yana's. Unlike Yana, Harry did not flee imminent persecution, but the long, slow, stultifying process of suffering as a member of a poor and despised minority Christian group.

Born in 1970 on the island of Makassar, the provincial capital of South Sulawesi, Harry was the fourth of Clara and Joce Pangemanan's six children. Clara's ancestral home, built in an ethnic Chinese style in a poverty-stricken, Muslim-majority neighborhood, was looted and vandalized more than once by Muslim extremist mobs during repeated periods of ethnic violence. When Clara's brother died, her sister-in-law and children joined the Pangemanan household. Twelve children and three adults lived on Joce's minimal salary as a postal worker. To feed so many people, Clara ran a catering business from her kitchen.[8]

In 1989, Harry's family's financial support system was threatened when Joce suffered a heart attack. His parents sent eighteen-year-old Harry to Jakarta to work to enable them to pay private school tuition for Harry's siblings, since public schools required all students, including Christians, to study Islam.

At a time when his peers set off for college, Harry cleaned oil drums by day in the sprawling capital city of Jakarta. The Indonesian economy had begun to collapse, and poor people like young Harry suffered most. By night, to pay for his father's increasing medical needs, Harry sold the residue of the tainted gas from the side of the road.

In 1993, Harry's aunt Nelly Pangemanan, a legal resident of California, visited her brother Joce and his family in Makassar and became upset when she learned that Harry no longer lived with his parents and siblings but had been sent to Jakarta to work. Nelly flew to Jakarta to rescue Harry and flew him back to live in her Los Angeles home.

In California, Harry worked for Nelly's husband, Harry's uncle, who published an Indonesian American newspaper. The work was demanding—making 4 a.m. deliveries, managing the office, and performing housework—but it enabled Harry to send vital money back home. For three years, Harry remained with his aunt and uncle as he overstayed his six-month tourist visa.

Back in Indonesia, disaster struck again in 1996 when the roof of Harry's family home collapsed. To pay for the repair, Harry took a contract job driving a truck across the United States. When he landed in New Jersey, Harry found a better job in a warehouse. The money

---

[8] Interviews with Harry Pangemanan, March 2009 and March 2017.

Harry made enabled Joce to undergo surgery in 1998. But while Joce recovered at home, he suffered another heart attack and died.

Meanwhile, in Central New Jersey's growing Indonesian community, Harry met Yana, who was working at a Burger King. Yana was renting a couch on which another Indonesian slept while Yana went to work.

In 2000, Harry and Yana returned to Nelly's California home to marry. Between them, they supported nineteen family members in Indonesia. Their first daughter, Jocelyn, was born in 2002 and was an American citizen based on the provisions of the Fourteenth Amendment.

During these years, Harry's sister Jessy attended college in Europe with Harry's financial assistance. After college, Jessy relocated to the U.S., where she married an American construction architect and became a U.S. citizen. When Jessy and her husband became parents, Harry's mother Clara arrived from Indonesia and moved in with Jessy to care for her grandchildren in their Ohio home. Thanks to Jessy, who applied for her mother, Clara received a green card.

From then on, Jessy and Clara were free from immigration worries. However, these close family connections were absolutely irrelevant to Harry's asylum case and provided no support for his desire to become a U.S. citizen.

After Harry and the other Indonesian men registered with NSEERS at the Newark office of ICE, they all filed cases requesting asylum status.

The definition of asylum status is bound up with the definition of a refugee, which is part of long-standing international law that stretches back to the end of World War II. Sixty million people were displaced in the war and international governments were overwhelmed. They created a global compact for safe, orderly, and regular migration, and that included an international agreement to offer asylum to people who qualify.[9]

Asylum status can be granted to people who are either already in the United States or seeking admission at a port of entry.[10] Anyone in the

---

[9] In the aftermath of World War II, refugees were defined and described as part of the *Convention Relating to the Status of Refugees*, United Nations General Assembly, July 28, 1951, https://www.refworld.org/docid/3be01b964.html. The United Nations High Commissioner for Refugees published an overview, "The Refugee Concept Under International Law: Global Compact for Safe, Orderly, and Regular Migration," March 12--5, 2018, https://www.unhcr.org/5aa290937.pdf.

[10] For the formal definitions of refugee and asylum, see "Refugees and Asylum,"

United States may apply for asylum in the United States regardless of their country of origin or their current immigration status. Requesting asylum entails making a case that you have suffered persecution. According to USCIS, asylum status is a form of protection available to people who meet the international definition of refugee—namely, someone who is unable or unwilling to return to their home country and is unable or unwilling to avail himself or herself of the protection of their home country because of persecution or a well-founded fear of persecution on account of race, religion, nationality, membership in a particular social group, or political opinion.

Anyone who is not in the U.S. may request refugee status. Refugee status is a form of protection that may be granted to people who meet the international definition of refugee and who are of special humanitarian concern to the United States. Thus, people who receive refugee status first wait outside U.S. borders to be vetted by the United Nations High Commissioner on Refugees and also by the U.S. Department of State. This "double-vetting" process seeks to ensure that no "closet terrorists" sneak into the U.S. while they pose as persecuted minorities.

These legal definitions confuse everyone who struggles to keep families together. To request the status of asylum, one must meet the definition of refugee. If you win asylum, then you are an asylee. The status of asylum is awarded by an immigration judge who is part of the Department of Justice.

Applying for asylum is risky for many reasons. Legal representation is expensive. The process can take years. You could be denied and deported. The notoriety of your case can endanger the safety of your family members in your home country. By filing for asylum, Indonesian Christians were claiming that their own government in Indonesia was unable or unwilling to protect them from persecution and mob violence. And applying for asylum also does not protect you from being detained or deported.

Though it is not illegal to request asylum in the United States, the Illegal Immigration Reform and Immigrant Responsibility Act

---

U.S. Citizenship and Immigration Services, last updated November 12, 2015, https://www.uscis.gov/humanitarian/refugees-asylum; and "What Is Asylum?" UNHCR: The UN Refugee Agency, accessed August 14, 2021, https://help.unhcr.org/usa/applying-for-asylum/what-is-asylum/. The formal definition of asylum is found in section 1101(a)(42) of Title 8 of the U.S. Code, https://uscode.house.gov/view.xhtml?req=granuleid%3AUSC-prelim-title8-section1101&num=0&edition=prelim.

of 1996[11] made it lawful for the federal government to detain asylum seekers in prison-like conditions in existing jails as well as in new stand-alone facilities for immigration detention.

In Central New Jersey, hundreds of Indonesian Christians who registered with NSEERS also applied for asylum.

Between 2002 and 2005, Pastor Seth periodically involved himself in the efforts of community members who were trying to reconcile their immigration status. He traveled to hearings in Newark with Indonesians from the congregation that worshiped in the Reformed Church sanctuary on Sunday evenings. Seth wrote letters of support to include in their asylum packets. He enabled a lawyer to work from a church office and offer a clinic on filing immigration claims on Saturday mornings.[12]

Why did Seth work so hard? "I did all this with the hopes of keeping intact a new immigrant community that had collectively faced many hardships," he explained. However, Seth had no sense of the challenges that he and his church would face while holding this community together over the next two decades.

For the Indonesians, life continued to go on, even in exile in the U.S. The community was young and growing. Because many people who had escaped Indonesia with visas were in their twenties and thirties, many marriages took place during this time. Other young families arrived in the U.S. and brought their small, Indonesian-born children with them. All these families continued to have children, and these children were born as United States citizens.

Occasionally, Seth shared with his Sunday morning congregation what was going on. Yet the main connection between the people in the two churches happened during two annual events.

Every year, in late winter, the nine or so interfaith congregations that worshiped at the Reformed Church of Highland Park joined together for a Saturday night potluck meal. They sang hymns for one another and offered communal prayers. The line of people waiting to serve themselves at the Indonesian table, loaded with fabulous seafood and Chinese-Indonesian hybrid dishes, was always the longest.

Then, each autumn, on the Sunday night before Thanksgiving, Indonesian Christian, Reformed Christian, Chinese Christian, Metho-

---

[11] The Illegal Immigration Reform and Immigrant Responsibility Act of 1996, Pub. L. 104-208, div. C, 110 STAT 3009-546 (1996) (codified in various sections of Titles 8 and 18 of the U.S. Code).
[12] SKD, 34-35.

dist, Jewish, Buddhist, and Muslim congregations filled the sanctuary of the Reformed Church of Highland Park, or perhaps another faith community, in a town-wide interfaith worship service of songs and prayers. People were friendly. They nodded hello. But language and culture divided them.

Meanwhile, in Indonesia, between 1998 and 2006, hundreds of Christian churches burned. The national unrest that had followed the end of Suharto's regime had gone underground, flaring up in local animosities between extremist Muslims and Christians.[13] When they weren't being attacked, Chinese Christians were discriminated against.[14]

There was no safe way to return to Indonesia with young families who had become comfortable living openly in expressing their vibrant Christian faith. Across the United States, not only in New Jersey but also in California, Washington, and Maryland, tens of thousands of Chinese Indonesian families, along with Harry and Yana, spent years with immigration lawyers and courts and tens of thousands of dollars on attorney and court fees.

And then, one by one, all Indonesian asylum cases were denied, without being heard. It turned out that, after one year had passed since an immigrant had entered the U.S., a judge could no longer consent to hear the immigrant's case for asylum.

The cases were denied because, back in 1996, the Clinton administration had changed the rules for asylum seekers, adding a

---

[13] While May 1998 has become infamous for the unleashing of religious acrimony throughout Indonesia, 145 churches were burned between 1992 and 1998 in anti-Christian violence (see John Sidel, *Riots, Pogroms, Jihad: Religious Violence in Indonesia* [Ithaca, NY: Cornell University Press, 2006], 73–78.) On Christmas Eve of the year 2000, thirty churches on multiple islands were bombed simultaneously, and Sidel identifies paramilitary assaults on Christian villages and churches and then, by 2004, secular targets. Sidel stresses the role of armed Christian groups in initiating violence and cautions against assigning Christian groups an "un-self-interested-victim or innocent bystander status" (222). Sidel shows that anti-minority violence increased when the political role of Islamic extremists waned in the Indonesian government.

[14] "Leaked diplomatic cables dating from 2006 allege that the Islamic Defenders Front, responsible for attacks on minority Muslims and Christians, receives funding from the police and acts as the police force's 'attack dog.' Senior officials at Jakarta Police and National Police levels have for years defended the Islamic Defenders Front as a 'partner' to the police and attempted to downplay its litany of transgressions" (Erwin Sihombing, "Police Say They're Too Scared to Fight Religious Hard-Liners," *The Jakarta Globe*, July 5, 2015, excerpt available at https://www.ucanews.com/news/indonesian-cops-too-scared-to-fight-religious-hard-liners/73883).

one-year "time bar" or deadline to the Illegal Immigration Reform and Immigrant Responsibility Act. This is the same act that had made it legal for the government to detain asylum seekers in prisons.[15] The one-year rule was poorly communicated to the population of undocumented asylum seekers.

Despite all the efforts that Indonesians made to right their status, immigration judges could not even hear the basic facts of their cases. Legislation pre-empted the possibility of mercy.

Two weeks after Harry and the other Indonesian men traveled to Newark to report for NSEERS, Harry challenged the leaders of the Indonesian congregation, insisting, "This is the time to join the Americans!" Then, Harry and Seth called a meeting where local leaders of the Reformed Church in America (RCA) encouraged the Indonesian church to join the denomination of their American ministry partners. Denominational leaders were excited to add this new community to their *classis*, or local group of churches. But the Indonesian leaders of the congregation that worshiped on Sunday evenings in the Highland Park sanctuary didn't welcome this change. They voted to remain an independent congregation.[16]

Nevertheless, Harry and Yana sensed that, at least for them, it was time to deepen their relationships with the American congregation that had already shown support and understanding of their situation.

During Easter week of 2003, Harry began to worship with the English-speaking congregation at 10 a.m. Then Harry returned to set up and then worship with the Indonesian service at 4 p.m. If the afternoon service finished sooner, he would mop the men's bathroom first, then the women's. Thinking "maybe I can help some way," Harry borrowed a floor machine to polish the linoleum floors in the church administration building. He went down to the basement and figured out how the boiler worked. Harry soon ran the boiler room.

---

[15] The one-year deadline to apply for asylum was part of the Illegal Immigration Reform and Immigrant Responsibility Act of 1996. To understand how this time bar impacted tens of thousands of asylum seekers, see Philip G. Schrag et al., "Rejecting Refugees: Homeland Security's Administration of the One-Year Bar to Asylum," *William & Mary Law Review* 52, no. 3 (2010): 651–804, https://scholarship.law.wm.edu/cgi/viewcontent.cgi?article=3369&context=wmlr. For current information on the one-year deadline or time bar for applying for asylum, see "Asylum Bars," U.S. Citizenship and Immigration Services, last updated May 31, 2022, https://www.uscis.gov/humanitarian/refugees-and-asylum/asylum/asylum-bars.

[16] Interview with Harry Pangemanan, March 2017.

The one person who worked more hours than Harry was Pastor Seth. Seth would find Harry cleaning up and say, "You're still here?" Sometimes they would talk. The two began a friendship that has spanned years.

In 2004, after every Indonesian in the community had had their asylum cases denied, they filed appeals at the Board of Immigration Appeals (BIA) in Falls Church, Virginia. The BIA functions as the Supreme Court for immigration cases. After a final determination by the BIA, there is no judicial avenue for appeal.

By early 2006, almost everyone had their BIA appeals denied too, because the one-year filing deadline had excluded everyone. Indonesians in Central New Jersey were now deportable.

On paper, most agreed to voluntary departure. But they didn't leave. Life was still very difficult for ethnic Chinese Christians in Indonesia, and families didn't want to go back. The poverty on the islands added another complicating factor. Many family members back in Indonesia who could not find work were already being supported by monies earned in America and sent back via Western Union.

After praying for direction, Harry and Yana decided to take a leap of faith. It was no longer safe for them to hide among their Indonesian community. Despite differences in language and culture, the Pangemanans asked to become members of the American congregation. Early in the spring of 2006, the Pangemanans and four Americans participated in a new member class with Pastors Seth and Stephanie.

A few mornings each week, before Harry set off for work, Seth invited Harry for coffee at Penny's, a family-owned luncheonette on the next block of the main street in their semi-urban town. Seth asked Harry to tell him his story, and Harry spilled his soul about everything—about Makassar, the ancient port city on the large island of Sulawesi where Harry grew up; about the extremist Muslim violence and discrimination against his Chinese Christian family; and about how, when Harry graduated high school in 1988 and his father became ill, his father sent Harry to Jakarta to clean oil drums to pay for his siblings' tuition.

Over weeks and months, Harry and Seth developed a sense of mutual trust. A hard-working, self-reliant person like Harry was not one to complain. To understand the turns in Harry's complicated life took time, patience, and friendship.

Harry's story helped Seth to see the raid on the Avenel apartments from the perspective of the Indonesian immigrants whom ICE targeted. It also enabled Seth to grasp the shocking reality that the Department of Homeland Security had turned Christian congregants into illegal fugitives and a new flavor of supposed terrorist: potential enemy combatants.

Seth began to perceive that the anti-terrorism tactics of the U.S. government had taken a sinister anti-immigrant, anti-family, and anti-community turn.

CHAPTER 3

American Ambivalence

In Highland Park, New Jersey, 2006

In the final tally, the federal government removed thirty-five parents, mostly fathers, from their families in the raid in Avenel on May 24, 2006. All thirty-five Indonesians were detained in the North Brunswick Correctional Facility, which is the official name for what residents call the Middlesex County jail. Within six weeks, every Indonesian there was deported. As many as seventy children who were living at Woodbine Apartments in Avenel lost a parent.

The thirty-five Indonesian parents who had resided in Avenel, New Jersey, and who were deported were among 640 residents of the United States who were rounded up that month in Operation Return to Sender because they had been issued final orders of removal by an immigration judge but failed to comply by leaving the country. The U.S. government cast these dire, family tragedies within a framework of despicable criminality.

"This is another example of a new and tough interior enforcement strategy that seeks to catch and deport criminal aliens, increase worksite enforcement, and crack down hard on the criminal infrastructure that perpetuates illegal immigration," said Homeland Security Secretary Michael Chertoff. "The fugitives captured in this operation threatened public safety in hundreds of neighborhoods and communities around the country. This department has no tolerance for their criminal behavior, and we are using every authority at our disposal to bring focus to fugitive operations and rid communities of this criminality."[1]

ICE Assistant Secretary Myers added insult to injury, saying, "America's welcome does not extend to immigrants who come here to commit crimes. ICE will leave no stone unturned in hunting down and deporting aliens who victimize our communities. Interior enforcement initiatives like Operation Return to Sender are a critical and necessary complement to our nation's border security measures."[2]

That June, ICE announced that Operation Return to Sender was complete, having arrested 2,179 individuals across the country, blatantly using immigration authority for purportedly crime-fighting goals. Immigration authority, as advocates at the Reformed Church would continue to learn, is far more flexible than criminal law, and as ICE stated, ICE officers arrested the majority of these individuals on administrative immigration violations and placed them into deportation proceedings.[3]

Immigration authority empowered an end-run around due process.

However, despite the announcement from ICE that it had ceased, Operation Return to Sender was far from complete in June 2006. It was a pattern that would play out again and again, terrorizing local communities and destroying families until the end of the second Bush administration in 2008.

Pre-dawn raids, even more ruthless and less ethical than the ones in May 2006 that included Woodbine Apartments in Avenel, continued to take place across the country.

At the Cardozo School of Law in New York, a professor of immigration law named Peter Markowitz directed his school's immigration legal clinic and began researching. Professor Markowitz and his students obtained internal ICE directives that laid bare the administrative framework underlying these raids. In 2009, Markowitz

---

[1] Qtd. in "ICE Apprehends More Than 2,100 Criminal Aliens."
[2] Qtd. in "ICE Apprehends More Than 2,100 Criminal Aliens."
[3] "ICE Apprehends More Than 2,100 Criminal Aliens."

and Cardozo students filed a Freedom of Information Act lawsuit to obtain the directives and shared them with the *New York Times*.[4]

They discovered a directive from the acting director of ICE, John Torres, from January 31, 2006, that raised ICE enforcement teams' "target goal" from 125 to 1,000 arrests per year and promised to "ensure the maximum availability of detention space for fugitive operations." The number of seven-member enforcement teams multiplied from 8 to 104. Meanwhile, congressional funding rose from $9 million in 2003 to $218 million in 2008, by which time the program had apprehended 96,000 people, three-quarters of whom had no criminal convictions. Many were ordinary violators of residency status—in non-compliance with civil statutes—people who did not at all fit the priority categories of the ICE program.[5]

Although pre-dawn raids on homes around America were billed as carefully planned hunts for dangerous immigrant fugitives, and although federal immigration officials repeatedly told Congress they would concentrate on the worst criminals and terrorists, the program went after far easier, far more vulnerable targets like the peaceful, church-going Indonesians of Avenel, New Jersey. Beyond raising steep quotas, subsequent ICE directives eliminated requirements that 75 percent of arrested people be criminals and allowed teams to include non-fugitives in their counts.[6]

The truth is that, in 2006 and still today in 2023, residing in the United States without authorization from the U.S. government is not and has never been a criminal offense. There is no criminal law against unauthorized presence. Overstaying one's visa remains a civil offense, no matter how strongly factions of the American public believe that unauthorized presence is illegal, nor how strongly members of the public believe unauthorized presence should be a criminal violation.

Yet, despite the overt duplicity of the U.S. government about ICE directives, one *New York Times* reporter on the immigration beat reported with dismay that too many Americans seemed to approve of the immigration raids.

"Many Americans have welcomed arrests of what the agency calls 'ordinary status violators'—noncitizens who have no outstanding order

---

[4] Nina Bernstein, "U.S. Immigrant Raids Went for Many Nonfugitives," *New York Times*, February 4, 2009, https://www.nytimes.com/2009/02/04/world/americas/04iht-immig.4.19929389.html.
[5] Bernstein, "U.S. Immigrant Raids Went for Many Nonfugitives."
[6] Bernstein, "U.S. Immigrant Raids Went for Many Nonfugitives."

of deportation but are suspected of being in the country unlawfully, either because they overstayed a visa or entered without one," she wrote.[7]

That reporter's name was Nina Bernstein, and she would eventually play a key role in the story of immigration at the Reformed Church of Highland Park.

Meanwhile, in the irrational exuberance of raids powered by quota systems, ICE agents committed countless outright injustices, though some facts took years to surface in public accounts.

Agents targeted immigrants by race. In Fair Haven, Connecticut, ICE officers went door to door asking not only how many people were inside each house but also what race they were.

In Willmar, Minnesota, ICE agents handcuffed and interrogated Latino residents whose presence was lawful but did not handcuff or interrogate white residents in the same home.

ICE admitted that its fugitive alien program mistakenly detained, arrested, and deported not only legal immigrants but also people who were U.S. citizens.

The stories were outrageous.

U.S. citizen Adriana Aguilar was sound asleep with her four-year-old son when ICE officers stormed into her bedroom in East Hampton, New York, pulled the covers off her bed, shined flashlights into their faces, and then interrogated Aguilar.

A citizen from birth living with his father in San Rafael, California, was forcibly removed from his home by ICE agents who pretended to be police and then confined him to a locked office for twelve hours.[8]

In Paterson, New Jersey, ICE agents barged into Ana Galindo's home, refused to accept her state driver's license as valid identification, interrogated her about where she was hiding "illegals," and pointed a gun at her nine-year-old son.[9]

Galindo and Aguilar sued ICE for violating their Fourth Amendment rights, among other lawsuits filed in ten states.[10]

---

[7] Bernstein, "U.S. Immigrant Raids Went for Many Nonfugitives."
[8] Jennifer Bennett, "Operation Return to Sender: The Government's Immigration Enforcers Run Amok," *Slate*, May 30, 2008, https://slate.com/news-and-politics/2008/05/the-government-s-immigration-enforcers-run-amok.html.
[9] Samantha Henry, "NJ Residents Reach Settlement on Feds' Home Raids," Associated Press, December 18, 2012, https://news.yahoo.com/nj-residents-reach-settlement-feds-135738017.html.
[10] Bennett, "Operation Return to Sender."

CHAPTER 4

Seeking Safety in Church

In Highland Park, June 2006

In Central New Jersey, the day after the Avenel raid on residents of Woodbine Apartments, the local newspaper ran a triumphant headline: "Feds Round Up Fugitives: Raids Net 35 Illegals."

As his sole information source, the *Home News Tribune* reporter relied on an Immigration and Customs Enforcement (ICE) supervisor. This staff writer, Rick Harrison, didn't question the federal supervisor's narrative nor wonder about the impact of the raid on the community. It would be the last time that paper would allow ICE to have the final word on an immigration action in Central New Jersey.

"Pastor Blasts Recent Raids on Indonesian Congregants," read the headline of Seth's op-ed reply. "When a man has spent $15,000 in legal fees to stay here legally, to support his nephews and nieces through Indonesian school, and he is held at gunpoint below the window of his apartment, while his 7-year-old daughter watches in horror from upstairs, there is something wrong with America," Seth's words seethed in newsprint. It was his first foray into advocating for undocumented Indonesians through the news media.

Seth emailed his op-ed to his Reformed Church congregation. Before the raid, only a handful at the church, along with Seth, knew that most of the Indonesians who worshiped in their sanctuary at four o'clock every Sunday were unauthorized residents. Now they learned that an immigration raid had happened near Woodbridge Center, a super-sized mall where they sometimes shopped. They were shocked to hear that the federal government considered their fellow Christians to be alien fugitives. Finally, congregants understood their pastor had no doubt that federal agents had perpetrated a grave injustice.

"For those of you who haven't yet heard," Seth informed his congregation during his sermon at the 10 a.m. service the next Sunday, "in the early hours of Wednesday morning, the Department of Homeland Security raided an apartment building near here.... They went door-to-door, kicking doors, yelling, 'Everybody out with your hands up!' They slapped handcuffs on fathers in front of their children. They took away a father who was home alone with a three-month-old- baby while his wife worked the third shift at a factory. They took a man away from his wife who is eight months pregnant. Not one of these people had a crime larger than overstaying their tourist visas.... The paper bragged of 797 'fugitives' caught in New Jersey since last October. I wondered if the other 762 were as harmless as these 35. I imagined so."[1]

It was Memorial Day weekend. Seth was preaching from the farewell prayer Jesus prays during his last supper in John's Gospel.

"I am not asking you to take [my disciples] out of the world," Jesus says to his father in heaven, "but I ask you to protect them from the evil one. They do not belong to the world, just as I do not belong to the world" (John 17:15–16, NRSV).

Seth told his congregation that they, too, did not belong to this country. "You are from God," he declared. Therefore, the members of his congregation also were not to be defined by government rhetoric, by public opinion polls, nor even by the laws of the land. "You have to abide by them, but you are not defined by them, and therefore you can always challenge them!"

To Seth, "you are from God" meant that the values of his community of faith, the well-being of their neighbors and families, came from the very source of life itself. Perhaps it was the congregants'

---

[1] Seth Kaper-Dale, *A Voice for Justice: Sermons that Prepared a Congregation to Respond to God in the Decade after 9/11* (Eugene, OR: Wipf and Stock Publishers, 2013), 114.

job to nudge their country to welcome their Indonesian siblings in Christ as neighbors and friends.

"I don't know what the Spirit of God has in mind in terms of the situation unfolding with the Indonesian community," Seth continued. "All I know is that this week, the Spirit of God told me this is the most important thing on my agenda, and I've seen the Spirit say the same thing to many others within our church."

Seth had often been on the phone since the raid, asking congregants if they could host women whose husbands had been detained in the raid. Their wives were too afraid to sleep in their own beds. Liz and Rob Roesner immediately opened their home. "I didn't do much," Liz said later. "The poor woman who stayed with me didn't know any English, and she didn't seem to want much attention at all. She was really shaken."[2]

Five days after the raid, a friendly ICE officer tipped off a probono immigration attorney that ICE was planning another raid. Panic spread across the Indonesian networks. The whole Reformed Church congregation got their chance to respond to the crisis.

"People were terrified," Harry said. "Everyone was certain ICE agents would return." No one felt safe at home. People called Harry. Please, they pleaded, please ask Pastor Seth if we can sleep at the church.[3]

Seth and Harry discussed the issues. The church was not zoned for overnight use. The borough had a new fire marshal who was threatening to slap code violations on the church kitchen for its industrial gas stove that was not protected by a firewall, and the wooden walls of its gymnasium-style social hall required fireproof varnish. There were other limitations. The church had ample bathrooms but no showers. The entire facility was rented out, seven days a week, as a kind of community center. Mondays through Thursdays, hundreds of senior citizens in Rutgers University's life-long learning programs spent hours listening to lectures by retired professors in Sunday school classrooms.

When Seth hung up with Harry, the next person Seth called was Patrick Beckford, the church elder who served as its vice president. "I said that any Indonesian who was worried about an immigration raid could stay in the church, and I take all responsibility personally," Seth informed Patrick. Not wanting to legally implicate anyone else in his

[2] Interview with Liz Roesner, August 2017.
[3] Interview with Harry Pangemanan, March 2017.

decision, Seth told the vice president clearly, "I invited the Indonesians, and I did not consult church leaders first."

Patrick, a naturalized U.S. citizen from Jamaica, gave Seth his unconditional blessing. Patrick understood this was a humanitarian crisis and the church could not look away.

Seth didn't know how secret living arrangements would work or how many Indonesians would take him up on his offer. Ten Indonesian families moved into the Indonesian Pentecostal Church of Perth Amboy. Another fourteen families moved into the Highland Park church.

Harry and Yana had left their apartment in Woodbine Gardens, too. They were hiding in the house of some friends in Edison who had called on the day of the raid and invited the Pangemanans to live with them. But Harry felt he must join the other families who were making do at the church.

"The rest of them will be at the church," Harry told Yana, "It's not fair. We need to be together." Harry and Yana had just become members of the American congregation, yet they retained their membership in the Indonesian Protestant congregation. All along, Harry took on the responsibility for maintaining good relations between the two congregations

Reluctantly, Yana agreed to join the group at the Highland Park church. At four months pregnant, she knew she would be more comfortable in her friends' home in Edison where they had their own guest room. But she felt obliged: Harry had called Seth and now the church was involved. Implicitly, Yana understood that she and Harry needed to be there, too.[4] The three Pangemanans packed up their belongings and settled into the twelve-by-sixteen-foot room that housed the Sunday school library in Highland Park.

As people moved in, Seth ran out to buy groceries, including cereal and milk for the children. Indonesian pastors arrived with cases of water and juice. For dinner, Indonesian friends dropped by and filled the industrial-sized church kitchen with food. Everyone ate together. Seth joined during one dinner and said, "Yana, you're pregnant, you can't sleep on the floor!" He then rushed out and purchased her an air mattress.

To complicate matters, the Reformed Church had always functioned as a kind of community center. On the first Tuesday in June, the social hall once again transformed into a polling place for primary

---

[4] Interviews with Harry and Yana Pangemanan, March 2017.

elections. Indonesian families hid their bedding and belongings on one side of the dining room wall, while on the other side the local board of elections installed voting machines and welcomed voters from borough precincts.

Finally, on Thursday, June 15, although all the Indonesians had already returned to their homes, Seth informed the church leadership team that Indonesians had hidden from law enforcement within the church. Three weeks had passed since the raid.

"As the pastor, I made an executive decision," Seth informed the church's *consistory*, a Protestant term for the group of ordained members who are technically Seth's and his co-pastor and wife Stephanie's employers. The biggest repercussion of Seth's unilateral action was that, as a team, church leaders had not been required to make a decision.

It is not clear they would have approved Seth's request if he had asked them first.

The leaders of the Reformed Church of Highland Park were an open-minded but cautious group. None of them knew anything about the country's immigration, detention, and deportation systems. Most trusted Seth to use his judgment in the heat of the moment. However, they were afraid.

"Seth was taking a risk," said Christy Van Horn, who was chair of the grounds and facilities committee. "Seth said he was willing to take that risk personally and he would go to jail instead of implicating the church," Christy explained. "But the consistory wasn't convinced that Seth could take on full liability. The church, too, could be in danger."[5]

For the American church, the stakes were high. As Seth and Stephanie entered the fifth year of their first call to ministry, they had begun launching ambitious plans.

Earlier that May, at its annual meeting, the congregation had agreed to sell the air rights above the first-floor offices, kitchen, and dining room of its administrative building for one dollar to a new housing organization that Seth led, a nonprofit called the Reformed Church of Highland Park–Affordable Housing Corporation, shortened to RCHP-AHC. This organization formed in May of 2006 to respond to a growing population of young adults who had aged out of New Jersey's foster-care system. RCHP-AHC planned to construct six units of supportive housing above church offices for young women who had grown up in foster homes.

[5] Interview with Christy Van Horn, December 2017.

The housing plan had already required the congregation to take on significant risk. To support a new second-floor structure, an engineering firm needed to sink support pillars from the roof into the seventy-year-old basement. At the church's annual meeting, ninety-four-year-old Fran Schell, baptized and wedded in the church and founder of the church's Tower Thrift Shop, was one of the last holdouts to voice her agreement. Only 4 out of 176 attendees voted against the building project.

Further, the plan to house women aging out of foster care met resistance in the borough. During the raid and while Indonesians were housed at the church, construction had not yet begun. However, neighbors of the church were alarmed by the change in zoning for the "Women Aging Out" project that would come to be known as "Irayna Court." In biblical Greek, *irayna* means peace.

One friendly neighbor, who lived across the street and who had spent part of her childhood in foster care, objected to building affordable housing for young, single women in her neighborhood. Based on her own difficult experience in the foster care system, she did not think the church could provide adequate supervision.

The building project already stretched the Reformed Church congregation. The immigration problems of the Indonesian Protestant congregation were not high on the consistory's list of priorities. They worried that if neighbors complained about the presence of undocumented people fleeing law enforcement, they might question the church's tax-exempt status. Some were concerned the borough might deny the zoning changes they were requesting for the housing project.

One long-time and deeply respected elder expressed major misgivings. "I feel Seth's action is unfair," she told fellow consistory members. "So many people are waiting to come here legally. They are paying fees and following procedures. They don't get to live here unless they receive prior approval. It just doesn't seem right for us to help people who are skipping the line."[6]

Others were more concerned about liability. They wondered, if someone breaks a law and we let them hide in the church, aren't we harboring fugitives? What happens when a church breaks a law? No one knew the answers. They decided to schedule a visit with an

---

[6] Discussion with elder Barbara Woodward at RCHP consistory retreat, January 2007.

immigration attorney. A group formed to study immigration law and how exactly to provide sanctuary from law enforcement.

Mostly, though, consistory members hoped the whole issue would simply disappear.

In June 2006, no one—except Seth—was willing to go to jail on behalf of the undocumented immigrants who were worshiping in their sanctuary.

CHAPTER 5

Life after the Raid

In Avenel and Jakarta, Indonesia, 2006

In May and June 2006, none of the American citizens at the Reformed Church of Highland Park grasped the full tally of the emotional, social, financial, and spiritual destruction that children, families, and marriages would face when the U.S. government deported fathers who were the sole wage-earners for their families. Their jobs had provided health insurance and leased apartments.

For families who lost someone in the May 24 Avenel raid, life changed forever.

Roslyn Pandeiroot and Franky Toar had been living in a building that adjoined Harry and Yana's. A few nights before the raid, they had argued because Franky had had a dream. "Something bad is going to happen," he told Roslyn. He wanted to move, but Roslyn refused. Roslyn's neighbors were her closest friends. Indonesian women in the complex helped her with cooking and exchanged rides and childcare. Franky told her, "If something bad happens, I do not want our kids to see." Franky was voicing the shame that many Indonesians felt because they were not able to resolve their immigration status.

In the late 1990s, Roslyn and Franky had left Indonesia after Franky had been involved in a confrontation with his Muslim neighbors. One neighbor claimed Franky had insulted him, and when word got out, Franky was verbally harassed and physically threatened on a daily basis. The couple felt they had no choice but to leave Indonesia.[1] In 1997, a sweeping financial crisis, triggered in Thailand, collapsed currencies in the Philippines, Singapore, Korea, and Indonesia and spread as far as Japan, Russia, and Brazil.[2] Indonesian students held demonstrations across Indonesia protesting steep fuel, food, and energy price hikes demanded by President Suharto's agreement with the International Monetary Fund. For decades, Suharto had consolidated power as an autocrat and was widely considered the world's most corrupt politician.[3]

On May 21, 1998, soldiers fired into a crowd at Trisakti University and shot four students dead. The Muslim population of Jakarta rebelled. Parliament called for the president's resignation.

After thirty-two years in power, Suharto resigned. But riots spread to North Sumatra, Central Java, and pockets of contention across Indonesia's seventeen thousand islands situated between the Indian and Pacific Oceans.

The Indonesian military, dominated by Islamic extremists, exploited long-standing hatred for ethnic Chinese businesses and exacerbated the violence in Chinese neighborhoods. Anger at the government was deflected by redirecting it to a despised minority. Mobs of Muslim extremists terrorized Chinese businesses, the majority of whose owners were outwardly Christian because Buddhism was not then a religion recognized by the Indonesian state.

As Chinatowns and churches burned, the BBC reported hundreds of rapes.

Systematic public gang rapes were documented. As many as 5,000 people across the country were killed in the violence.[4]

---

[1] Interview with Roslyn Pandeiroot, February 2017.
[2] For a helpful timeline of events of the 1997–98 worldwide financial crisis, see "The Crash: Timeline of the Panic," *Frontline*, PBS, http://www.pbs.org/wgbh/pages/frontline/shows/crash/etc/cron.html.
[3] "The GCR 2004 details funds allegedly embezzled by political leaders of the two previous decades. During his misrule, Mohamed Suharto, President of Indonesia from 1967-98, is alleged to have stolen US$15-US$35 billion in a country where the GDP per capita hovers at around US$700," ("Press Release: Plundering Politicians and Bribing Multinationals Undermine Economic Development, says TI," Transparency International, March 25, 2004, https://web.archive.org/web/20070621044111/http:/www.transparency.org/content/download/4450/26759/file/GCR_2004_press_release_FINAL.pdf).
[4] *AsiaWeek,* an online publication of *Time* magazine and CNN, conducted an

Indonesia is home to 231 million Muslims, 87 percent of the country's total population, the largest Muslim population of any country in the world. Yet Indonesia has had a Christian presence since its time as a Dutch colony, which began in 1816 and ended with Japanese occupation in World War II.

In Central New Jersey, before 1997, only one Indonesian Christian congregation had formed. By 2002, there were nine Indonesian congregations in adjoining towns: Perth Amboy, Woodbridge Edison, Metuchen, South Plainfield, Piscataway, and Highland Park. The churches were denominationally different, but culturally, socially, and emotionally their members were closely entwined in supportive relationships outside worship.

Many of the 1,200 or so Indonesian Christians who settled in Central New Jersey—including Franky and Roslyn and Harry and Yana—were ethnic Chinese.

Like other Indonesian men who fled anti-Christian violence and then registered with the Department of Homeland Security, Franky Toar filed for asylum. In 2004, his case was denied without being heard because he had missed the one-year filing deadline. In 2005, Franky's appeal was denied and he was ordered to deport. With his job in a restaurant supply warehouse, Franky was the family's sole financial support. His teenage children attended school in Avenel. Obeying the court order was not a viable option.

The day before federal agents raided his apartment complex, Franky lay in bed, stricken with flu. On the night of the raid, Roslyn was shocked that, even though he was so sick, Franky did not wait for a

---

investigation of events in Indonesia in May 1998, and the results appear in Susan Berfield and Dewi Loveard, "*AsiaWeek* Investigation: Ten Days That Shook Indonesia," July 24, 1998, http://www.cnn.com/ASIANOW/asiaweek/98/0724/cs1.html.

bang on his own door. When he heard the commotion in the courtyard, Franky was so mortified to be arrested in front of his children that he jumped out a window into the front parking lot and injured his leg. He was wearing no shoes or socks. Agents chased him. When they caught him, they brought Franky home anyway. His wrists were tied with plastic rope because the agents had not brought enough pairs of handcuffs. They picked up Franky's socks, his shoes, and his ID. Amanda, 16, and Vaidioll, 18, hugged their father for the last time.

"That scene will hurt us all for the rest of our lives," said Roslyn.

On the morning of the raid, Jane Massie had opened her front door. The week before there had been a fire in her building and the police had woken up her and her husband to get them outside to safety. That time, opening their door saved their lives. This time, ICE agents entered and took both Jane's passport and her husband Johan's. Then they tied plastic rope around Johan's wrists.

From their balconies, Jane, Roslyn, Amanda, and Vaidioll watched as ICE agents loaded their husbands and fathers, Johan and Frankie, into vans full of Indonesian men and drove them away.[5]

Because federal agents took Jane Massie's passport, and her other ID had expired, she could not visit her husband Johan during the weeks he spent in the Middlesex County Jail. Visitors must surrender valid IDs to enter the facility.

"When he called me to say he was deported to Indonesia," said Jane, "my heart broke." Jane's son Ryan insisted they talk with his father every day, just as other children insisted on speaking daily with parents who were detained on May 24, 2006, and who were then deported back to Indonesia.

"Sometimes it is too much to bear," Jane cried.

Like Johan, Franky Toar was also deported to the capital of Jakarta. Franky then traveled 2,000 miles west to be near his few remaining relatives in Langowan. To feed himself, Franky sold firewood. During his first Christmas in Langowan, a Muslim extremist killed a Christian and carved a cross in his body with a knife. Franky worked during the holidays as a guard to protect local churches from robbery and arson, as dozens of local churches had been burned between 1998 and 2006.

When Franky became desperate for food, he asked Roslyn to send him money, even though she had two teenagers to feed, and even

---

[5] Interview with Jane Massie, February 2017.

though these same teenagers, Amanda and Vaidioll, and their mother now faced deportation themselves.[6]

When she should have felt safe at home, Amanda refused to answer knocks at the door unless the visitor had called ahead first. "We're just here to work and live," Amanda said. "We are just hoping for the day when we can be normal as well."

Roslyn and Jane, along with other Indonesian women whose husbands were detained that day and then deported, took the only job they could find with their lack of skills and limited English. They filled cosmetic bottles with nail polish for minimum wage, in a warehouse that housed a factory in Edison, New Jersey. They could no longer afford the rent at Woodbine Gardens. When the women moved, they lost their ability to share cooking, driving, and childcare.

The now-single mothers illegally sublet single rooms in other people's apartments in different towns. Often a mother shared one bed with all her children. When the official renter whose name was on the lease broke the lease, single-mom families had to move again. Living without leases, in new towns, mothers could no longer prove local residency, so their children missed countless days of school. While their husbands' employers had provided health insurance for their families, undocumented Indonesian mothers making minimum wage had to enroll their children in Medicaid, public assistance, and food stamps.

With the gradual erosion of the vibrant community of Indonesians in Avenel, the human and financial costs of detention and deportation accrued slowly.

Looking back, Seth grew sad when he remembered that time. "I was so busy trying to figure out how to fix things that I didn't get a chance to visit those thirty-five people who were detained," he regretted. "Then they were all gone."

By December, many Indonesian families canceled their Christmas celebrations as they mourned their broken homes and the 9,000 miles that separated them from peace. In Avenel, at the Woodbine Gardens Apartments, no decorations were hung in the windows which were kept shut with the shades drawn.

---

[6] Group discussions at the Reformed Church of Highland Park with women whose husbands had been deported, January–March 2017.

CHAPTER 6

Building a Responsive Community: The Background

In Highland Park, 2001 to 2008

The deep and abiding friendship between Seth and Harry formed the center around which the Reformed Church's care for immigrants revolved. Yet, in the first years, no one realized that keeping the Pangemanan family and other Indonesian families together would require the involvement of the entire church and the creation of a far-reaching community to respond to the dire situation that was about to unfold.

From Sunday school teachers to deacons and worship leaders to elderly worshippers to occasional visitors, hearts and minds throughout the congregation would need to soften, listen, and see through the eyes of our friends and neighbors before the congregation could grasp the full measure of the impending disaster.

From the very first day of their ministry at the Reformed Church of Highland Park—ironically, Tuesday, September 11, 2001—Seth and Steph had begun building this kind of responsive community.[1] In their

---

[1] Seth writes, "Our official office hours at our first church began the morning of September 11, 2001. My wife and co-pastor Stephanie and I had only recently

first week, the twenty-five-year-old, newly ordained pastors pivoted from their centuries-old church's "Sunday-only" worship routine and offered a candlelight vigil for terrorist victims as soon as that Thursday.

Lee and Neil Selden, artists and therapists in their early sixties who lived two blocks away, felt drawn to this new kind of church community in its very first days. In their married life they had never attended any church regularly. But before they moved to Highland Park, the Seldens had lived in Lower Manhattan, in the apartment of Lee's sister who had recently died. Rattled and feeling on edge, Lee began calling local churches in hopes that she would find one that was holding a service that addressed the concerns of people affected by the terrorist attacks of 9/11. Stephanie was the only pastor who called her back. Stephanie invited Lee to a vigil the next night in the church that was around the corner from the Seldens' Highland Park apartment. Lee and Neil had often walked past the old brick church, across from their dry cleaner and a convenience store. Never before had they stepped inside.[2]

When the Seldens opened the doors of the church's square bell tower, they walked through an entranceway filled with choir robes hidden behind curtains and found seats in a sparsely populated sanctuary where the sunlight illumined nineteenth-century stained-glass windows. Seth was up front, wearing a black, academic-style minister's robe, and he began the service from a Victorian pulpit. Right in front of Seth, a woman in the first row began to sob uncontrollably. Seth stepped down, sat next to her on the pew bench, and put his arm around her as her shoulders continued to shake. Lee Selden didn't know if the woman was a recent acquaintance—Seth and Steph had just been installed at the church that prior Sunday—or if she was someone who had just walked in from the neighborhood, as Lee had.

Stephanie kept the service going from the lectionary stand. For what seemed to Lee to be about ten minutes, Seth simply sat with the woman. The Seldens had never seen such a demonstration of care in the middle of a worship service. From that point on, they rarely missed a Sunday. Neil, a secular Jew and confirmed Buddhist who would never

---

finished seminary.... We entered the church building just as the director of our seniors program yelled, 'My God, one of the Trade Center towers has been hit. Somebody flew a plane into one of the towers!' Moments later he yelled again down the hall, "It happened again—another plane!—we're under attack!'" (Kaper-Dale, *A Voice for Justice*, xv).

[2] Interview with Lee Selden by phone, April 2017.

formally join as a church member, became one of the church's main recruiters for new members.

The next Sunday, September 16, Carol and Charlie Page, a couple in their late fifties who were nearing early retirement, became discouraged when the new minister of their long-time Episcopal church in their hometown of Piscataway, three miles from Highland Park, failed to mention the terrorist attacks of 9/11 even once during the hour-long service. Carol and Charlie walked out and never returned.

As a strong soprano member of the Highland Park Community Chorus, Carol had been invited to sing in the installation service of the new Reformed Church ministers. She had missed the installation service but she picked up the excited buzz about the young Princeton seminarians, now pastors. The following week, Carol and Charlie worshiped in Highland Park. From that moment on, they became dedicated and beloved congregants. Charlie, a biology professor at nearby Rutgers University, joined Carol, a lifelong singer, as the Reformed Church choir's only male member, standing right next to Seth. Charlie joined the consistory and the church finance team. He and Carol would support the immigration ministries especially at pivotal junctures.[3]

Wendy and Colin Jager had started visiting the Highland Park church in the fall of 2004. They were looking for a community of faith that was dedicated to justice. They drove thirty minutes from their hometown in Plainfield, New Jersey, where Wendy taught English as a second language (ESL) in a public library program called Literacy Volunteers of America.

That was Wendy's first experience with people who didn't speak English. In the first activity Wendy assigned, she asked new students to provide their contact information. If students didn't want to divulge personal information, most likely because they were undocumented, they didn't have to. As a teacher customizing her lessons to the needs of her classroom, it became clear to Wendy that first and foremost her students needed jobs. But because of their immigration status, they had to rely on informal networks. Many worked, as Wendy put it, "around the house" as cleaners, painters, masons—especially the men who came from Mexico.[4]

Colin worked about a mile from the Highland Park church on the College Avenue campus of Rutgers University in New Brunswick

---

[3] Interview with Carol and Charlie Page, April 2017.
[4] Interview with Wendy Jager, March 2017.

where he was a professor of English. As they planned to join the church, they sold their large Plainfield home and purchased a more compact home a few doors from the church.

In early 2005, Wendy and Colin Jager met Harry and Yana Pangemanan at a class for people inquiring about becoming new members. The Jagers' neighbors, Kathy and George Besterczie, an elderly mother and her adult son who lived across the street from the Jagers' new home, also joined the class.

Wendy had learned from her students in Plainfield that new immigrants find great comfort in sticking close to people from their home country. This enabled Wendy to appreciate the tremendous effort and commitment it took for the Pangemanans to communicate with people more broadly than just in their national group of origin.

"As an ESL teacher, I recognized the bravery of Harry and Yana to step away from worship and life that was centered around Indonesians," Wendy explained. "In joining us, Harry and Yana were saying, this is where we live, this is our church, we need to worship in English. And they brought gifts—they didn't just ask for help. They were very generous with their time and talents. They always brought food. When others left straight after worship, Harry and Yana stayed and cleaned up. What they could give they gave with pure generosity. They gave way beyond anything they received."

Wendy felt the Pangemanans' loyalty to the concept of church was remarkable. Harry would shampoo carpets, polish floors, and do any odd jobs that needed to happen. The Pangemanans felt as Wendy did: that church is something very special to care for.

On a June Sunday in 2005, six new congregants stood at the front of the Reformed Church sanctuary, promising to be faithful members who "through worship and service, seek to advance God's purposes here and throughout the world."

CHAPTER 7

Converting Hearts

In Highland Park, 2006 to 2008

It was after the ICE raid in Avenel, sometime later in the summer of 2006, that I became aware of thirty-six-year-old Harry and thirty-eight-year-old Yana sitting in a back pew during a sparsely attended Sunday service at the Reformed Church of Highland Park. Though they had joined the congregation as members the year before, the family sat alone. The parents, Indonesian citizens, were attractive and well-groomed, singing and praying aloud with intensity. Four-year-old Jocelyn, their U.S. citizen daughter, nestled in between.

After the gospel and the sermon, the collection of offerings, and hymns of praise, Pastor Stephanie looked out and asked, "Congregation, what shall we pray for?"

Rev. Stephanie Kaper-Dale, whose name is often shortened to "Steph," grew up in southwest Michigan, in an area densely populated with Reformed churches. Her own family was deeply involved in their Reformed church, attending worship services and multiple programs each week. The churches in her town served as hubs of the community, central to the lives of those in the neighborhood, and in that context a seed for a call to ministry was planted.

A passionate feminist and advocate for justice, Steph got to know the families in the community of central Michigan's migrant workers through her summer jobs. Through those relationships, she worked on her Spanish and became familiar with their struggles.

As the co-pastor of the Highland Park church, Steph took the first rotation as the president of the consistory leadership team. She was especially talented at adapting the intricacies of polity and procedures to enable effective ministry. Steph organized pastoral care and visitation to shut-ins, directed Christian education, oversaw fellowship activities, and provided a steady, non-anxious presence that enriched church functions.

While Stephanie solicited prayers from the congregation that morning, her husband and co-pastor Seth scribbled notes on a prayer list. He had met Stephanie at Hope College, a school in Holland, Michigan, affiliated with her Reformed Church in America denomination. Unlike Stephanie's Michigan family, Seth's Vermont family didn't have strong denominational ties and were more likely to choose a church by the quality of the community than by their denomination.

Toward the end of each service, this ritual of open-ended, spontaneous, and public prayer and petition, the "Prayers of the People," was the main reason many members showed up in the pews of this Highland Park sanctuary.

On that mid-summer Sunday, Harry stood up from his back pew and spilled his immigration nightmare like an inky black stain all over the sanctuary. ICE agents had tracked down his friends. He knew he was next on their list. At every stoplight he feared a police officer would ask for his papers. If he were deported, he couldn't bring Yana and Jocelyn with him. Back in Jakarta, churches were burning. Attorneys took their savings, but nobody had been able to help them.

In the congregation, we Americans had been lulled back into a sense of normalcy since we had no news of ICE since the Avenel raid the previous month.

Despite Harry's thick accent, no one in the mostly white congregation misunderstood. The air dripped with his fear. "I am asking you and I am asking God. I need help," Harry implored us.

"Pray for me. Pray for Yana. Pray for Jocelyn."

I was sitting up front, on the sanctuary's right-hand side, in a pew I had become accustomed to. As Harry spoke, his voice filled me with dread, though I didn't fully grasp how precarious his situation had become. Harry was being pursued by the full force of the federal government. A five-billion-dollar budget fueled the division of Enforcement and Removal Operations (ERO)—the network of agents, detention centers, and airplanes that managed deportations on behalf of ICE, which was part of the Department of Homeland Security. The DHS had been organized with ERO at its center precisely to trap Harry and others like him. U.S. law offered no protection from removal.

To me, Harry sounded like someone caught on the tracks of an approaching train that had lost its brake system. Disaster loomed. I did not want to be there when it happened. A cotton scarf hung about my neck, and I fought a bizarre impulse to stuff my scarf into Harry's mouth. I wanted to do anything to stop Harry from asking for help. Illegal immigration was the last topic I wanted to open in worship.

I was still getting used to my new church and denomination. I had formally joined the church in 2004 and had become a consistory member on June 26, 2006. I was Roman Catholic from birth, and my Christian faith was formed during twelve years of parochial school and three years of graduate school at the Catholic University of America in Washington, DC.

But I owed my life to my new church. So I was in trouble.

Back in 2002, Neil Selden, the wizened poet and social worker who had first come to church with his wife Lee in the first days after 9/11, was my Jewish therapist. In the middle of a counseling session, Neil pushed me to visit the church. We were working on improving my parenting skills with my eighteen-year-old son, Michael. I had never married Michael's father. When Michael was eleven years old, I married my husband, Mark. Now Michael was struggling with severe mental illness. Formerly a top student, Michael refused to complete the basic requirements to graduate from Highland Park High School.

"I feel so alone!" I complained in therapy to Neil.

I can still see the shards of late afternoon sun that cut the Berber carpet between my cozy beige armchair and Neil. Sitting Buddha-style, legs drawn up on the opposing couch, Neil stretched his neck across the divide between us and mapped my expression onto his face. The corners of his mouth, his eyebrows, the creases of his eyes sagged downward in a self-pitying frown.

"I'm so alone!" Neil mimicked me.

I laughed. Neil inhaled and drew his head back.

"OK, Liz, tell me: Where are your people?" Neil asked, his eyes squinting at me.

"My people? You mean, my family?"

"Not your family," Neil responded. "Your people. Where is your church?"

"I have none."

Another glimpse into my personal faith journey: Before Mark and I married, local Catholic churches had shunned Michael and me. I had never married Michael's father, so my son and I did not share a last name. After I taught religion classes for children for a year, I asked the leaders to correct my last name. The nun who ran the Confraternity of Christian Doctrine (CCD) program at Highland Park's Catholic church exclaimed, "You mean Michael is not your brother?" I am a single mom, I replied. I never married Michael's father. When I asked if that was a problem, she expressed her concern about allowing an unmarried mother like me to teach Catholic doctrine. Next, I tried to join a thriving Catholic church in another town, but the pastor required me to get a letter of transfer from the first church. Neither church felt like a community where I wanted to fight for my place. I needed support, not a battle.

Neil was undeterred by ornery Catholics. "You better get yourself over to that little church on South Second Avenue," my therapist scolded. "I go with my wife every week. Those two young blond pastors write some pretty mean sermons. I could sit and listen to them all day long."

Pushing me to attend his church was clearly against therapy protocols, but traditional boundaries were never Neil's strong point. Yet, after years of therapy and multiple therapists, I thought, how often does a therapist throw you a lifeline?

In the spring of 2002, alongside Neil and Lee, I began sporadically attending church services at the Reformed brick church with the tower across the street from my dry cleaner. My young adult son rarely joined me. Instead of participating in worship, Michael would show up afterwards and hang out at coffee hour or pass through the hallways on weekdays. When Michael needed someone to talk to, he hit up Pastor Seth for a cup of coffee. Michael discoursed, somewhat obsessively, with Neil and Seth and any number of elders and deacons about theology and obscure bits of philosophy, ethics, and politics. Everyone at the Reformed Church made time for Michael.

Michael was always welcome.

As Michael turned twenty years old in 2004, his brain disorder exploded. He left home and lived, homeless, on various couches in nearby New Brunswick. When Michael became addicted to marijuana, I feared for his life. In January 2005, Michael's mental state collapsed and, with my assistance, he checked himself into an in-patient facility.

By this time, I was helping to run a home Bible study, and the group prayed for us. When Michael emerged from his program, social workers in that study group counseled him. A year later, Michael was hospitalized again.

During the time for congregational prayers and petitions at the close of worship services, I spoke up often, pleading repeatedly, "Please pray for Michael."

One Sunday after the service, another therapist and social worker whom I had come to know during that in-home Bible study approached me in the pews. He said he couldn't be specific because of privacy regulations, but he had participated in a meeting at Michael's facility.

"I want you to know," he said, holding my hands in both of his to reassure me, "everything is going to be okay."

When Michael left his second in-patient stay, Middlesex County assigned him a case worker who would do all the running around and appointments I had been responsible for. And just in time. By this point, I was a forty-four-year-old mother with a four-year-old daughter and a young baby with extreme colic. I was also the sibling living closest to my elderly father, who was indigent and bipolar, whose health was failing, and who needed permanent, government-supported assisted living.

Michael received a housing voucher, and to me, this seemed miraculous. I will never know how his name was selected from the mass of people whose names filled county waiting lists. But I believe that the prayer and support of my church lifted Michael's case. He was assigned a case worker, a deeply caring social worker named Jim McGovern, who helped Michael rent an apartment, purchase furniture, enroll in Medicaid, apply for food stamps, and sign up with a paralegal to file a claim for Social Security Disability Insurance. Michael's road back to sanity and independence would take another ten years. But there was a road. And we weren't alone.

In the meantime, I had stood in front of the church twice and made commitments. In 2004, I became a member. In 2006, I was ordained to the role of elder on the church leadership council. I had agreed to be "set apart for a ministry of watchful and responsible care for the welfare and order of the church." I would "serve all Christians with advice, consolation, and encouragement."[1]

And, just like Harry, when Michael and I needed help, I had stood up and asked for prayer. Now Harry needed help.

So, what did the church require of me? I was too afraid to find out.

Our hallways had reverberated with immigration crises since 2002, when the Indonesian men asked if they should trust the U.S. government's National Security Entry-Exit Registration System program. Seth had taken me along into the dining hall discussion with Indonesian men, immigration attorneys, and civic leaders. Though I had nothing to offer, I could never forget that night. Then, after the 2006 early morning raid in Avenel, Seth had informed the leadership council, of which I was now a member, that he assumed all legal responsibility for harboring Indonesians in the church. And when the Indonesians returned to their homes with no legal incidents, I felt we had dodged a bullet.

Nevertheless, Harry's desperate prayer of petition from his seat with his family in a back pew of our church was the first time an undocumented person pleaded for help in our English-language worship service. It was a warning sign of terrible things to come. It broke through my wish to maintain a low level of obliviousness. Still, I did nothing, besides hoping it would all blow over.

Then, in 2007, Harry and Yana asked to baptize their second daughter, Christa, in the American congregation. In the Reformed tradition, baptism is part of the public Sunday service. In a key part of the rite, the entire congregation stands and promises to help the child and her parents to keep their baptismal vows. On the day of the baptism, American congregants met Harry's sister Jessy, his mother Clara, and his niece and nephews who lived with Jessy's husband in Ohio. The extended Indonesian family was resplendent in custom-tailored batik dresses and shirts from Indonesia. Yana catered a beautiful Chinese Indonesian lunch for the congregation. The pickiest Americans loved her skinny deep-fried egg rolls and yellow sticky rice.

While Yana and Harry's English was halting, they certainly understood far more than they were comfortable speaking. Congregants got to know them because they would lead heart-rending songs of faith during worship services and because they poured themselves into

---

[1] Reformed Church in America, "Ordination and Installation of Elders and Deacons," accessed August 7, 2023, https://www.rca.org/liturgy/ordination-and-installation-of-elders-and-deacons/.

serving the church. Harry polished floors and repaired buildings. Yana hosted funeral repasts, fundraising dinners, and coffee hours.

Immigration started to feel more personal.

But ICE did not go away. By the fall of 2008, ICE began to arrest people while they were at work, shopping in the grocery store, or dropping off their children at school. While there seemed to be a respite from large raids in people's homes, we regularly heard about individuals being picked up outside buildings before they arrived at work and home. This happened to a dozen people between the raid in 2006 and the end of 2008. Our congregation began to feel like a family experiencing a shared crisis.

In a meeting of elders, Pastor Stephanie shared her deep concern that the Pangemanans were experiencing incredible stress. Harry and Yana had requested someone to meet with them on Sunday mornings before worship to pray with them. Praying aloud with people was not my thing, I rationalized. I was relieved when I didn't need to at that point.

Wendy Jager, now one of our new elders, volunteered. Wendy prayed aloud with clarity and fervor. Somehow, she seemed to spontaneously capture the most important matters that weighed on everyone's hearts and minds.

Wendy, the former ESL coach, was now also the director of the Sunday school program, after having taken the church membership class with Harry and Yana. Each Sunday, twenty minutes before service, Wendy met with the Pangemanan family in a small nook off the main hallway that we called the prayer room.

When it came to their immigration crisis, Wendy didn't try to talk with Harry and Yana about their complex and demanding situation. Wendy said praying is hard when you are overwhelmed by fear. You don't know what to pray for. You can't utter a prayer. So, for Wendy, a lot of prayer is listening and then putting feelings, fears, and anxieties, not situational details, into words, so people feel a connection with God.

"I don't need to have any specific expertise or advice," Wendy explained. You make yourself available, Wendy said, and you try to remain present amid pain and fear and to verbalize what you've seen in your prayer partners as a means to communicate with God. It helps to affirm the things we know to be true first, and then ask for things.[2]

---

[2] Interview with Wendy Jager, March 2017.

Wendy was wary of over-promising. You don't want to set up prayer to provide false hope, she insisted. Instead, through verbalizing, Wendy tried to give her prayer partners something that was very intimate, because they were allowing her to sit with them in weakness and vulnerability.

For Wendy, the act of prayer is the prayer—it's the practice. We wait for something magic to happen, but the prayer itself is the magic. When Wendy prayed with someone, first she quieted down and surveyed her surroundings. "I listen," she said. "I do not ask questions, except this one: What do you want me to pray for?"

Sometimes Yana would say, I'm scared, I'm so scared for Harry's safety. I'm scared about what will happen to my kids. Wendy focused on noticing, listening, and reflecting back what she heard.

When thinking about her experiences praying with others, Wendy recalled a vivid moment in the sanctuary during one of the congregation's monthly healing liturgies. An elderly leader, Delores Van Liew, raised her hand for Wendy to come over and anoint her husband with oil that had been blessed by the congregation.

Poor Joe Van Liew was bent over in their pew. Wendy saw he was holding in his hands the picture of his deceased son in formal dress as a fireman. Wendy started crying. She couldn't pray, she said. "I was supposed to be offering a blessing, but I couldn't offer anything besides presence."

It's hard to overestimate the value of physical presence. Wendy believes we have a real need to develop a responsive community, where each person is trying to look beyond their own lives, working to be attentive to others.

"I've become more comfortable with moments of silence in the prayer," Wendy explained. "This is a time to allow God's presence to be felt. Deep listening is almost a withdrawal. Then, we verbalize our fears and state God's relationship to us: God, you know Yana is really scared right now. She cannot quiet her thoughts."

The goal, Wendy said, is to hand over the troubles by putting them into words that ask for God's presence. You must be careful, she warned. Yana still might be scared both when we pray and after we pray. It's not that the fear goes away. But it is shared. A prayer is a shared complaint made to heaven.

"The next step," according to Wendy, "is then to add the backdrop of all the things we know." God, we know you are stronger than our fears, Wendy would say. We do not know what comes next, God, but you always have good plans for our lives. God, your ways are loving ways. After all, Wendy said, God knows our fears and God is always with us. There is nothing you can do to separate yourself from God.

Finally, then, there is giving thanks—and giving thanks, according to Wendy, is your chance to remember all the evidence. Actively remember, together, to see the hand of God in our lives—even in the times when we cannot feel or see the hand of God. You don't feel God working now. Yet we can still affirm: even though I don't see how, God is at work in my life. Even when I don't see or feel God, it's important to say these things aloud. This gives you the courage to keep going.

Wendy kept circling back to the importance of the physical act of being silent together. Focus on your presence. Put yourself in God's presence, Wendy advised, and try to be a link for another person who has so much anxiety or pain or loss that they feel they just can't be with God.

One Sunday after the service, during coffee hour, Wendy could tell Yana was experiencing a lot of anxiety. She asked, Yana, would you like to pray with me? Knowing that Yana was close with another congregant, Wendy asked her, "Mary, would you come with us?"

But Mary McLaine was nervous and replied, "I can join you, but I don't want to do the praying." For Wendy, though, that was fine. Mary had been worried that her presence would be distracting, but Wendy felt that Mary's very presence was a kind of prayer that said, I'm sitting with you, Yana, I am with you in your unease.

Mary, a professional researcher and paralegal, had taken the lead in investigating the legal ramifications of sanctuary. Mary spent time visiting with Yana every week, and the two women developed a deep friendship. Horrified by Harry and Yana's precarious position, Mary created a display board that introduced the Pangemanans and their plight. She visited local churches to explain their complicated story and seek their support.

Alongside Mary, a growing group of congregants began meeting as the immigration committee. Rev. Patty Fox, our new associate minister, led worship services and education sessions on the biblical imperatives to welcome refugees. At one service, Pastor Patty handed out a list of Bible verses that specifically address the welcome of foreigners and strangers. The length of the list astounded me. The biblical evidence of God's love for foreigners was overwhelming.

As we learned to rely on one another, our faith, courage, and community was evolving and changing.

CHAPTER 8

Caught

In Avenel, January 12, 2009

On winter mornings, Yana would return home from her third-shift, night-time job where she operated a factory machine just as Harry was leaving for his first-shift, day-time job where he managed shipments in a warehouse. Their habit was to meet outside their new first-floor apartment to say hello and goodbye in the parking lot. The morning ritual enabled them to seamlessly exchange parental duties without waking up their kids. Yana might even get to close her eyes before the day began for her daughters, six-year-old Jocelyn and two-year-old Christania, whom everyone called Christa.

On Monday morning, January 12, as Yana arrived home from her night shift and Harry Pangemanan prepared to get into his car and leave for work, ICE agents were waiting outside their Avenel apartment.

They were hiding in plain sight.

Yana looked up and saw two agents approach Harry from behind, a man and a woman. "Do you have an immigration problem?" the male agent asked Harry.

Before Harry registered with the Rumsfeld-Ashcroft NSEERS program, he and Yana had filed for asylum. But incompetent attorneys, on whom they had spent thousands of dollars, had compromised their legal status.[1]

In the cold morning light, ICE agents led him and Yana back to their apartment. Entering the home, they told Harry and Yana to sit down. But Yana didn't sit. She was searching for her phone. The female agent raised her voice in irritation and abruptly yelled, "Sit now!"[2]

Yana clutched her phone in one hand and with the other hurriedly scrolled through her contacts.

"I am looking for my pastor's phone number!" Yana exclaimed as she took a seat. But before she could hit dial, the agent barked again.

"Who's in the house?"

"Nobody! Just me and the kids. They are sleeping," Yana pleaded, hoping to keep their voice levels low so the girls wouldn't wake up.

Both agents looked into the room where the girls slept peacefully. The female agent told Yana to wake up her daughters and get them dressed. Besides Yana and Harry, the agents would take the girls with them, too.

"No," the male agent instructed his partner. "Those children are too little to take with us." Turning to Yana he said, "When your kids wake up, get them ready and come see us at the ICE office in Newark." Then he told Harry to stand up and put his hands behind his back. The agent shackled Harry's hands in cuffs.

At that moment Jocelyn ran into the room, her eyes full of sleep, and wrapped her arms around her father's waist. Because of the cuffs, Harry couldn't hug back. Harry bent down and looked into his daughter's eyes. "I am leaving," he told his daughter.

The agents led the way and Harry walked out backwards, facing Jocelyn the whole time, hoping he could spare his four-year-old the sight of his hands in cuffs behind his back.

From their apartment window, Jocelyn and Yana watched ICE agents load Harry into the back of their black sedan.

---

[1] Interview with Yana Pangemanan, February 2017.
[2] Interview with Yana Pangemanan by Jocelyn Pangemanan, January 2023.

CHAPTER 9

Resistance is Futile

In Central New Jersey, January 2009

God's call is irresistible, according to the witness of unwilling prophets like Jonah, Isaiah, Hosea, Micah, and Jeremiah from the Hebrew Bible. According to a central tenet of Reformed doctrine, God's grace is irresistible, too. It took three years of stress, terror, and pursuit by federal agents before many members—including me—came to understand that the very immigration ministry we resisted, feared, and fled was in fact our own flavor of irresistible grace.

In January 2009, the entire Reformed Church congregation received an unmistakable call to help an undocumented immigrant who had become part of our family of faith. In the wake of the imminent destruction of a church family who had become central to our community, I was one of many church members who found we could no longer resist getting involved in our country's broken immigration system.

Agents drove Harry to the Elizabeth Detention Center, a warehouse just outside Newark Liberty International Airport that had been converted into a privately run prison for hundreds of immigrants.

They had instructed Yana to report to the Newark immigration office within two hours. Members of the church intervened and Yana was able to stay home to care for her daughters, provided she reported to ICE monthly. [1]

The next Sunday, Seth's voice broke as he told the congregation how Harry had been wearing a blue coverall as they visited through a Plexiglass visitor window at Elizabeth Detention Center. "Our congregation made a sacramental vow," Seth reminded us. At Christa's baptism, Harry and Yana had promised to nurture her in our church. As a congregation, we had stood up in our pews and promised to give them the strong support of God's family. Harry and Yana need a lot of help, Seth explained. To get to work, Yana needed childcare. To hold on to the Avenel apartment, somehow, they would need to replace Harry's salary.

I don't remember that Sunday's sermon. I was thinking about a story about an onion that I'd read in *The Brothers Karamazov* by Fyodor Dostoevsky. It went like this: One day, a nasty old woman, who had never been kind, dug up an onion and gave it to a beggar. When she died, an angel pitied the old woman and asked God to rescue her from hellfire. The angel mentioned the onion. Offer her an onion, God suggested. The angel held out the onion and the woman hung on for dear life. Others arose from the deep and clung to the old woman. But the nasty old woman kicked them off, lost her grip, and fell to oblivion.

I was wondering if I had been given an onion.

My mind floated back to a year or two before, when a leader named Jean Stockdale, who was a true saint of the Reformed church since well before Seth and Stephanie arrived, had hired me to set up thirty-minute interviews with first-generation immigrants around town. The goal was to capture the life stories of neighbors who had global roots. The project was the brainstorm of a local philanthropist named Ralph Voorhees, who was also a church elder. Ralph hoped that after we collected stories, we could then recruit interviewees to become volunteer interpreters for patients at Robert Wood Johnson University Hospital, where he served on the board of the hospital's foundation.

I was a stay-at-home mom, and with Ralph's financial support, I received seventy-five dollars per interview. It was a great way to get to know my neighbors and make some cash. A Danish mom who was a fine artist agreed to be interviewed if I paid her seventy-five dollars

---

[1] SKD, 36.

for one of her paintings—a deal I could not refuse. The elderly woman who doled out generous portions of Sedutto ice cream at the Corner Confectionery at Raritan Avenue and North Third had always rubbed me the wrong way until she agreed to tell me the story of why she left Ukraine. We cried together.

I completed nine interviews, but the overall project went nowhere. First-generation immigrants had no energy left over to volunteer as hospital translators. Nevertheless, I gained experience that would serve me well. All those interviews taught me that there was no easy way to encapsulate a life story in a half-hour interview. People who had lived through a major life-change like immigration left behind all they knew for everything they hoped for. A full and complete life had been interrupted. A terrible decision had been reached: to cut oneself off from everything one knew and then start all over again with nothing. Loved ones were lost. Careers abandoned. And then a brand-new life started from scratch.

My interviews began to focus on one question: Why did you leave? That question was a magic key that revealed treasures. Even if you talked to people from the same country, from the same time, their answers were completely different.

Among the neighbors I interviewed was Jack, who had run a large hardware store a decade earlier in Bergen County in northern New Jersey. Though Jack had retired, the hardware business was in his blood. Slowly, Jack was transforming the garage of his Highland Park home into a depot where local contractors could pick up supplies.

Jack lived in a corner house at a busy intersection. For a year, the school district's "purple bus" picked up my kindergarten-aged daughter and dropped her off in Jack's driveway. To my chagrin, Jack handed my girls lollipops. Jack and I had shared more than a year's worth of sidewalk chats. But as our first formal interview progressed, I was shocked to discover that Jack was a survivor of the Holocaust. While Americans his age were heading to college, Jack went to a work camp run by an invading army. Every detail was like pulling teeth. Jack wouldn't tell me the name of his home country. "Country, what country?" Jack asked me. "I didn't have any country. I was Jewish," he balked. I could only guess that he had left Poland.

"Language, what language? I spoke Jewish." Jack meant Yiddish. He became talkative only when I asked about his life in the United States. In the late 1940s, he began his hardware business in North

Jersey suburbs. Because he had no car, Jack used mass transit to get to his clients' homes, carrying lumber and building supplies on city buses. That interview went nowhere. Jack cut it off after ten minutes. But it gave me a sense of the territory.

Immigrants were survivors. And I had no idea what kind of trauma they had experienced.

That Sunday after Harry was detained, immediately after service, an ad hoc team met around the shiny grand piano in the front of the sanctuary to address the challenges of Harry and Yana's situation: paying rent without Harry's salary, providing childcare so Yana could go to work; ensuring a steady flow of visits for Harry in detention; collecting donations to pay a retainer for a new attorney.

I volunteered for nothing. But I watched from my pew.

After the next week's service, Seth reported that the biggest need the lawyers had was to ask someone to write two detailed narratives of Harry and Yana's life stories—how they grew up, why they left Indonesia, why they can't go back—and to list the steps taken in their legal cases. Their stories needed to be logically separated in case their legal cases went in different directions.

Yikes, I thought, different directions? I feared that Harry could be deported while Yana remained here, a single, working mother with two U.S.-citizen children. By 2009, three years after that Avenel raid, we had come to understand how deportation played out, breaking community ties, destroying families, and putting children at risk.

Finally, this was a job that I felt suited for and perhaps even called to do. Instead of joining the procession into the dining hall for coffee hour, I approached Seth. "I would like to write the personal narratives," I volunteered.

Before staying home with my second daughter, I was an independent consultant for the back offices of the New York Times Company. I didn't work in the newsroom, but I visited it to interview their staff members. My job was to make a case for enormous infrastructure projects that would enable departments to go paperless. An otherwise tedious task was laced with terror. Employees were haunted by images of reams of paper endlessly floating a thousand feet downwards against a brilliant blue sky in the demise of the Twin Towers. Then, for months after 9/11, all U.S. mail and packages received by the Times were steam-boiled amidst widespread mailings of white powder that contained deadly bacteria called anthrax. Finally, Times reporter Jayson Blair faked interviews and easily falsified paper travel vouchers.[2] The lengthy reports I wrote won corporate buy-in for electronic systems.

Surely, I could make a case for Harry and Yana.

Seth looked at me dubiously. "Are you sure?" he asked. "Harry's story will be tough. You'll have to visit Elizabeth Detention Center. Maybe hang out with Harry's mother and sister."

"I'm sure," I affirmed.

Maybe writing these stories would be my onion.

---

[2] Dan Barry et al., "CORRECTING THE RECORD; Times Reporter Who Resigned Leave Long Trail of Deception," *New York Times*, May 11, 2003, https://www.nytimes.com/2003/05/11/us/correcting-the-record-times-reporter-who-resigned-leaves-long-trail-of-deception.html.

CHAPTER 10

A Light in the Darkness

In Elizabeth, New Jersey, January to March 2009

Just off Exit 13A on the New Jersey Turnpike, a group of nondescript warehouses holds FedEx packages, Peterbilt truck parts, paving equipment, and lumber. Nearby stands a windowless industrial building that the U.S. government adapted to hold up to four hundred people in indefinite immigration detention.

On every trip I had made to Newark Liberty Airport, I passed this house of horrors without knowing it. And until I stepped inside, I couldn't believe a place this inhumane could exist so close to my own backyard.[1]

My friend José Morais, who led our church's immigration committee, had already visited several times. When José offered to drive me, I accepted, grateful and relieved. Never before had I visited a prison. We chose a blustery night in early February. The gate in the chain-link fence surrounding the visitor parking lot swung open. As

---

[1] This account is drawn from two articles about my visits to Elizabeth Detention Center that I contributed to a local newspaper called *The Mirror: Reflecting Highland Park's Community* in March and April 2008.

José pulled into a parking space where the initials CCA were the only visible markings on the big box building we were about to enter. CCA, or Corrections Corporation of America, the country's largest private jailor, ran this holding center on behalf of U.S. Immigration and Customs Enforcement.

As José instructed me, the essentials—water bottle, notepad and pen, cell phone—stayed in my purse, locked in his car. Visitors were allowed to carry only ID inside. We crossed a road and entered a large, harshly lit hall full of stackable plastic chairs that scraped against dirty linoleum tinged with the night's ice, snow, and mud. We stood in line behind the winter coats of other visitors to reach a number dispenser, deli-counter-style,[2] next to the visitor window.

Ahead of us, people turned in money orders. Yana had warned me that detainees couldn't receive toiletries or goods from outside. Everything they needed had to be purchased from the center, including snacks and phone cards to contact their lawyers and loved ones and to raise funds for their legal battles. José and I each took a number and sat down.

More than once, José said, when he had been there before, so many people came to see their loved ones that visitors from our church never made it inside to see detainees. But that night, we were lucky. Severe weather had deterred visitors from coming out. An officer called our numbers right away.

We approached a "customer service" window where a form asked us to list our names and addresses and then add the A-number, the Alien number, of the people we hoped to visit. I wrote Harry's A-number. José wrote the A-numbers of Harry's newest friends. We handed over our IDs.

I pulled open a door to a new hallway populated by armed guards. José and I deposited our coats on a conveyor belt and walked through a metal detector. A sign warned: Be prepared to be frisked.

Once through the detector, our path stopped short. We stood facing what I thought was a wall until a guard pulled out a key on a chain and a sliding security door opened slowly. We walked into a chamber that felt like an elevator to nowhere. From outside the chamber, the guard warned us to be patient—a second door would open when the first door sealed shut.

---

[2] Jocelyn Pangemanan noted while editing this chapter that the description of that deli-counter number dispenser brought back a lot of memories of visiting her dad.

A Light in the Darkness   65

As the first door closed, my pulse raced. I closed my eyes and muffled an urge to cry out. My shoulders tightened in a shiver of fear. But the second wall opened as promised and we emerged into the visitors' hall.

An amateurish mural splashed garish blue paint across a back wall, depicting the New York City skyline, including the World Trade Center towers targeted on 9/11. In the places where cartoonish airplanes crashed into the towers, tongues of fire licked the buildings. It gave me the creeps. Jean Stockdale later told me she heard that detainees had painted this mural. After all, the terrorist events of 9/11 had been used to justify not only that warehouse but the building of the entire behemoth Department of Homeland Security.

Most people inside had not been charged with a crime. Living in the U.S. without papers that authorize your presence was a civil offense. Entering without a visa or overstaying a visa was a misdemeanor. Nevertheless, living conditions for people in the Elizabeth Detention Center exceeded the severity of a federal prison.[3]

Forty men at a time shared what was called a dorm room: a wide-open space with exposed toilets and showers along the back wall. Each dorm room held ten "bed sets" where four men lay separated by knee walls. There was a bank of tables with chairs. The lights never dimmed. There was no privacy. At all times, men were completely exposed. Each detainee was permitted an hour each day in a room with a skylight and another hour in the visitors' hall, but only if someone came to see them.

The dismal visitors' hall had no more than twenty stalls. On a more crowded night, all the visitor stalls were occupied, and, as José had experienced previously, some visitors who traveled a long distance did not get their turn to see their loved ones before the detainees' 9 p.m. curfew.

The facility housed more than 300 men and only a few dozen women. Genders were separated, except in this receiving hall. On my first visit, a large Muslim family that included young girls wearing

---

[3] The ways in which immigration detention centers exceeded the punishing conditions of the federal prison system are documented by Dora B. Schriro in "Immigration Detention Overview and Recommendations," U.S. Department of Homeland Security, October 6, 2009, https://www.nytimes.com/interactive/projects/documents/immigration-detention-overview-and-recommendations. This report was the most comprehensive review of the immigration detention system to date. See especially the sections on Detention Management, Programs Management, Medical Care, and Special Populations, pages 22–28.

hijab headscarves and plaid school uniforms crowded around a visitor booth. They were talking by phone with a female detainee who was visible on the other side of the Plexiglass. The girls were crying.

In another stall, a woman with a toddler, an infant, and two elderly people whom I imagined could be grandparents visited a man who might have been her husband. The toddler grew upset and began to throw the kind of fit I was used to at home. I fought an urge to ask if I could hold the little one and try to entertain her. Their language sounded foreign to me, but the toddler's frustration was perfectly clear. Who could blame her? She voiced the agony none of us dared speak aloud.

Since I had written down Harry's A-number when I requested to visit, I was surprised when another detainee, in the same kind of faded blue coverall that Seth had described during his sermon, appeared before me. He introduced himself as Peter from Kenya. "This is the worst thing that has ever happened to me," Peter complained over the intercom phone that enabled us to speak across a Plexiglass divider. "And I have seen many atrocities," he added. Peter had been detained in Elizabeth for ten months. He was scared to go home, but he felt he could not endure life in detention much longer. To me, Peter seemed to show signs of mental decompensation. I tried to imagine ten months without sunshine, fresh air, or darkness.

When Peter moved over to speak with José, I sat in my booth alone and waited. In the gap between visitors, I remembered a scene from the classic tale by the ancient poet Homer. In that story, Odysseus digs a pool where he can pour libations and visit with souls who had departed to the underworld. Like Odysseus peering into the shadows, I wondered who would appear next behind the Plexiglass. It would be a complete surprise.

A man from the Congo approached my booth. He didn't speak English, but his French was flawless. José had hoped that, with my paltry school-girl French, we might bond. We did our best.

Toward the end of the night's visitor session, finally Harry approached my Plexiglass booth. I almost didn't recognize him. He looked frail and haggard in his dismal blue prison jumpsuit.

Harry said he couldn't sleep with the lights on all the time. Just to get his blood flowing again, he had started exercising in his "dorm." He did calisthenics in place. He jogged along the chamber's perimeter. A yoga teacher in our congregation had mailed him a yoga routine he could do in a tight area. In prison you can learn a language or get a GED.

But in Elizabeth detention, there were no classes. No activities. Harry said he and his bedfellows made up games they could play together.

Visits with Harry's daughters, U.S. citizens who were two and six, were difficult for Harry, behind the Plexiglass, speaking over the intercom phones. He didn't really want his daughters to see him that way. But Yana couldn't stay home. Jocelyn would stand on the small table provided in front of the Plexiglass and place her hand over the glass. On the other side, her father would place his hand on top of hers.

"I would often keep my hand on the glass for the entire fifteen minutes that were allotted," Jocelyn remembered fourteen years later.[4]

Yana was also in danger of deportation, but she was permitted to continue to work. Even so, the family could not subsist on her salary alone. If Harry were deported, Yana might be forced to rely on public assistance and Medicaid for her daughters. If Harry and Yana were both deported, Yana thought it most likely that their girls would go with them to Yana's mother's poverty-stricken hometown on the island where Yana had grown up. Once there, Yana knew they would receive inadequate healthcare (none of Jocelyn's asthma treatments would be available) and education and live as members of a minority subject to intense discrimination. Their Christian faith would be their greatest liability.

Decades later, I have yet to meet a persecuted Indonesian Christian who was especially subdued about their faith.

A few weeks before my visit to the Elizabeth Detention Center, Pastor Seth had visited Harry and found a palpable change in Harry's always-positive demeanor. He wondered: how could he help Harry keep hope alive? Then Seth got an idea. Seth asked Harry to do him a favor. "Would you do something for me, Harry?" Seth asked, knowing that Harry was almost incapable of saying no to his pastor and friend.

"Be a light for everyone inside."

By the time I visited, Harry was getting busy, encouraging others, finding out their stories, seeing who needed visitors. Harry decided to invite men who did not share a single common language to join in a Bible study. This reminded Harry of Seth's Wednesday morning Bible study in the church parlor, where, despite the language divide, he had shared questions and faith experiences with other members. The detainee group grew from an initial few to sometimes as many as fifteen men whom ICE had deposited in Elizabeth as they arrived from home countries around the globe.

[4]   Notes provided by Jocelyn Pangemanan on a draft, February 2023.

Harry was one of the lucky ones at the Elizabeth Detention Center. Every day he received at least one piece of mail. He had the support of a church community, friends, employers, and a legal team. Many, many others arrived at the Newark airport all alone. In Bible study, Harry would talk about his faith, his family, his church, and the congregants who visited him nightly. Detainees who had no visitors asked if Harry's church members would visit with them, too.

One of Harry's faithful visitors was elder Franco Juricic. Franco had a demanding job in the finance department of a large pharmaceutical company and a crazy commute along New Jersey's clogged roadways. He was the father of one-year-old twins, volunteered at the church, played ice hockey, and trained for marathons. That winter, it was a stroke of fate that Franco happened to have the time to travel to Elizabeth Detention Center to visit with Harry.

Two and a half months before Harry was detained, Franco had been training for the New York City Marathon when he was diagnosed with pancreatic cancer. Instead of running the marathon on that first November Sunday in 2008, Franco stood up in his pew during the Prayers of Petition. Wearing a drab trench coat, looking frail and jaundiced, Franco explained to our congregation that he had just been handed a deadly diagnosis.

Like Harry, and like me, too, Franco used this time during the prayers of the people to plead aloud with God and his church to help him.

Afterwards, Franco said his mother, who had been born and raised in Croatia, was mystified. "Why do you have to share such private information with everyone?" she asked Franco. But Franco did not hesitate to entrust the whole congregation with his intensely private health situation. In this public moment, Franco shared both his extreme vulnerability and his absolute trust.

After investigating treatment options, Franco and his wife Jacquelyn opted for aggressive surgery. Just before his scheduled procedure, Franco invited all his friends and family to join them at the next week's Eucharistic service at the Reformed church. When that Sunday arrived, the church was packed. Coffee hour was the closest to the miracle of the loaves and fishes that I have ever witnessed. Jacquelyn's dear friend Cathy Proctor showed me the plates she had set aside in the kitchen to ensure Franco and Jacquelyn would get something to eat. Just like a wedding, I thought.

That January, while Harry was detained, Franco was still recovering from the surgery that seemed to have been successful in rooting out his cancer. As Franco started a regimen of chemotherapy and radiation, he remained on short-term disability. Congregants would spy Franco walking very slowly to services and meetings at the church on South Second from his house a few blocks away on North Third. Though his abdominal muscles needed to knit back together, Franco steadfastly refused car rides. He was planning his next marathon training. Thoughtfully and carefully, Franco used this span of time to reflect on his recovery from illness and how he wanted to live the rest of his life. That time of reflection included frequent visits with Harry.

Later, when Franco thought about why he was drawn to those wintry visits at Elizabeth Detention Center, Franco realized that he had just experienced the scare of his life. In his battle with pancreatic cancer, Franco grappled with the fact that he might not be around to care for his twin children, a beautiful son and daughter, whose first birthday he and Jacquelyn had just celebrated. Harry also had two children. Harry's daughter Christa was the same age as Franco's twins. Harry was imprisoned, worrying about his children and unable to care for them in any way. If he were deported, he might never again hug his children. Franco completely related to Harry's predicament.[5]

---

[5] Interview with Franco Juricic, August 2017.

CHAPTER 11

A Wing and a Prayer

In New Jersey and Washington, March 29, 2009

At 5 a.m. on Harry's sixty-eighth day in the Elizabeth Detention Center, he was awoken by an agent from ICE who told him to gather his things in a bag. The agent then handcuffed Harry and put him on a plane at Newark Airport. Harry called his wife and said he was afraid he was being deported. Then he called Seth, who was in the middle of an early morning breakfast meeting.

"Pastor, I think my time is up," Harry told Seth.

Seth called Stephanie, who told him to stop at the house for his clerical collar before heading to Newark. He hated wasting an extra three minutes, but he guessed Steph was right. He put on his clerical collar and, along with the person he was meeting for coffee, sped to the airport. He was dropped at the door, then ran through the airport lobby.

Like Harry, Seth assumed Harry was being deported. Strangely, though, he could find no flights scheduled to depart for Indonesia. Then Seth's phone rang. It was Harry, boarding a plane for Seattle-Tacoma International Airport in the west coast state of Washington.

Seth reached the airport security line and begged to be let through. Quickly and desperately, he explained, "The U.S. government is breaking up a family, and I need to tell the father that we love him and that we'll do everything in our power to be supportive of their girls." The woman at security told Seth to go to the information booth and ask to get a special visitor's pass. Seth did as he was told and was granted the pass.

By the time Seth arrived at the right gate, the plane doors had closed. He asked the agent at the desk if Immigration had gotten on the plane with anyone. She said they had.

"I pleaded with her," Seth explained later, "I told her that I was Harry's pastor, and that after sixteen years in this country he was being pulled away from his wife and his two little girls. I explained that when we baptized the little one we made vows to her, saying that we would support her parents as they raised her in the faith." Seth begged the manager to let him on. She responded: "FAA rules prohibit anyone getting on a plane without a ticket."

Another airline employee approached Seth and commiserated. "I know what they're going through," she said with a strong Irish brogue. "My brother was here for years and then he was deported. It's terrible what we're doing to people."

Seth thanked her for her concern and said that he was just going to stand by the window, praying for the plane and praying for Harry. He stood there and prayed while intermittently dialing Yana and Harry's attorney to let them know what was happening.

"Father," the Irish-American employee interrupted Seth. She seemed to mistake Seth, with his clerical collar, for a Catholic priest. "Follow me," she said, and walked him to the plane doors, which opened from the inside. The plane was full. Harry sat at the very back, handcuffed between two ICE agents, and watched his pastor walk down the aisle. When Seth caught his eye, a look of great joy came over Harry's face.[1]

"How the hell did he get in here?" one agent asked Harry.

Harry kept his eyes riveted on Seth, lifted his handcuffs, and pointed to heaven.

As Seth drew nearer, the two big men on either side of Harry stood up and retreated to the area near the bathrooms, making room for Seth to sit down with Harry. Immediately Seth clasped Harry's hand and told him that he knew Harry was losing hope. This is so hard, Seth

---

[1] Interview with Harry Pangemanan, February 2017.

said, but if Harry landed in Seattle and was put in another facility, he needed to stay strong and keep up the fight for at least two weeks.

"Harry, you are going to Tacoma," Seth told him. "It's a very large detention center with up to 1,500 detainees. They are going to pressure you into returning to Indonesia."

Press releases from ICE boasted about its cost-saving measures to rent 747 planes at SeaTac Airport, fill them with deportees, and skip across Asia, dropping people off in capital cities.[2]

"I know that," Harry replied.

"All I'm asking is that you give me two weeks. Just two weeks," Seth begged. "Can you hold on for two more weeks, Harry?"

Immigration detention was designed to snuff out hope, as the church immigration team had begun to learn. More than one detainee whom church members visited had been discouraged from exerting their rights and had succumbed to pressure to return to their home country.

The first person I visited at Elizabeth Detention Center had just given up. In Kenya, Peter had been caught up in the political, economic, and humanitarian crisis that erupted after his country's former president was declared the winner of a highly contested election. To escape, Peter flew to the U.S. with a work visa and a committed employer. He worked legally for one year until his employer laid him off. When Peter walked into an immigration office to find out how he could protect his status while he looked for a new job, he was slapped into handcuffs and driven to the windowless Elizabeth Detention Center, where conditions felt like torture. After ten grueling months of isolation, helplessness, monotony, and humiliation, Peter dropped his asylum case and begged his ICE officer to arrange for him to go home, even though it entailed great risk. ICE flew Peter to Nairobi and left him without any money or shelter. When he landed in Nairobi, Peter called the church's immigration team leader, José Morais, from a borrowed cell phone. He was penniless and homeless but relieved to breathe fresh air and feel the sun on his face for the first time in almost a year.

Conditions in Tacoma would be challenging. Harry would live among strangers. There would be no more church visits. Harry would lead no more multilingual Bible studies as he did in Elizabeth, where

---

[2] "ICE Air Operations Fact Sheet," U.S. Immigration and Customs Enforcement, May 6, 2022, https://www.ice.gov/factsheets/ice-air-operations.

not only the detainees but also the guards had taken to calling Harry "the mayor." Worst of all, Harry would never see his family.

But Harry agreed to wait in Tacoma for two weeks before giving up. It was his only chance if he ever wanted to parent his daughters and live with his wife again. Later, Seth recalled thinking, "If two weeks came and went, and we couldn't find a solution for Harry, we would help him in whatever way possible to start life again in Indonesia."[3]

On the plane, Seth and Harry prayed aloud together, for Harry's kids, for his wife, for his spirit. They prayed that God would open some door that they hadn't yet thought of.

Then Seth walked off the plane. Harry flew off into oblivion and Seth began the struggle of his life to find one person in the U.S. government who could reverse Harry's trajectory.

Already, he and other church members had reached a dead end with U.S. congressmen. Frank Pallone, U.S. Representative (Democrat) for the church's district, and Leonard Lance, U.S. Representative (Republican) for Avenel, both were sympathetic and supported the church's advocacy for Harry. But they said they were powerless at this point to reverse the ICE process. Both told Seth, "My hands are tied."

Seth figured his only chance was to find someone in the Obama administration who would listen to his story and set Harry free. But it didn't help that this happened to be every pastor's busiest season: the week before Palm Sunday.

While Seth drove to the airport that day, I joined church members who rushed to Yana, surrounding her with love and support. From the place where we found her, lying on a mattress on her bedroom floor, we used my laptop to Google the Tacoma facility to see where Harry was going. I contacted my younger brother who lives in Seattle to let him know Harry was on his way.

My brother Robby had never met Harry and Yana, but at that moment, it felt important that Harry would know one caring person in the state.

Jocelyn was at school in Avenel, so I drove two-year-old Christa to Highland Park where Jacquelyn Juricic offered to care for her and where Christa could play with Jacquelyn and Franco Juricic's twins.

After noon, the church newsletter arrived by email, announcing the church would hold a prayer vigil at Elizabeth Detention Center that evening where they would celebrate communion.

---

[3] SKD, 38.

ICE had broken our body of Christ, and church members scrambled to the place where they had ripped Harry from the middle of our community.

Members of other immigration advocacy organizations, including First Friends of NJ and NY and the American Friends Service Committee, would join church members there to protest, sing, pray, and share in communion.

CHAPTER 12

A Broken Communion

In Elizabeth and Highland Park, March 29, 2009

It killed me, but on the evening that our church protested against ICE moving Harry to Tacoma, I could not go to the detention center.

The Reformed Church had helped me and other local parents with a student-led project to raise money for a school in Zambia. In that south-central African nation, a women's farming collective ran a school for AIDS victims and orphans just outside of Lusaka, the country's capital. Several fifth graders had taken ownership of the project and dedicated the elementary school's annual talent show that night to raising funds and educating Highland Park families about the Zambian school.

That night, I had to be in Highland Park.

During the afternoon, I sat at Bartle Elementary School with a team of students who were painting Project Zambia posters, wracking my brain for how I could help get the word out about Harry.

I thought about immigration detention stories I had been reading in the *New York Times* by a reporter named Nina Bernstein.

That past Christmas, Nina published a terrifying story about Central Falls, Rhode Island, and the Donald W. Wyatt Detention

Facility, an institution that Nina described as "built on the hope that it would revive the city's economy." Nina described how people who lived nearby detention centers were apathetic about who was housed inside them until they turned out to be neighbors:

> Few in this threadbare little mill town gave much thought to the Donald W. Wyatt Detention Facility, the maximum-security jail beside the public ball fields at the edge of town. Even when it expanded and added barbed wire, Wyatt was just the backdrop for Little League games, [the facility's] name stitched on the caps of the team it sponsored. Then people began to disappear: the leader of a prayer group at St. Matthew's Roman Catholic Church; the father of a second grader at the public charter school; a woman who mopped floors in a Providence courthouse. After days of searching, their families found them locked up inside Wyatt only blocks from home, but in a separate world. In this mostly Latino city, hardly anyone had realized that in addition to detaining the accused drug dealers and mobsters everyone heard about, the jail held hundreds of people charged with no crime, people caught in the nation's crackdown on illegal immigration. Fewer still knew that Wyatt was a portal into an expanding network of other jails, bigger and more remote, all propelling detainees toward deportation with little chance to protest.[1]

It occurred to me that our church's story was an antidote for the kind of listlessness that worried Nina. Our local community had finally risen in protest. A church believed the wanton destruction of the Pangemanan family was a kind of cruel crucifixion.

Emboldened by my congregation's courageous protest that I could not join, I called the main number of the Times. I imagined the phone ringing in the central marble entrance on 42nd Street where I used to enter, even though, since 2007, the paper had moved its operations to a brand-new building on Eighth Avenue.

I told the operator the name of the CTO I had worked for—Harvey Morgenstern, a man beloved throughout the company—and that I was calling with an immigration emergency. It was a long shot, but I asked if I could speak with Nina Bernstein. The operator put me through to Nina's voicemail. I left a desperate message. Nina called back a few moments later.

---

[1] Nina Bernstein, "City of Immigrants Fills Jail Cells with Its Own," *New York Times*, December 27, 2008, https://www.nytimes.com/2008/12/27/us/27detain.html.

I left a faculty meeting where teachers were planning the night's event. Nina's interest was piqued. A devoted veteran of the immigration beat, she wanted to know: Would there be interesting visuals? From past days in corporate public relations, I knew a compelling photo could guarantee inches of column space. I promised there would be Americans and Indonesians wrapped arm-in-arm, with protest signs, babies, and small children. Two young, charismatic pastors would pass a chalice and break apart a crusty loaf of bread. Nina sent a crew of photographers. The photos were taken. The relationship with Nina would become an important one, but that was months away. Eventually, those photos would be published and they would break hearts.[2]

But other items were more pressing. Nina did not file our story that day.

---

[2] Nina Bernstein with photos by Hiroko Masuike and Suzanne DeChillo, "Taking a Risk and Hoping for the Future," *New York Times*, December 8, 2009, https://www.nytimes.com/slideshow/2009/12/08/nyregion/20091207INDONESIANS_index.html.

CHAPTER 13

Imprisoned on the Far Western Tip

In Tacoma, Washington, March 2009

When Harry's plane finally touched down at Seattle-Tacoma International Airport, ICE agents drove him twenty-five miles south to the Northwest ICE Processing Center—a name which sounds as if its purpose is to move people, instead of holding them indefinitely.

More conventionally, ICE also calls this mega–immigration prison, run by the for-profit Geo Group, the Tacoma Northwest Detention Center.

The Tacoma center opened in 2004 under a contract with the Department of Homeland Security with a capacity for 500 inmates. But unlike Elizabeth, the site offered the possibility for tremendous expansion. The single-story complex rests on reclaimed tidal waterfront land in Commencement Bay, the southern inlet of Puget Sound, which also contains a major oil refinery, a superfund site for a Kaiser Aluminum plant, and the third largest shipping gateway system in the U.S.[1]

---

[1] Steve Wilhelm, "The Northwest Seaport Alliance Just Became the Third-Largest Cargo Gateway in the U.S.," *Puget Sound Business Journal*, August 4, 2015, https:/

As Mount Rainier loomed ever larger on the southeastern horizon, the ICE vehicle with Harry inside approached the Tacoma waterfront. Harry noticed that huge areas of the center were under construction. By 2010, the latest expansion of the Northwest center provided space for 1,600 detainees, making it four times the size of the warehouse that Corrections Corporation of America (CCA) had transformed into Elizabeth Detention Center beside Newark Liberty Airport.[2]

Yet below the surface details, the two centers shared significant similarities.

Both Geo Group and CCA were funded by the Vanguard Group, in which former U.S. President Dick Cheney had invested $85 million.

While Cheney was still vice president in late 2008, a Texas grand jury indicted him and U.S. Attorney General Alberto Gonzales for contributing to prisoner abuse in privately run prisons and for covering up abuse by interfering with investigations. The indictment alleged that the two men, along with CCA and Geo Group, engaged in a for-profit scheme in which federal prisoners were neglected by being allowed to be assaulted by other prisoners and then denied proper medical care.

In a matter of weeks, a U.S. district judge dismissed the charges, ostensibly for procedural issues in seating jury members. But jury members had written that they were appalled "to find that numerous elected officials from different levels of our government throughout our country to our U.S. Vice President Richard B. Cheney, defendant, are profiting from depriving human beings of their liberty."[3] Over the next years, detainees in facilities run by both entities would join in protests, riots, and hunger strikes to publicize and improve dehumanizing conditions.

As Harry tried to adjust to life in Tacoma, he felt extremely agitated. He worried gravely about his children and his wife, though he knew there was absolutely nothing he could do for them.

---

www.bizjournals.com/seattle/news/2015/08/04/the-northwest-seaport-alliance-just-became-the.html.

[2] Lael Henterly, "ICE Contract to House Immigrant Detainees Opening This Summer," *Seattle Globalist,* June 2, 2014, https://seattleglobalist.com/2014/06/02/ice-contract-to-hold-immigrant-detainees-opening-this-summer/25639.

[3] Matthew Clarke, "Cheney and Gonzales Indicted in Connection with Private Prison in Texas," June 15, 2009, *Prison Legal News,* https://www.prisonlegalnews.org/news/2009/jun/15/cheney-and-gonzales-indicted-in-connection-8232with-private-prison-in-texas/. See also Paul R. La Monica, "BlackRock and Vanguard Are the Biggest Investors in Private Prisons," CNN Business, July 1, 2019, https://www.cnn.com/2019/06/28/investing/prison-stocks-mutual-funds/index.html.

When he felt helpless and distressed, to calm down and re-focus his thoughts and prayers, Harry read postcards and Bible passages he received, not only from New Jersey but from all over the country, from people whom he had never met.

In Michigan, Wendy Jager's mother had mobilized a team of long-distance letter-writers who faithfully maintained contact with Harry throughout his detention. Would they ever know how each page they wrote and every card they inscribed saved the life of this family?

My mother and I convinced my brother Robby, who lives in Seattle and who had never met Harry, to visit him in detention.

At first Robby resisted. He had never been to a prison before, and Tacoma was a long, unpleasant drive through Washington's most crowded corridor from his comfortable, fifth-floor Queen Anne apartment that overlooked snow-capped mountains on the Olympic Peninsula and illumined cruise ships at night crossing Puget Sound.

But Father Ryan, the Jesuit monsignor of Robby's downtown church, St. James Cathedral, had delivered fiery sermons about Christ's radical welcome of immigrants and strangers. In the summertime, Robby volunteered at a camp for migrant farm workers.

As Robby worried about what to do next, his friend Amy, whom he considered a church "partner in crime," offered to accompany Robby for the drive that, with traffic congestion, could sometimes last three hours.

His reservations melted away.

Harry was shocked when utter strangers came to see him in such a desolate place. "I didn't know Robby for my life," said Harry. "He and Amy came because of you, his sister," Harry told me later. "Like he knows me for years."

"Pray for me, I asked Robby. We prayed together."

After Robby's second visit, Iska, Harry's cousin who lives in California, traveled to Tacoma to surprise Harry. Iska had assumed Harry would be on the next plane that ICE rented to drop deportees across Asia. Later, Iska admitted to Harry, "It was my mission to see you for the last time in the United States."

On Good Friday, Robby returned to visit Harry again. Before he left Robby told Harry, "This is it, Harry. You've done all you can do. Now it's God's turn to take over."

Harry said that meeting with Robby left him feeling a deep, spiritual peace.

CHAPTER 14

Hope Stirs in the Dark

In New Jersey, Holy Week, 2009

When ICE moved Harry to Tacoma, they forced Seth to completely change his strategy.

Rather than work with the local ICE office in Newark and plead for help from U.S. congressmen, Seth knew the only hope for Harry would be if the newly elected Obama administration were to respond in a humanitarian way, reaching down from the highest levels to direct the local office of ICE.

Time was tight. Easter season is a pastor's busiest time of year. And at the Highland Park church, the season became jam-packed as Music Director Brian Katonah directed a large cast of church members—including Seth—in ambitious performances of the Broadway musical *Godspell* on Good Friday and Holy Saturday evenings.

Nevertheless, Seth committed himself to push harder in Washington, DC.[1]

At first, trying to imagine where to start, Seth made random calls in the dark. He tried the White House and different constituent

---

[1] Seth describes the steps he took after Harry was moved to Tacoma in SKD, 38–40.

hotlines. He continued to ask representatives in the U.S. Congress to intervene. Finally, Seth sat up one night and called every one of forty phone numbers listed on the ICE website. He begged and pleaded on the telephone, asking that someone please call him back.

The Wednesday night before Easter, Seth's phone was on mute during *Godspell* rehearsal, so he didn't see that someone had left a message.

On Maundy Thursday morning, Seth listened to what sounded to him like the kindest recorded voice he had ever heard. A woman in Washington, DC, had just returned from visiting detention centers, and she was responding to his call for help.

The voice belonged to Dora Schriro, who had been appointed by President Obama a few weeks earlier.

Schriro had earned a law degree from Saint Louis University, a doctor of education from Columbia University, a master's from the University of Massachusetts, and a bachelor of arts from Northeastern University. She was the first woman to direct two state corrections departments.

For eight years, Schriro led the Missouri Department of Corrections. Then she served six years as the director of the Arizona Department of Corrections. As special advisor to DHS Secretary Janet Napolitano, who was a former governor of Arizona, Schriro's job was to review the way that immigration detention was happening nationally and to make suggestions to overhaul the system.[2]

Seth called back and immediately Dora answered her own phone.

Seth made the call from the church's front office. Lisa Berman, the church office manager, listened as Seth sat there, in her office, explaining the situation to Dora.

Lisa watched tears stream down Seth's face when Dora said, "I'm sorry. I'm so sorry that we are doing this to this family." Dora apologized five times in the course of that call.

Unlike every other government person Seth had talked to over those eighty or so days, Dora didn't say, "My hands are tied." Instead, she said, "Let me see what I can do."

The next time Seth spoke to Harry he told him about his breakthrough with Dora Schriro. Two weeks had passed since they prayed on the plane. Seth had heard how ICE officers put steady pressure on detainees to give up their cases and voluntarily deport.

---

[2] SKD, 38-40. See Schriro, "Immigration Detention Overview and Recommendations."

Seth still couldn't make a promise, but Harry needed to stay strong for a few more days. Seth and Harry prayed Dora would come through with humanitarian aid.

All day Maundy Thursday, there was no further word. But on Good Friday, Dora Schriro called Seth back.

She had reviewed a great deal of paperwork from Seth and she wanted Seth to confirm something.

"The Pangemanans went all the way to the Board of Immigration Appeals in Virginia?" Schriro asked. The Board of Immigration Appeals, or BIA, is the final arbiter in all immigration cases, much as the U.S. Supreme Court is the final court of appeal for criminal cases.

The Pangemanans' case had been denied by the BIA, Seth confirmed.

Then Schriro said, loud and clear, "Hmmm... not much I could do."

And at first, when he hung up, Seth was incensed.

Later, Seth shared with Harry that in the waiting space of that Holy Saturday, Seth felt like he had hit a true emotional low point. Yet, somehow, it didn't feel quite like the dead-end experience of helplessness he had felt when other leaders had told him that their hands were tied.

Seth struggled to hold on to hope.

CHAPTER 15

The Mystery of Easter

In Washington, New Jersey, and Ohio, April 12, 2009

Suspended in the limbo of the Northwest Detention Center in Tacoma, Harry described himself undertaking a spiritual journey of letting go and trusting God.

It was Holy Saturday.

He called his mother Clara and apologized for all the trouble he had caused her as a rambunctious youth. Then he asked her and his sister Jessy to find a sunrise Easter service in Ohio and attend, in person.

He imagined it must have sounded like a last request. They promised Harry they would find a service and go to it.

Next, Harry called Yana and asked her to worship with the Reformed Church's Easter sunrise service in Donaldson Park alongside the Raritan River.

It had been Harry's custom to go to this service alone. He had kept up this tradition in honor of his father Joce, who had insisted all his children walk in the dark to worship together before sunrise every Easter in Indonesia.

At first, Yana couldn't imagine, with two young children, how she could possibly get to the riverside service in Highland Park before sunrise. But she called deacon Mary McLain, who woke up extra early that Sunday morning and drove thirty minutes in the dark to pick up Yana and her girls in the Avenel section of Woodbridge.

As the early morning sky lightened on the East Coast, Yana and her daughters climbed into Mary's car and drove to the banks of the Raritan in Highland Park so they could worship outside with their church family.

The morning was just brightening at 5:30 a.m. when Seth walked down to the bottom of his street to enter Donaldson Park.

Harry was on his mind as he prepared for the daybreak service. He knew this service was a favorite of Harry's. Harry always came alone. Seth remembered that Harry had told him about Easters when he was a child in Indonesia, how he had worshiped at sunrise with his father and all his siblings.

Because the service started so early and Harry's girls were so small, it made perfect sense to Seth that Yana would stay home with them until the later Easter service in the church sanctuary.

So that morning, when Mary McLaine's car drove up in the dark and Yana, Jocelyn, and Christa ran over to join the church group, Seth was overwhelmed with gratitude.

A couple dozen faithful church members sang and worshiped together down by the river in the chilly park as the sky turned a brilliant blue.

As God had given resurrected life to his son Jesus, the worshippers by the river asked God for new life for Harry.

Sunrise in Ohio found Harry's mother and sister on their knees at a church service, asking God's mercy to keep Harry and his family together as they faced permanent and irrevocable separation.

Finally, Easter morning light stretched to a corner of concrete in an outdoor recreation yard surrounded with barbed wire on a spit of reclaimed tidal land in Puget Sound, where a compassionate guard allowed Harry to experience the sunrise, alone, for ten precious minutes of silence.

Later that Easter Sunday afternoon, Robby called Harry to tell him he was coming, but he was stuck in traffic.

"No worries," Harry replied. "Let go, brother, and let God."

CHAPTER 16

Loosened Chains

In Tacoma and Avenel, April 15, 2009

Three days after Easter, a guard in the Tacoma detention center woke Harry up before 6 a.m. and told Harry to pack all his belongings in his bag.

Harry gathered his clothes and his Bible. Then he filled a black garbage bag with all the envelopes and cards he had received through the mail while he was detained in Newark and Tacoma.

These messages had helped preserve his spirit. Harry could not leave them behind.[1]

The agent told Harry to make his way to the visitors' room. Unlike Elizabeth Detention Center, where guards supervised detainees outside their dorm rooms, in Tacoma, detainees roamed long, winding corridors on their own. Color-coded stripes painted on the floor directed them to one of the several locations where they were authorized to go.

---

[1] Harry described the story of his departure from Tacoma in an interview in February 2017.

The processing room was empty at that hour of the morning, but Harry thought he heard strains of the hymn, "How Great Thou Art," coming from somewhere.

An agent handed Harry a paper. Harry signed without reading it and then followed the agent outside. This seemed strange to Harry. agents typically walk behind the detainee.

Outside a car was waiting. The agent opened the front door and sat in the driver's seat. Harry opened the back door and sat in the back seat. Between the driver and the backseat passenger, there was no Plexiglass barrier. It was just a regular car. They passed the gate. The agent got out of the car and left the engine running with Harry sitting in the back. This time, there were no handcuffs.

To Harry, his situation seemed surreal.

A crazy thought ran through Harry's mind. He imagined he could jump into the driver's seat and take off, right there and then. He thought, I could drive for five miles and abandon this car. Then he thought better of it. Maybe it's a trap!

The agent returned and drove Harry to the tarmac at Sea-Tac Airport. He parked the car near a jet plane. From the parking lot, the agent stepped into an airport building door while Harry stayed in the car. There was no delay for processing. The agent returned with a piece of paper. He said, follow me.

Together, Harry and the agent walked up the steps into the plane. Before Harry sat down, the agent gave him a ticket. The agent told Harry, "Here's your paperwork. Have a nice flight."

Harry didn't know where he was going. When the agent left, Harry opened the ticket. To his amazement, Harry read that the plane was bound for Newark, New Jersey.

Before take-off, Harry plugged in the battery of his cell phone. It had been more than two months since he last used it, but somehow it had remained charged. His wife Yana did not pick up. Seth did not pick up. Finally, Pastor Stephanie picked up.

Harry told Stephanie, "I am on a plane to New Jersey."

When he hung up, Harry pulled out his Bible and randomly opened it up. On the page before him, Harry read Paul's story about how he and Silas had been imprisoned and then, during an earthquake, their chains somehow mysteriously loosened. Paul and Silas were freed from prison, yet they remained and talked with their prison guards.

When his plane arrived in Newark, Harry was the last one off. Agents were waiting for him—the same agents that, a few weeks earlier, had taken him from Elizabeth Detention and brought him to the airport. Harry didn't say anything. They didn't ask who Harry was. They just said, Follow us.

Harry walked straight behind them, but they did not go through the airport terminal. Instead, they took secret doors that led to their car. Again, there were no handcuffs. When Harry reached Elizabeth, there were three gates. Two led in and out for detainees. One is for the visitor's room.

This time Harry didn't go to the processing room but instead, he went to the main office. He waited.

After ten minutes, an agent came back and told Harry, Sign this. Harry hesitated. It said, "Order of Supervision." Harry asked, "Excuse me, officer, what is this for?"

"You are going home," the agent replied.

CHAPTER 17

Hope Returns

In Highland Park, April 15, 2009

Three days after Easter, Seth was touring a county jail, the North Brunswick Correctional Facility, with a group of regional immigration advocates. The jail contracted with ICE to house undocumented immigrants whose cases were under investigation. The advocates feared the county was still proactively locking up immigration violators, even though most immigration infractions are civil offenses—not criminal.[1]

The warden showed off newly refurbished cells for ICE detainees and boasted that his facility only detained immigrants who were criminals. When he heard the warden say these words, Seth exploded in anger.

"Warden, how dare you tell me that you only detain criminal immigrants. In 2006, I know for a fact that you detained thirty-five Indonesian parents here for six weeks. Not one of them had a criminal violation. All of them were deported from your jail."

The warden's face turned red. Seth had disrupted his public relations tour. "Pastor, are you calling me a liar?" the warden retorted.

---

[1] Seth describes his visit to the county jail on the day Harry returned in SKD, 39-40.

Seth said that he was just stating the facts. The lives of those Indonesian men, their wives, and children, had been destroyed. Now, for the sake of public relations, the warden had brushed it off as if the incident had never happened. The same falsehoods that had shielded the local community in Rhode Island from uncomfortable truths, as Nina Bernstein had written that past December, were now being applied in New Jersey.

Seth hadn't been allowed to bring his cell phone into the county facility. By the time he exited the jail, he had nine voice messages. As he drove back to Highland Park, Seth listened to them.

The first message, at 9:30 a.m., was from Yana. In a hysterical voice she cried, "Seth, they're taking Harry away." He calculated that would have been 6:30 a.m. in Seattle.

Yana's second message said, "They are taking him somewhere, but we don't know where."

Stephanie left a message that said, "Harry just called, he said they are putting him on a plane to Newark!"

In the ninth message, Yana said, "Harry is getting on the plane now, but he thinks they might be sending him back to Elizabeth Detention Center.

Seth called key congregants and strategized about what to do. By this point, they had generated so much media attention around this story that if they made some phone calls, the TV and newspapers would have been at the airport waiting for the plane.

They wondered, should they hold another worship service there, this time in thanksgiving? Because they were not sure what was happening, they decided to lay low and not risk "ruffling feathers." They were thrilled to have Harry back on the East Coast. They didn't want to jeopardize any goodwill by aggravating ICE at such a sensitive time.

While Harry's plane was crossing the continent, congregants waited for what felt like an eternity.

Finally, that afternoon, Seth's phone rang again. This time he heard Harry's voice, he was in Elizabeth. "Pastor, someone can come and get me. They are releasing me to my family."

Seth and Harry realized that the quickest way for Harry to get home was to take a taxi. Harry asked the agents for numbers to call a cab. His wallet still contained the cash he had put into it that morning in January when he was first detained on his way to work.

Seth quickly called several church members and set a phone chain in action. They called the journalists who had publicized the Pangemanans' dire situation.

I called Nina. She couldn't believe that ICE was sending Harry home after shipping him to the major hub that ICE used to redistribute deportees across Asia. Nina knew this was an unheard-of aberration in typical ICE practices.

"You know, Liz, I am kicking myself that I didn't file Harry's story when ICE shipped him to Tacoma," Nina regretted.

I hung up knowing that because Nina didn't file that first story about Seth and Harry in the airport, the second story, the miracle of Harry's release, would also not make it into the *New York Times*.

But I understood Nina's dilemma. A few days before, Nina had published a major front-page immigration story that featured a holocaust survivor from Paterson, New Jersey who had tried for four years to raise an alarm about deaths occurring in detention centers that ICE failed to report, investigate, and track.[2]

Tens of thousands of similar dramas were taking place every day. No one had a crystal ball to tell when one of those stories would shed the most light on the plight of so many.

Thirty minutes after he spoke with Seth, Harry walked into his Avenel apartment. His daughter Jocelyn was waiting for him, but to Harry, she looked totally different. She was only seven, but she seemed much older.

Jocelyn didn't come straight over to Harry. Instead, she ran out to the balcony. Yana ran out and hugged Harry. Christa hugged Harry.

When Jocelyn returned, Harry asked his eldest daughter, "Why did you go outside?"

Jocelyn told him, "I prayed outside."

Such a grown-up little girl, Harry thought, and then he asked, "Jocelyn, tell me, what did you pray?"

She said, "I knew you were coming. But I didn't believe it until I saw you here. Then I had to thank God for answering my prayers."

The news got out. By 3 p.m. many Indonesians overran the apartment. Seth called and asked Yana if the Pangemanans would come to the church.

---

[2] Nina Bernstein, "Immigrant Detainee Dies, and a Life Is Buried, Too," *New York Times*, April 3, 2009, https://www.nytimes.com/2009/04/03/nyregion/03detain.html.

Harry took a shower. All his clothes were in boxes that Yana had assembled to send to Indonesia. Yana had been preparing to ship his belongings to his family, she was so certain that her husband would never again need them in New Jersey.

Harry rummaged in the boxes until he found a batik dress shirt from Indonesia. Yana drove Harry and her daughters to the Reformed Church of Highland Park.

By 8 p.m. that evening, a hundred people gathered in the Highland Park sanctuary, singing and praying. Then in through the door walked Harry, carrying Christa in his arms as Yana held tightly onto Jocelyn. Harry looked pale and gaunt, exhausted and elated.

Besides Seth, no one in the sanctuary that night, three days after Easter, had really believed they would have ever seen Harry in the flesh again. Not even Yana, with her boxes packed for Harry in Indonesia.

For the first time in more than sixty-eight days, the whole Pangemanan family sat together in the front pew.

Joe Van Liew, the elderly gentleman for whom Wendy Jager had offered prayers in his pew during a healing service, loved Harry and Yana so much that he had walked several blocks from his home to the church, despite his worsening emphysema, carrying his supplemental oxygen.

Joe's wife Delores was working and couldn't get away. "You'd better get yourself over to the church!" Delores urged Joe.

Sadly, Joe would die, too soon, after that day, but thankfully, I snapped a blurry picture of Joe beaming, his arm wrapped around Yana as she sat next to the husband she thought she might only see again in Indonesia, their daughters piled on their laps.

For years, Yana and I shared that blurred image on Facebook, a sign to us of God's working the impossible in our lives.

That night, many church members said that participating in Harry's release was the most impressive miracle they had ever personally experienced. To see a hopeless situation utterly reversed, due to the tenacity of love expressed by the people of God, transformed their experience of faith.

A few days later, Seth called Dora Schriro and asked if she was responsible for Harry's homecoming.

Dora responded, "I may have sprinkled a little pixie dust…"

CHAPTER 18

An Extraordinary Agreement

In Highland Park, June to December 2009

In the Edison distribution warehouse where Harry had worked faithfully for years, Harry's supervisor had kept Harry's job open for him, even though he knew the federal government had detained Harry because of his immigration situation.

After his boss called him five times asking him to return, Harry finally felt ready to go back to work.

The deep rupture Harry and his wife and children had experienced in their family life began to heal.

But Harry and Yana still faced a complex legal situation. They received only temporary stays of removal. Despite the ordeal, they had not won a permanent reprieve.

Seth was surprised when Harry's release did not end the church's involvement in broader immigration issues.

Harry had connected with many fellow immigrants as he strove to provide a loving presence inside the detention center walls. He shared his concern for fellow detainees with his friends on the outside.

Church members continued weekly visits to men who weren't as lucky as Harry, men who did not have a church family pulling for them, men who were still inside. On a second night, another group, mostly women, began weekly visits to the much smaller group of female detainees. Twice weekly visits would continue until 2020, when the Covid-19 pandemic closed visitation to detention centers.

Church members could now appreciate the immense threat that their government posed to undocumented people, and they felt compelled to invest time and energy helping people escape detention and deportation.

Congregants took turns standing in the detention center's Plexiglass visitor cubicles, listening to harrowing stories of death-defying journeys. Ebeneezer Mercer, a soccer star from Ghana who was accused of being bisexual and therefore threatened, crossed the Atlantic in a shipping container, armed with only a box of crackers. He drank rainwater he collected from a leaky ceiling. Once the detention center released him, Ebeneezer called the only people who had visited him: the Highland Park church.

French-speaking Claude Kabila, a relative of the infamous Congo dictator, Joséph Kabila, explained how he had operated a successful business until he was pressed into service as a driver for executive leaders of the Democratic Republic of Congo. To save his own life, Claude fled on a flight to the United States, abandoning his wife and children. With no pre-arranged visa, Claude climbed aboard knowing he was bound for detention as soon as his plane landed. Just before he left, Claude said that his superiors gave him an order he refused to execute. He never told church members what that order was. But the immigration judge was convinced and immediately granted asylum status to Claude. With a grant of asylum, eventually Claude would be able to welcome his wife and children to reside in the U.S. with him. When he was released from detention, Harry and Yana gave Claude a couch to sleep on. Church members helped Claude file visa applications for his family.

My son Michael spent time with Harry and Claude. He convinced me to take Claude to New York City to visit the Metropolitan Museum of Art. "I have known these paintings all my life," Claude said in rooms filled with French impressionism. "Today is the first day I can stand in front of them."

Shocked by the stories of injustice that detainees suffered at the hands of the U.S. government, congregants joined Seth in advocating not only for individuals but also for the entire congregation of Indonesians who shared their space.

Congregants began to interview Indonesians and other undocumented immigrants. They recorded these stories with the hope that they could show ICE the humanitarian catastrophes that led people to come here and overstay their visas.

In July 2009, Harry, Seth, and a dozen church members drove the church van to Washington, DC, to visit ICE headquarters and meet with Dora Schriro. Selma Colmant, an elder who led the church's prayer shawl ministry, brought a powder-blue, hand-knit shawl for Dora.

Church members waited for hours in the ICE office reception area. When Dora finally appeared, she looked exhausted. But the visit delighted her. She told them that this gesture—the prayer shawl combined with finally meeting Harry, after all she had heard about him—was the nicest thing that had happened to her since she took the job.

Seth handed Dora 300 pages of interviews with undocumented people who were in serious immigration trouble. Five women had authored this massive document, led by Jean Stockdale and Rev. Linda Lachesnez, a Reformed pastor who had joined the church as a member while she awaited her next call to a church.[1]

That summer, the immigration committee organized a series of weeknight potluck suppers in the social hall. They asked Harry and Yana to encourage undocumented Indonesians to gather after work. During extra-long summer days, dozens of parents left work, picked up their children, and drove them another forty minutes to the church.

At these suppers, Americans and Indonesians finally came face-to-face to share real-life problems. In discussions over yellow rice, steamed vegetables, chicken nuggets, and slices of local pizza, church members learned that most undocumented Indonesians lived in constant fear of ICE. They moved often and sometimes used the mailing addresses of friends instead of their own addresses. They never put their contact information in school directories. If they suspected that their location may have been given to ICE, they uprooted their families and established a new household somewhere nearby.

Based on interviews with Harry, Yana, and other women whose husbands had been deported, the church developed a questionnaire to collect data and find out who needed what kind of help. Data could help communicate the dire situation to lawyers, journalists, and advocates. But for undocumented people who had survived for years by living

---

[1] SKD, 40.

underground, providing their contact information and immigration stories was a great challenge.

At first, no one who was living below the radar felt comfortable sharing. The information forms remained blank and conversation felt stilted until church members brought out the social hall sound system and a roving microphone.

After everyone had found something to eat on the potluck table, the microphone was passed to Indonesian pastors from congregations in Central New Jersey and as far away as New York City.

One well-known Indonesian pastor from Queens came because he heard the story of Harry's release. "This never happens," the elder gentleman assured everyone. "Harry is the only immigrant I have heard about who returned home from Tacoma."

Undocumented Indonesians passed the microphone and told their stories. They did not have to write anything down, nor did they share their names or addresses. They simply explained how their lives had become impossible. Many expressed shame for being undocumented. Many said how much they loved America.

A few said how disappointed they were. "We came to America because it is a Christian country!" one man exclaimed, pointing out how he had once been persecuted in Indonesia for being Christian and now he was persecuted by Christians in America for being Indonesian.

Church leaders quickly realized the potluck dinners were not the place to fill out forms. Yet they were a terrific forum for sharing stories and raising laments to God. Advocates started making appointments for one-on-one sessions to fill out the forms. They began interviews with the kicker question: Tell me when and why you left Indonesia? This one question unlocked the key to every undocumented person's challenging life story and current legal predicament. Ask that question, church members learned, and you open a door for a relationship of mutual respect and deeply held trust.

I kept in touch with Nina Bernstein. When Harry asked me to make a flyer for an Indonesian food bazaar that the combined group of Indonesians planned in the courtyard of Woodbine Apartments that August, I forwarded it to Nina and invited her to come and meet everyone. Yana assigned me the job of bringing a football cooler full of lemonade. While my daughters and husband helped serve lemonade on the shared green lawn of Woodbine Apartments, I received an email from Nina. She couldn't make the picnic because she had to care for her elderly father who was having a health crisis in a nursing home.

In late August, Dora Schriro called Seth. When she read the massive documents that church members had left when they visited her office in July, she noticed a pattern in some of the stories. There were situations that she believed should have been dealt with by the *citizenship* side of the Department of Homeland Security, the organization called U.S. Citizenship and Immigration Services or USCIS. This government agency oversees lawful immigration to the United States.

Dora felt some cases had been turned over to ICE for removal by mistake. She wanted Indonesians to meet with a woman named Ellen Gallagher, an immigration attorney at USCIS, in September.[2]

Over the course of the summer, the church developed a relationship with First Friends of New Jersey, a group that was holding eight rallies throughout the state called "A Children's Vigil." In September, the Reformed Church of Highland Park hosted one of the rallies.

A group of congregants developed artwork for the event, lined up speakers and singers, and prepared candles and signs. Seth engaged his contacts in the media.

The purpose of the Children's Vigil was to drum up public support for H.R. 182, the "Child Citizen Protection Act," a bill that would allow immigration judges to take into consideration the needs of an undocumented person's family members, especially their U.S. citizen children, when deciding whether to deport them.[3]

The vigil started at 3 p.m. on one of the first days of the 2009–2010 school year. Two hundred people and dozens of members of the press, including cameramen, participated. During the vigil, the church turned a spotlight on local families who were devastated after the deportation of a parent or spouse.

The very next morning, disaster struck for two Indonesian fathers as they took their small children to school in Woodbridge. Each had dropped his kids off at the door to their school and started walking

[2] SKD, 40.
[3] James Queally, "'Children's Vigils' Call for Widespread Reform of Federal Immigration Policies," *The Star-Ledger*, September 16, 2009, https://www.nj.com/news/2009/09/childrens_vigils_call_for_wide.html; Bridgette A. Carr, "Incorporating a 'Best Interests of the Child' Approach into Immigration Law and Procedure," *Yale Hum. Rts. & Dev. L. J.* 12 (2009): 120–59, https://repository.law.umich.edu/articles/533; Olga Byrne, "Promoting a Child Rights-Based Approach to Immigration in the United States," *Georgetown Immigration Law Journal* 32, no. 59 (2018): 60–98, https://www.law.georgetown.edu/immigration-law-journal/wp-content/uploads/sites/19/2018/05/32-1-Promoting-a-Child-Rights-Based-Approach-to-Immigration-in-the-United-States.pdf.

away from the building. But ICE agents had been waiting for them. The fathers were immediately handcuffed, put in an ICE vehicle, and taken to Elizabeth Detention Center.

Many people who had organized the Children's Vigil the day before felt that this was government payback. But Seth could not let himself believe that the local ICE office could be so purposefully malicious. He imagined it was rather a matter of coincidental timing.

Nevertheless, Seth's righteous indignation over the entrapment of fathers at their children's schools drove him to immediately re-engage with the people in Washington whom he had found so helpful in Harry's case.[4]

Seth called Dora Schriro's office in Washington and was shocked when he learned the news: Dora Schriro had just resigned. Six months after taking her high-level post in the Department of Homeland Security, Dora Schriro walked away. Nina Bernstein wrote that DHS announced Schriro would lead New York City's troubled corrections system.[5]

Seth tore through various numbers of ICE offices in Washington that he had collected over the past few months, leaving messages in each voicemail box.

Time after time, Seth's message was the same: "If there is anyone on the other end of this phone who has the same heart as Dora Schriro, please call me! We have trouble here in New Jersey, and she's been the only one to take us seriously."

That same afternoon, a woman called Seth back. "I am one of Dora's people," she said. "What can I do for you?" Seth quickly explained the whole situation. She asked Seth to give her a day.

The next day, the woman from ICE called back and asked Seth to join a conference call at 4 p.m. There were several officials she wanted Seth to talk with whom she believed needed to hear our story.

Seth called and found that on the other end of the phone were some of the highest-level immigration officials in the country.

Seth explained how and why Indonesians came to this country, why they didn't apply for asylum right away, and how it was that they had all turned themselves in for NSEERS in order to help their adopted country to identify terrorists. He begged the leaders to do whatever

---

[4] SKD, 40–41.
[5] Nina Bernstein, "Immigration Official to Run New York's Jails," *New York Times*, September 8, 2009, https://www.nytimes.com/2009/09/09/nyregion/09detain.html.

was in their power to work for the release of the two fathers who had just been detained, as well as two other Indonesian men also recently detained.

To Seth's surprise, before the call was over, he was linked to the ICE director of the New Jersey Field Office. For months while Harry had been detained, Seth had tried to reach this field office director, Scott Weber.

On the teleconference, officials gave a quick synopsis of the situation and Director Weber said, "Reverend, would you please come up to Newark to meet with me and my staff?"

Absolutely, Seth replied. Scott Weber apologized for the lack of communication from his office and said he wanted to hear Seth's suggestions.

Two days later, Seth and Rev. Linda Lachesnez, who had collected the immigration stories given to Dora Schriro, traveled to Newark. At the Rodino Building on Broad Street in Newark, they took the elevator to one of the highest floors. An office manager led them to a large corner office, where five stern-faced officials were seated around a table.

Scott Weber asked Seth to describe the situation facing the Indonesians in New Jersey. Seth started in 1998 with the fall of the Suharto regime, sharing details about the persecution of ethnic Chinese Christians in Indonesia. He described how the vast number of Indonesians in New Jersey had fled Indonesia to start a new life of safety in the United States. He questioned why the U.S. State Department granted so many visitor visas to poor, frightened Indonesians who were clearly fleeing for their lives. He explained that there had been just one small Indonesian church in New Jersey in 1997, and by 2001 there were nine. Hard-working Indonesians then melted into holes in the labor market that a booming, Clinton-era economy could not otherwise fill.

Seth explained how, after 9/11, the Indonesians registered with NSEERS, hoping for a path to citizenship, and then they filed for asylum even though they missed the one-year filing deadline. He told them how families had been devastated in the ICE raid of the Avenel apartments in 2006.

To explain his own motivation, Seth told them about Christa Pangemanan's baptism. He said it was unethical and unchristian to baptize children and then not fight to keep their families together.

At the end of Seth's story, Director Weber informed him, in front of his staff, that he was going to do something totally unusual. He told

Seth to meet with the Indonesian community and to let them know that anyone who was living in fear of deportation and had been given final orders of removal was invited to come in to meet with ICE.

Pending a review to ensure they had no criminal record, Indonesians would be given a two-year stay of removal, according to Weber. This would allow them to get a driver's license and a work permit and to live without fear of deportation.

Director Weber made sure that Seth knew he was not talking about amnesty, only a temporary stay. However, throughout the conversation, Scott Weber and Seth discussed a hope that everyone seemed to share that the Obama administration would usher in new laws to help immigrants like the Indonesians of Central New Jersey.

"I cried, right there in the office," Seth admitted later. "It was such shocking news, to hear that ICE was going to work with our church. I was so amazed that they had heard our story, not only about Harry, but now about the entire Indonesian population in New Jersey!"

Seth had come into the meeting with the names of the two fathers who had been arrested a few weeks earlier while taking their children to school. He asked Director Weber if he might release them to their families as a sign that he was serious about not deporting Indonesian men and breaking up families.

Not only did Weber agree, but he also promised to release five other Indonesians who were currently detained. Weber informed Seth that it would take a couple of days, but that all seven men would soon return to their families.

On the way home, Seth called Harry and asked him to call an emergency meeting with the entire Indonesian community.

That night, 140 Indonesians packed the church sanctuary and listened as Seth told them the good news: They were highly favored by ICE! No one could quite believe it. With Harry translating, Seth shared the whole story.

Then, Seth told the families of the seven men who were currently detained that their loved ones would be released in the next forty-eight hours. Their wives were skeptical but hopeful.

Two days later, the seven men were released, verifying Seth's story that the church's relationship with ICE Newark had changed.

Linda Lachesnez, Harry Pangemanan, and Seth started to design processes and documents that would allow the church to supervise Indonesians on behalf of ICE Newark.

Working more closely with ICE was a risk. But the people who would participate in this program were not just currently targeted for deportation. They were being hunted down.

Seth remembered that the church had developed an ongoing relationship with Times reporter Nina Bernstein. When ICE transported Harry to Tacoma, Washington. Seth had met the photographers Nina sent to capture the protest the church held at Elizabeth Detention Center. Seth, too, was disappointed when Nina filed no article for publication at that time.

Nina had followed the story of Harry's miraculous release, but she hadn't written about it, and she admitted her regret.

Now Seth called Nina and informed her that ICE was showing favor to an entire group of people because of the advocacy of his church.

Finally, he captured Nina's undivided attention.

Nina set up a date to visit the church and meet with the Indonesians who were in desperate trouble and with the Americans in Highland Park who were working so intently to help them.

The meeting took place that same week in November.

"I'm in totally uncharted waters," Seth admitted when Nina asked him about the risks. The arrangement might buy the Indonesians a year or two. For some, new grounds might be found to reopen their cases. Congress could change immigration law.

If nothing about the situation changed, one immigration advocate cautioned, Indonesians who sign up could find they just moved up from "not known" to "on the list," to "you're taking the steps onto the airplane."

On Sunday, December 19, 2009, below the fold on its front page, the *New York Times* published Nina Bernstein's article, "Church Works with U.S. to Spare Detention."[6]

Earlier that month, Nina had accompanied Pastor Linda as she drove a van full of wary Indonesians to ICE Newark to sign papers allowing the church to supervise them for two years. The first people to step forward had to overcome terror born of experience.

Augus (Teddy) Assa told Nina the whole experience for him was "Very, very scary." He fought tears as his five-year-old daughter, Cristia Celine, who happened to be my daughter's Sunday school classmate,

---

[6] Nina Bernstein, "Church Works with U.S. to Spare Detention," *New York Times*, December 12, 2009, https://www.nytimes.com/2009/12/13/nyregion/13indonesians.html.

clung to him in the van on the way to the immigration enforcement unit in Newark.

Teddy told Nina, "In my heart, I hope I will stay in the United States."

Everyone like Teddy who signed the order received a two-year stay of deportation, authorization for work, and a New Jersey driver's license. The families of parents who participated could finally come out from the shadows and live normal lives.

"I'm proud of my church," Harry Pangemanan told Nina. "Not just the pastor, the whole church."

It was an unprecedented step. The actions of extreme solidarity that the Reformed Church of Highland Park took on behalf of undocumented Indonesian congregants became well-known among immigration advocates.

Amy Gottlieb, immigrant rights director for the American Friends Service Committee in New Jersey, who had been dealing with the ICE field office in Newark since 1996, called it "an amazing moment."

Rex Chen, the supervising lawyer at Catholic Charities of the Archdiocese of Newark, said he remained pessimistic. Chen was disproven in the short run, but later, his comments would prove prescient.

Melinda Basaran, participating lawyer and chairwoman of the New Jersey chapter of the American Immigration Lawyers Association, had worked directly to represent undocumented congregants from the church in their legal proceedings. Melinda was amazed and greatly relieved.

Like Rex, Melinda also cautioned that with the federal government, there are no guarantees.

CHAPTER 19

Changing National Priorities

In New Jersey and Washington, D.C., 2010

When Ellen Gallagher, the USCIS attorney, reconnected with Seth, she told him that Dora Schriro had been mistaken. There were no Indonesians whose cases proved to be wrongly in the ICE "enforcement" side instead of the CIS "citizenship" side.

Nevertheless, Ellen was able to help the church win the release of six members of another targeted group who were wrongly detained. The six men were Filipinos whom Harry had met through his Bible study and whose cases clearly belonged on the citizenship side.

The immigration advocates felt emboldened to ask for more people to be released.

In January 2010, the White House released an executive order that asylum seekers who are not a threat to national security should not be detained for more than thirty days. At that point, the church visitation team knew many individuals in the Elizabeth Detention Center who had been there for months or longer, despite pending cases.[1]

[1] SKD, 43.

At the end of that January, Seth, Jean Stockdale, Pastor Linda, and José Morais, the congregant from Colombia who helped lead the immigration committee, traveled to Trenton for an appointment with Chuck Richmond, the director of community affairs for the State of New Jersey.

They hoped to create a community supervision program as an alternative to detention. They made a case that it was important for the State of New Jersey to care for the housing needs of asylum seekers who had no American contacts.

As one of the Northeast's main ports, New Jersey was adding many "high-needs" people to its population, with no safeguards in place to assist with their transition from detention. The team hoped that Governor John Corzine, a Democrat, who was about to be replaced by Governor Chris Christie, a Republican, might take one positive action on behalf of immigrants. Corzine had formed a blue-ribbon committee on immigration reform for the state.

Sadly, by the time he left office, Governor Corzine's commission never took any action.[2]

With a positive reception from Chuck Richmond—but no promises—Seth called ICE in Newark to set up a meeting with Field Office Director Weber and shared the church's proposal for an alternative program to detention.

Seth and Jean refused to believe that ICE wanted to keep people who had no criminal record in detention. Scott Weber agreed. He explained that the new mandate from the White House would be a difficult one to follow. At that point, his only alternative was to open the door of Elizabeth Detention Center and let undocumented immigrants and asylum seekers, some of whom had no contacts in the U.S., fend for themselves.

The church proposed that ICE pay the Reformed Church of Highland Park–Affordable Housing Corporation a small daily fee, fifteen dollars per individual per day, to house, feed, transport, and offer social services to people who required ICE supervision. They included a more elaborate proposal to oversee non-detained individuals who were not homeless through community supervision. Weber promised to take the proposal to Washington for consideration.[3]

Soon after that meeting, Field Office Director Weber was mysteriously transferred. None of the programs Seth, Jean, and José presented to him were considered.

[2] SKD, 43.
[3] SKD, 43.

Nevertheless, hoping to model its care for detainees, the church provided the new director of the Newark Field Office with the names of three detainees from Tajikistan, Ghana, and India whom church members had been visiting for many months and asked ICE to release them.

Church leaders promised that, without any funding, the church could pilot the success of their program.

Within a week, all three detainees were released. Church members stepped up and offered guest rooms in their houses.

Nothing had been more of a stretch for church members than inviting individuals to come straight out of immigration detention and to move into their homes.

As a pastor, Seth could not promise anything about these individuals, other than that the government did not find them to be a threat. He could not even promise a length of time that the individuals would be needing housing. He did, however, make it clear that the church would not abandon anyone who volunteered for this ministry. If someone stepped forward to host a former detainee in their home, the church would walk alongside them, offering financial support, time, and backup plans if needed.

As a church elder, I convinced my husband and my elderly mother that we could offer temporary housing for a twenty-year-old asylum-seeker named Aziz from Tajikistan. Aziz spent the first two days sleeping in our basement guest room. Aziz loaded the Skype application on my work laptop so he could make free international calls. On the second night, Aziz went out to visit local bars with my twenty-six-year-old son who had an affinity for Russia and Russian literature. The two young men enjoyed lively conversations. But on the third day, a Monday morning, Aziz informed me and Pastor Seth that he had located friends who were staying in Brooklyn, and they were coming to pick him up. He gathered his belongings and I drove Aziz to the church where people gathered to say goodbye with the orange juice and mini donuts they had quickly assembled. Once there, Aziz told everyone that he was leaving immediately for a flight to Moscow. His friends showed up in a car and Aziz left with them.

An hour later, investigators from the FBI knocked on Seth's office door. They wanted to question Aziz about a smuggling ring they believed Aziz helped to operate. No one heard from Aziz again. Aziz from Tajikistan was the first and last detainee that my family would house in our basement.

While its members visited detention centers and helped immigrants with their cases and basic needs, the church was holding out hope for a package of federal legislation that lawmakers referred to as "comprehensive immigration reform."

It's hard not to look back on those days with amazement as leaders at the highest level of the U.S. government were working together, across partisan divides, to provide a path to citizenship for America's undocumented residents.

On March 18, 2010, Senator Charles Schumer, Democrat from New York, and Senator Lindsey Graham, Republican from South Carolina, jointly published an op-ed that presented a broad plan for fixing our "badly broken" immigration system.

"Our plan has four pillars," the senators wrote. First, requiring biometric Social Security cards to ensure that illegal workers cannot get jobs; second, fulfilling and strengthening our commitments on border security and interior enforcement; third, creating a process for admitting temporary workers; and fourth: implementing a tough but fair path to legalization for the eleven million immigrants in the United States illegally.[4]

On March 21, 2010, Seth, Harry, and a van full of church members were invited to speak at a nationally televised rally for comprehensive immigration reform in Washington, DC.

From the parsonage in Highland Park, Pastor Stephanie and her two youngest daughters watched CNN's coverage and snapped a photo of Seth and the church team when they appeared on stage on the National Mall.

On CNN, Harry and Jocelyn, now nine, held hands with Seth and his eldest daughter. Behind them stood a host of Reformed Church families with their young children.

"Keep hope ALIVE!" Harry shouted to the crowd.[5]

President Obama had been scheduled to make an appearance and talk about immigration reform. However, soon after they arrived, church members heard that the president's remarks were canceled.

---

[4] Charles E. Schumer and Lindsey O. Graham, "The Right Way to Mend Immigration," *The Washington Post*, March 19, 2010, available at https://www.lgraham.senate.gov/public/index.cfm/op-eds-columns?ID=8BA44F52-802A-23AD-4AΓ5-129EAA561923.

[5] Mary Snow, "NJ Indonesian Immigrants Targeted by the INS," CNN, December 11, 2011, https://www.cnn.com/2011/12/11/us/nj-indonesian-immigrants-targeted-by-the-ins/index.html.

Hope would need to wait for another day. The rally had been upstaged by a surprise announcement by the Obama administration.

Instead of comprehensive immigration reform, the U.S. Congress had reached a deal with the Obama Administration about the Patient Protection and Affordable Care Act, also called the ACA or Obamacare.

That same Tuesday, March 23, President Obama signed the healthcare bill into law. Unlike comprehensive immigration reform, when it came to the Affordable Care Act, there had been no bipartisan effort. In the Senate, the Democratic majority had dwindled to 59 when a Republican won the seat vacated when Massachusetts Senator Ted Kennedy died. The Senate resorted to using budget reconciliation to pass its bill, since it required only a simple majority. In the House, all 178 Republicans voted against the ACA bill. So did 34 Democrats.[6]

Republicans not only fought against the healthcare bill, but they also bitterly resented its unilateral passing.

From the perspective of advocates of bipartisan immigration reform, despite all its benefits, the ACA seemed to come at an unholy price. Eleven million people resided in the U.S. without authorization, and as both Janet Napolitano, the Secretary of Homeland Security, and Lindsey Graham agreed, no one believed that attempting to deport or jail all of them was reasonable. In fact, Graham stated, "seventy percent of Americans are in the camp that illegal immigrants need to be fairly and firmly dealt with." Graham was concerned about ensuring that the number didn't grow to twenty million, and for that he said the country needed to secure borders and a system to control visa overstays.

Two years later, Lindsey Graham looked back and voiced his disappointment at this failed bipartisanship opportunity.

"I don't believe there was much of an effort to deliver comprehensive immigration reform in the first [Obama administration] year. And I don't think it's Congress' fault," Graham stated. "I think the president failed the country by not making this a priority. He had a large majority he could have worked with, and he chose healthcare over immigration. And here we are."[7]

Good government is about impossible choices. The bipartisan possibility of immigration reform had been sacrificed for a quickly

---

[6] "H.R. 3590 (111th): Patient Protection and Affordable Care Act," as reported by Govtrack, a free legislative tracking tool provided by Civic Impulse, LLC, March 21, 2010, https://www.govtrack.us/congress/votes/111-2010/h165.

[7] In oversight hearings, Lindsay Graham implies that the Obama administration chose healthcare over immigration reform (CSPAN, April 25, 2012, 34:55 to 35:12, https://www.c-span.org/video/?305606-1/homeland-security-oversight#).

vanishing, completely partisan chance to change healthcare for all American citizens.

And the country's anti-immigrant venom continued to grow. That year, Congress funded the Department of Homeland Security to carry out 400,000 deportations per year. In 2012, ICE deportations would increase to 1,000 a day. By the time Janet Napolitano left office in 2013, *Time Magazine* reported that the number of deportations under her leadership rose from 389,834 in 2009 to 409,849 in 2012.

That yearly total exceeded the number of deportations in George W. Bush's two terms in office.[8]

Instead of ushering in a new era of comprehensive immigration reform, after eight years in office, President Obama would end up deporting 3,118,927 people,[9] removing more human beings from the country than all other presidents combined.

As 2010 progressed, Seth began to feel like he had become a first responder for immigration emergencies.[10] That role had been developing since Harry was released in 2009. His successes, and the publicity about them, meant that people who were desperate for immigration assistance were finding their way to him.

Each week Seth would receive requests from individuals around the country to please help them win the release of a beloved church member. In addition, every week, church members would return from detention center visits with new, tragic stories of people from many countries who needed advocacy.[11]

For a while, in hopes that funding would soon arrive, Seth or Jean Stockdale would call up the Newark office and request the release of someone the church was getting to know.

It amazed them how often the advocacy calls worked.

Quickly they learned to focus on the release of people who already had family and friends in the U.S., because in those cases, someone else besides the church was already committed to housing and caring for

---

[8] Michael Scherer, "Janet Napolitano Leaves Office with Her Border Security Efforts Incomplete," *Time*, July 12, 2013, https://swampland.time.com/2013/07/12/janet-napolitano-leaves-office-with-her-border-security-efforts-incomplete/.

[9] "Fiscal Year 2016 ICE Immigration Removals," U.S. Immigration and Customs Enforcement, updated February 2, 2023, https://www.ice.gov/remove/removal-statistics/2016#_ftnref4; full report available at https://www.ice.gov/sites/default/files/documents/Report/2016/removal-stats-2016.pdf.

[10] SKD, 43.

[11] SKD, 45.

them. Individuals with no U.S. connections at all were very hard to serve.

Church members with available guest rooms were already booked up with other asylees.

Language was a tremendous barrier. One asylee named Domingo, who lived in rooms at the church for months, described his loneliness and depression in extremely broken English.

"I was happier in Elizabeth Detention Center," Domingo told Seth. "There was always someone there I could talk to."

During the summer of 2010, at least twenty individuals were released due to church visits, the church's growing reputation, and ICE's desire to release people somewhat responsibly.

In addition to Indonesians, the church was able to win the release of people from many different countries whose families were already established in the U.S.

Meanwhile, as the news media spread encouraging reports of the new orders of supervision program, Seth pushed especially hard for the release of Indonesians around the country.

Seth found himself speaking on behalf of Indonesians with field office directors in Los Angeles, Seattle, Cleveland, Boston, Maryland, Philadelphia, and New York.

CHAPTER 20

A Grim Discovery of Human Trafficking

In Elizabeth and Highland Park, 2010

No release in 2010 was more significant than the release of a young German graduate student named Karsten, according to Seth. Karsten's release from Elizabeth Detention Center led to an amazing new ministry.[1]

Karsten was a theology student from Germany studying at Princeton Theological Seminary while his wife, an American woman named Diana, worked on completing her PhD in psychology at a Princeton hospital. One morning in May 2010, after Diana left for work, there was a knock at their door. When Karsten answered it, two men with badges grabbed him, put him in handcuffs, and led him away to an unmarked car.

A few nights later, the church visitation team was at the detention center when Dolores Ranghelli, a most caring and intuitive church member, saw a young woman, Karsten's wife Diana, crying in the waiting area. Delores approached Diana and asked what was wrong. Diana explained that she and Karsten were married and that they had filed immigration forms, but they must have done something wrong.

[1] SKD, 46–48.

Three weeks earlier, Karsten and Diana had gone to the citizenship organization of DHS, USCIS, to correct their mistakes. At the time, the couple thought everything had been worked out. Instead, USCIS turned Karsten's case over to ICE. And as the church had come to learn by this time, all ICE does is detain and remove.

Seth emailed Nina Bernstein to let her know that there was a German seminary student with a U.S. citizen wife sitting in Elizabeth Detention Center. Then he called the field office director in Newark to let him know that a reporter from the *New York Times* was on her way to talk with them about Karsten.

Before Nina reached the detention center, ICE released Karsten.

The few days Karsten spent in detention had a profound effect on him. Karsten was shocked that his had been the only white face in a sea of brown and black faces from around the world. While inside, Karsten had met some wonderful people, including many who had come to the States seeking sanctuary and protection and now, instead, were languishing in jail.

When Seth met with Karsten, Karsten exclaimed, "If you think my story is terrible, you have to hear what happened to my friend Roy George!"

Then Karsten specifically asked Seth to work for the release of Roy George from India. Seth was moved by Karsten's concern and set about requesting the release of Roy George.

In June 2010, after many days of calls and requests, ICE finally released Roy George under the supervision of the church. Temporarily, Karsten and Diane hosted Roy in their small Princeton graduate apartment. Roy met Seth and then joined the church for Sunday worship.

As Harry and Franco had done before him, Karsten stood up during the prayers of the people at the end of Sunday worship. He thanked the church for helping to win his release and for winning the release of his friend, Roy George.

As happened on any Sunday when some major victory like this occurred, the whole congregation stood up, applauded, and gave thanks to God.

A few days later, Roy sat down with Seth and Jean and unraveled his complex story.

Back in 2006, Roy George had come to work with a major U.S. shipping company in the Gulf of Mexico. He had been promised a green card that never materialized. He'd also been promised that he could bring his family to the U.S. eighteen months after he arrived.

Instead, years had gone by, and Roy found himself without proper work authorization. He realized he would never be permitted to bring his family.

Roy explained that he was one of as many as 525 men from Kerala, India, who had signed up to work with a corporation called Signal International.[2]

Like Roy, each man had taken a test before he left India to certify that he was an experienced pipefitter, welder, or shipbuilder. When Roy learned he passed the test, he had been hoodwinked into paying a tremendous sum of money, up front, to secure employment in the United States.

Between 2004 and 2006, hundreds of Indian men paid the agents who served as recruiters for the U.S. oil and shipping industry as much as $11,000 to $25,000 each for travel, visa, recruitment, and other fees after they were told it would lead to good jobs, green cards, and permanent U.S. residency.[3]

Many of the workers sold their houses and other valuables and took out high-interest loans to come up with the money.[4]

Hoping to provide a better future for their families, Roy George and men like him took a tremendous risk. They sold their wives' gold jewelry. Then they sold the land their parents had saved for them. And, for the remainder of the sum, they took out loans—even though India lacked regulation to ensure fairness and justice in lending.

---

[2] "Top U.S. Law Firms Files Multiple Human Trafficking Lawsuits against Signal International, LLC.," ACLU, May 21, 2013, https://www.aclu.org/press-releases/top-us-law-firms-file-multiple-human-trafficking-lawsuits-against-signal. See also Liam Stack, "Indian Guest Workers Awarded $14 Million," *New York Times*, February 18, 2015, https://www.nytimes.com/2015/02/19/us/indian-guest-workers-awarded-14-million.html.

[3] Michelle Chen, "These Workers Came from Overseas to Help Rebuild After Hurricane Katrina—and Were Treated Like Prisoners," *The Nation*, February 20, 2015, https://www.thenation.com/article/archive/these-workers-came-overseas-help-rebuild-after-hurricane-katrina-and-were-treated-prison/.

[4] We helped tell the stories of perpetrators including Signal International, New Orleans lawyer Malvern C. Burnett, and India-based recruiter Sachin Dewan. In 2015, the jury in this case ruled that Signal International, Burnett, and Dewan engaged in labor trafficking, fraud, racketeering, and discrimination. See "Exploited Indian Workers in US Awarded $14 Million," *The Hans India*, February 20, 2015, https://www.thehansindia.com/posts/index/NRI/2015-02-20/Exploited-Indian-workers-in-US-awarded-14-million/132642.

Many men—but not all—were recruited in India after 2005, in the wake of the immensely destructive category 5 Atlantic hurricane named Katrina that caused over 1,800 fatalities and $125 billion in damage in late August, especially in the city of New Orleans. At the time, Katrina was the costliest tropical cyclone on record, in terms of loss of life and critical infrastructure.

Most important to Roy George's story, Katrina disabled the oil and gas industry in the southeast of the United States, especially in Louisiana and Mississippi. More than thirty oil platforms were damaged or destroyed, and nine refineries were damaged and shut down for weeks following the storm.[5]

For Signal International, Hurricane Katrina scattered its workforce. Signal used the U.S. government's H-2B guest-worker visa program to import employees to work as welders and pipefitters.

When the men arrived at Signal in late 2006 and early 2007, they discovered that they would not receive the green cards that recruiters in India had promised. Instead, Signal forced the men to pay $1,050 per month to live in isolated, fenced labor camps. Often, as many as twenty-four men shared a single trailer with only two toilets. Signal officials told the guest workers that they would still deduct the "man camp" fees from the workers' paychecks even if they found their own housing elsewhere. Visitors were not allowed into the camps. Company employees regularly searched the workers' belongings. Workers who complained about the conditions were threatened with deportation. Some men were deported.

In India, they had been skilled pipe fitters and welders, and they were put to work in the Gulf of Mexico under dangerous conditions on oil rigs damaged in Hurricane Katrina. Until the work ran out. They were now in the U.S. as skilled workers without work and without work authorization. Without jobs, the men fell behind in the repayments of terrible debts to creditors back in India. Their creditors were harassing their devastated South Indian families. The men were stranded in the U.S. without legal support.

Soon Roy moved to Maryland, into an apartment with a few other men from Kerala who had overstayed their visas, all of whom had come to the U.S. through legitimate means but who had also been tricked into this same raw deal.

---

[5] "Service Assessment: Hurricane Katrina, August 23-31, 2005," National Oceanic and Atmospheric Administration, June 2006, http://www.nws.noaa.gov/om/assessments/pdfs/Katrina.pdf.

Then, one afternoon in September, there was a knock at the parsonage door. When Seth opened it, Roy George was standing with eight friends. These nine men had driven from shipping centers in Maryland, Mississippi, and Texas to see if the church might be able to help them with their human trafficking dilemma.

Serendipitously, that autumn, a seminarian intern working with the church had just started chairing a group at New Brunswick Theological Seminary called the Human Trafficking Round Table of Central New Jersey. For the first time, Seth learned about the various types of trafficking. The student, Marie Mainard-O'Connell, had been especially concerned about sex trafficking and had brought together experts from government agencies and nonprofits to meet for a monthly forum on the subject.

When Marie, Jean Stockdale, and Seth met with Roy and his friends, they could clearly identify their situation as an instance of human trafficking. Using contacts Marie had established through the Round Table, they set up a meeting at Seton Hall Law School for the very next day.

The nine men slept in the church. In the morning, Jean and Seth drove them to Newark.

Lawyers from Seton Hall listened respectfully, but they informed the church delegation that while they might be able to provide one person with legal support, they could not help nine, and certainly not dozens of trafficking victims.

The nine men belonged to a sub-group of eighty-five men who shared a more complicated employment history that had led to their being left off the list of hundreds of victims whom the Southern Poverty Law Center was already assisting to file for human trafficking visas.[6]

Colloquially known as T-visas, human trafficking visas enabled victims to receive green cards and permanent residency status in the U.S. In time, T-visa recipients could apply for their immediate family members to come to the U.S. with green cards as well. Eventually, victims, their spouses, and children could apply for U.S. citizenship.

The Reformed Church delegation walked out of the meeting at Seton Hall feeling dejected.

---

[6] Memorandum to Ellen Gallagher, USCIS Special Council, from Rev. Seth Kaper-Dale, regarding T-visa applications for 85 trafficking victims from Kerala, India, February 3, 2011.

Seth and Jean looked at the men, and at each other, and both agreed. "Maybe Seton Hall Law can't help," they said. "But our church will give it our best shot."

In the weeks that followed, Jean Stockdale and Marie Mainard-O'Connell studied the situation with other congregants. More than anything, each trafficking victim needed someone who could write in English to help him fill out a T-visa application with a solid affidavit that explained the complications and risks of his own situation. Jean and Seth set a date in mid-October and invited all eighty-five men from Kerala, India, to come to the church on a weekend for assistance with their applications and affidavits.

For a few weeks during worship services, Seth recruited volunteers who could commit a few hours each to meet in person with one individual who wished to file a T-visa application.

From October 21 to 23, seventy-four men from shipping ports around the U.S. arrived in Highland Park. It became clear that all the men had been conned under similar circumstances, falling for false promises of green cards made by the principals of a recruiting firm in India, assisted by a U.S. attorney in Louisiana named Malvern C. Burnett, and a local sheriff named Michael Pol. A wide assortment of disreputable Indian loan sharks profited from the scheme.[7]

Church members and staff were not attorneys. Volunteers would assist each man to "self-file" their own applications.

Marie and Jean paired the men from Kerala with U.S. citizen volunteers. Seth had recruited undergraduates from Rutgers who agreed to serve as scribes for the men. They joined church members and neighbors of Indian descent who offered to translate from Malayalam and Tamil.

Over the long weekend, volunteers received training in understanding the basic fact pattern and timeline that applied to all the men. Then they interviewed the men, listening, understanding, confirming, and then writing down each man's particular story.

---

[7] Michael Pol received more than $1 million between 2006-7 by importing 590 skilled welders and pipe fitters to U.S. shipyards, see Lisa Olsen, Susan Carroll, "Labor trafficking scheme reaped millions," Houston Chronicle, June 6, 2013, https://www.houstonchronicle.com/news/houston-texas/houston/article/Labor-trafficking-scheme-reaped-millions-4585015.php. After a four-week trial in 2015, a federal jury ruled that Signal International, New Orleans lawyer Malvern C. Burnett, and India-based recruiter Sachin Dewan engaged in labor trafficking, fraud, racketeering and discrimination, see the ACLU summary of David, et al. v. Signal International, LLC, et al., https://www.aclu.org/cases/david-et-al-v-signal-international-llc-et-al#summary

Volunteers could not promise anyone success, but they tried to give these men hope.

At the end of the weekend, the men departed. Volunteers stayed in touch by email and cell phone until every visa application was filled out and a narrative support letter written that explained who the helper was and how they helped the men to file the application for their T-visas.

The initial results were disappointing.

Within the next two months, every application submitted with the help of church volunteers received an "Intent to Deny" letter from the U.S. government arbiters located in the Vermont Service Center of USCIS. The Vermont Service Center was the central location for the federal employees who decided whether to accept or deny T-visa applications.

Community volunteers became discouraged. Many volunteers dropped out. A small group of church and community members then committed to help Jean oversee the next massive project: to respond to the issues listed in the Intent to Deny notices that the men from Kerala received from USCIS arbiters, and, if necessary, appeal each denial.

For the next four months the group met weekly. They conducted legal research, reached out to area attorneys, worked with national nonprofits that had expertise in human trafficking, and spent hours thinking through new approaches.

Jean made the boldest, most direct effort when she drove to Vermont with two of the men, to visit the Vermont Service Center, on a day that the adjudicators had set aside for visiting with members of the public who wanted to ask questions about the T-visa process.

During the public comment session, Jean asked the people invested with the power of granting T-visas if they would like to hear directly from one of the trafficking victims about how they got into a terrible situation and why they couldn't extricate themselves.

The decision-makers surprised everyone when they welcomed the chance to hear directly from the victims of this exploitative scheme.

The men explained how when they worked for Signal International, they had been confined in terrible living conditions and forced into dangerous work situations, but many of their fellow workers protested, and eventually law enforcement enabled them to leave Signal's employ.

However, instead of returning to their homes in India, the eighty-five men who sought help from the church immediately went to work for a second consulting agency, called J&M Contracting, which was even more devious.

Once released from camps run by Signal, the men were no longer kept under lock and key with armed guards. In principle they were free to return to their homes in India at any time. To U.S. regulators in Vermont, the switch of employers looked as if the men had taken on new work willingly, so therefore they could no longer be considered "enslaved."

But the men explained how the second company had "leased" their group of eighty-five men to Signal International before the men ever arrived in the U.S. Then, after the men were released from Signal, the second company hired them back directly while promising to finally make good on the promised green cards.

Victims who had only been employees of Signal received T-visas, while men who were victims of both Signal *and* the second company were summarily denied.

The eighty-five men that the Reformed Church helped were trafficked into working impossible, dangerous jobs—but not because they were being imprisoned by the second company.

The bonds that chained these men to their perpetrators were invisible, induced by crushing debt and financial and physical intimidation of their families back home. These men undertook terrible work under dangerous conditions for low wages because their wives, children, and parents were being harassed and extorted for the debt they had taken on. They wagered that working for the second exploitive company might be the only way to obtain a green card.

Some of their colleagues who returned to India had died by suicide because their debt situation had become insurmountable.[8]

By introducing real victims and enabling them to tell their own stories in person and answer questions directly, Jean helped adjudicators understand the extreme emotional and financial stress these "doubly trafficked" victims endured.

Eventually, every man Jean worked with received a T-visa, and as word of mouth spread, the final number nearly doubled the original number of eighty-five. National experts in the human trafficking arena told Jean that this result was unprecedented.

---

[8] Michael Kunzelman, "Lawsuit Accuses Oil Rig Construction Firm of Violating Indian Guest Workers' Rights," *SouthCoast Today/The Standard Times*, March 11, 2008, https://www.southcoasttoday.com/story/business/2008/03/11/lawsuit-accuses-oil-rig-construction/52489661007/.

Throughout the process, a few trafficking victims stayed in the homes of church members, sometimes for months, as they finished their paperwork. Seminarian Marie Mainard-O'Connell, and her family were leaving the area, and instead of selling their vacant home, they rented it to the church at a very reasonable price so that victims of trafficking could reside nearby.

Another church family allowed their family's financial assets to be included in a request to bring one deported man back from India.

What no one anticipated at the time was that Jean Stockdale would give her life to this project from that day onward. Jean moved to Texas to help repatriate additional victims who had been deported because they had not received assistance from groups like the Reformed Church, the ACLU, or Southern Poverty Law Center. Back home in India, because of the tremendous debt they had accrued, deported trafficking victims continued to be susceptible to violence, murder, and suicide.

Jean had been a critical member of the Reformed Church of Highland Park since before Seth and Stephanie were installed as pastors in 2002. Single-handedly, she started a summer camp in the church basement for girls with working parents. She led the Who Is My Neighbor? Inc. nonprofit, which expanded the summer camp and then established an after-school program and homework help center. Jean had started a free-trade collective retail store that joined forces with the national Ten Thousand Villages chain, run by the Mennonites, resulting in a retail outlet on Highland Park's main street. Jean visited detainees in jails and detention centers. She coordinated ICE visits for Indonesians, helped organize their legal paperwork, and became an extended family member for the Pangemanans, eventually moving in with them to provide childcare.

For years to come, on an occasional Sunday morning, a visiting Indian family would stand up in worship, and the husband, who was one of the men Jean and her team had helped, would introduce his newly arriving wife and children. He would give thanks for all the help that enabled their family to be finally reunited in the United States after years of desperate struggle.

And the people of the Reformed Church would applaud and praise God who had helped liberate one more family from economic, emotional, and physical devastation.

And, as the Psalmist says, redeemed a few more lives from the pit.

CHAPTER 21

Betrayed

In Highland Park, October 2011

When an immigration judge issues an order of deportation, a period passes while the U.S. government arranges travel documents and transportation back to a person's original country.

Negotiations between countries can trigger delays. After international arrangements are made and the U.S. government is ready, it sends a letter, called a "bag and baggage" letter, to the U.S. mailing address that an immigrant has already provided to the court. The letter describes when and where to report for their trip out of the country, as well as the minimal cash and the pounds of baggage they are permitted to bring along.

If someone ignores a bag and baggage letter from Immigration and Customs Enforcement and fails to show up on the appointed date, then ICE refers their file to its fugitive unit that tracks people down, arrests them, and then detains them until travel arrangements can be made.

Fugitive listings reach local law enforcement offices. That means, if you are stopped for speeding or a broken headlamp, you can be arrested and held for ICE.

Ignoring a bag and baggage letter can buy you more time in the U.S.; however, you could end up in jail or prison awaiting removal. You could be charged criminally. Your friends or family could be charged with harboring a fugitive. You could be arrested in public, in front of your family, or in your bathrobe. The arrest could be embarrassing, frightening, or dangerous.

Ignoring an order of removal also counts against you if you apply to return to the U.S. to reside as an authorized alien.

In October 2011, all seventy-two Indonesians in the Reformed Church's order of supervision program received bag and baggage letters ordering them to report to the local ICE headquarters in Newark on December 10. They were to bring airline tickets for irreversible deportation.

Seth called his ICE contacts and was told that the Indonesians of the Reformed church, formerly considered model immigrants, had been reclassified and were now considered alien fugitives.[1] All orders of supervision had been cancelled.

The order of supervision program had been a bold success, a model program with the promise of reforming the government's practice of detaining people in prisons, but everyone knew it was also a terrible risk.

Faith meant walking forward and putting hope in unlikely possibilities. Now the worst-case scenario, one that Seth had foreseen

---

[1] In the effort to effect the annual removal of 400,000 people, which DHS was funded for, the line between civil and criminal penalties blurred. In 2014, DHS Secretary Jeh Johnson (who succeeded Janet Napolitano and served from 2013 to 2017) established Policies for the Apprehension, Detention, and Removal of Undocumented Immigrants Civil Immigration Enforcement Priorities (CIEP) in a November 20, 2014, memorandum. A 2016 report stated that these CIEP priorities "intensified ICE's focus on removing aliens convicted of serious crimes, public safety and national security threats, and recent border entrants." Failure to abide by a final order of removal was stipulated as a priority for enforcement in that 2014 memo, as the 2016 report explains: "More specifically, DHS's priorities establish three civil immigration enforcement categories, in descending order of priority. These priorities are: 1) national security threats, convicted felons or "aggravated felons," criminal gang participants, and illegal entrants apprehended at the border; 2) individuals convicted of significant or multiple misdemeanors, or individuals apprehended in the U.S. interior who unlawfully entered or reentered this country and have not been continuously and physically present in the United States since January 1, 2014, or individuals who have significantly abused the visa or visa waiver programs; and 3) individuals who have failed to abide by a final order of removal issued on or after January 1, 2014. ICE may also include individuals not falling within the aforementioned categories if their removal would serve an important federal interest."

back in December 2009 when he helped set up the order of supervision program, was about to take place.

For a few weeks, there was a lull in the church's advocacy. No one, including Seth, could grapple with this information.

All along, Seth's strategy had been to work to bring out goodwill among various members of the federal administration. He thought of his approach in biblical terms.

Some of the most dramatic conversion stories in the New Testament were those of Roman military leaders. Even Pontius Pilate, the Roman prefect or governor of Palestine, had his own form of a "come to Jesus" moment, when he told the crowd of Judean leaders, "Take [Jesus] yourselves and crucify him; I find no case against him" (Luke 23:4, NRSV).

But for the immigration advocates at the Reformed Church, the writing was on the wall. Seth's days of "redeeming Caesar"[2] were over. It was the first time anyone at the church had seen Seth stymied. He did not have a new tactic that he could pull from his back pocket.

I had become even more personally invested in the situation.

Back in the fall of 2010, Seth had asked me to accompany an Indonesian family who had newly arrived in New Jersey. Rita and Harry Tuwo were undocumented and had owned a home in Georgia. When ICE pursued them for deportation, they abandoned their home and sent their U.S. citizen daughter, who was eight years old, to live with relatives in Indonesia. Now the Tuwo parents were living in Edison, New Jersey. Rita had just delivered an infant named Georgia who was born with Down syndrome. The Tuwos were waiting for an official diagnosis.

Rita and Harry spoke poor English and were confused by the diagnosis of Down syndrome. They told me that no one in Indonesia had Down syndrome. Online research showed that it had been a long-term practice in Indonesia to institutionalize children with Down syndrome, though a few nonprofits were trying to reverse the practice and the cultural stigma.

I accompanied the family to doctor visits and helped them create a notebook that would provide a medical journal for Georgia. Every visit had its own page where Georgia's parents stapled the doctor's

---

[2] There is a long line of people who write about the sanctuary movement in the United States through a gospel lens, including Hilary Cunningham, *God and Caesar at the Rio Grande: Sanctuary and the Politics of Religion* (Minneapolis, MN: University of Minnesota Press, 1995).

report. The next doctor could page through the journal and see Georgia's medical history.

When DNA results verified Georgia's diagnosis, she was entered on the State of New Jersey's list of children born with birth defects. She would receive social-work supervision and intensive therapy, courtesy of her state, as would every other U.S. citizen child with her diagnosis.

In October 2010, Georgia was almost a year old. Her sister, now nine years old, had returned from Indonesia and was enrolled in public school in Edison, New Jersey. The girls' father Harry worked as a hibachi chef and brought home a comfortable income. But I was terrified about what would happen to the family if ICE deported Harry Tuwo. Rita did not speak English, and while she was caring for Georgia, Rita could not work.

Meanwhile, I had been working as an assistant to Seth and Harry Pangemanan while they joined in drafting a federal bill with a spirited pro-bono attorney named Bob Boneberg from Lowenstein Sandler, a premier law firm in New York and New Jersey. The bill would enable Indonesian families to re-apply for asylum.

Seth had undertaken this extraordinary and massive project in 2009 to provide a safeguard in case the orders of supervision backfired.

If enacted, the legislation would allow undocumented Indonesians to resubmit their asylum cases by giving them a reprieve from the one-year time bar.

Because of the time bar, immigration judges had denied their cases without ever hearing them.

The justification for the bill was that the time bar had been poorly communicated and had just gone into effect in 1998, the same year as the Suharto regime collapsed and spurred persecution of ethnic Chinese Christians living in Indonesia. Without the time bar, many Indonesians had excellent cases for asylum.

U.S. Congressman Frank Pallone, who represented the church's district, introduced the bill along with a congresswoman from New York City, Carolyn Maloney, a close friend of attorney Bob Boneberg. It was entered in the docket of the House of Representatives as HR-3590 and entitled, "The Indonesian Family Refugee Protection Act."[3]

Seth and Harry took a church delegation to visit congressional offices in DC and successfully lobbied twenty Democratic lawmakers to sign on.

---

[3] The full text of the bill, the Indonesian Family Refugee Protection Act, is found in the registry of Congress at https://www.congress.gov/bill/112th-congress/house-bill/3590?s=1&r=43.

Everyone acknowledged that passage was a long shot. There was zero likelihood that the Republican-led House Judiciary Committee would ever bring the bill to the floor for a vote.

Yet Bob Boneberg had studied an old bill, written to protect Chinese refugees from a ship called the *Golden Venture*, and the legislative team hoped that, like the special legislation for *Golden Venture* passengers, the chance of relief from an active bill in committee might forestall deportations.

Seeking to learn more about how such special legislation might protect my friends, I contacted the office of U.S. Representative Todd Platts in York, Pennsylvania. I spoke at length with a staff member who, since 2003, had helped lead efforts for refugees who had arrived in the U.S. aboard the *Golden Venture*, which had run aground in 1993.

The staff member told me a story of decades-long, impassioned advocacy. It foreshadowed the many years that lay ahead for everyone who cared about Central New Jersey's undocumented Indonesians. Like the people who devoted countless hours in York, Pennsylvania, we, too, might never find a kind of "golden ladle" that would scoop up hundreds or, we dared hope, thousands of Indonesian families living across the U.S. all at once. No matter how much we sought a single approach, a single solution might never emerge that would save all ethnic Chinese Indonesian Christians living in the United States without authorization to do so.

On June 6, 1993, the *Golden Venture* cargo ship ran aground near Rockaway Beach in Queens, New York. Its passengers, nearly 300 migrants primarily from Fujian Province, China, were being smuggled into the U.S. by a Chinese crime syndicate. Desperate to reach shore, ten passengers jumped ship and drowned. The federal government apprehended the others and either deported them or confined them to prisons throughout the U.S.

This incident established a new precedent for detaining asylum seekers through a presidential decision directive by President Clinton that stated, "INS will detain illegal aliens entering the U.S. with the assistance of criminal syndicates. Absent a credible claim for asylum, smuggled aliens will remain in detention pending final determination status so as to ensure repatriation if asylum is denied."[4]

---

[4] William Jefferson Clinton, "Presidential Decision Directive 9: Alien Smuggling," Clinton Digital Library, June 18, 1993, https://clinton.presidentiallibraries.us/items/show/12740.

A journalist named Patrick Radden Keefe tracked the international smuggling conglomerate that brought the *Golden Venture* to American shores, as told in his book *Snakehead*. In an article in the *New Yorker* magazine, Keefe explained how pivotal this incident became for immigration policy.

Before 1993, people who immigrated to the U.S. without proper documentation and then claimed asylum received a court date and then, most often, they were released. A good number vanished into the general population and never appeared in court.

But the *Golden Venture* incident marked a turning point. Decision makers at the highest level feared this "catch-and-release" system would become a "magnet" for future illegal migration that would exponentially increase, so penal detention of undocumented asylum seekers became policy.[5]

More than 100 passengers from the *Golden Venture* landed in York County Prison in York, Pennsylvania, an under-utilized facility that contracted space out to the U.S. Immigration and Naturalization Service—the organization that morphed into ICE in 2002 as part of the creation of the Department of Homeland Security.

These Chinese immigrants were so desperate for American freedom that they went into debt to pay their traffickers more than $30,000, enduring near-starvation and horrible shipboard conditions in hopes of a way out.

Deep in Republican territory, a local coalition sprang up to help the new arrivals. Lawyers with no experience in immigration law volunteered to take on the cases. Volunteers included Jews, Christians, Republicans, Democrats, and even factory workers who had little in common except their devotion to the cause.

A reporter interviewed one thirty-nine-year-old mother of three. "When we started," she said, "it kept running through my mind: How can I work on the same side of an issue with these crazy, left-wing, liberal wackos?" And, conversely, she believed others were thinking of

---

[5] The sheer magnitude of China's population was enough to fluster even the most ardent of refugee advocates. When Jimmy Carter admonished Deng Xiaoping in 1979 for not allowing more of his people to emigrate legally, Deng is said to have replied, "Why certainly, President Carter. How many millions would you like?" Before 1993, immigration detention was relatively unknown, "but after the decision to confine the *Golden Venture* passengers, the practice took root" (Patrick Radden Keefe, "A Path out of Purgatory," *New Yorker*, June 6, 2013, https://www.newyorker.com/news/daily-comment/a-path-out-of-purgatory).

her, "How can I work on the same side as this dittohead Rush Limbaugh conservative?"[6]

In the county prison in York, Pennsylvania, sixty asylum cases were denied on a single day. To me, this was a stunning prelude to the blanket denial of asylum cases of the Indonesians in New Jersey in the early 2000s.

In York, pro-bono lawyers had educated themselves on immigration law and they felt they had substantiated abundant, credible evidence of forced sterilization and abortion among the Chinese cases. They felt this evidence warranted the granting of asylum.[7]

Pro-bono lawyers were shocked into action when all cases were denied. Pennsylvanian advocates doubled down and approached each person's case individually.

One by one, loopholes and circumstances enabled unique solutions. For example, one person had a serious health condition, and a judge determined that this warranted a grant of withdrawal of removal. After many years in the U.S., another passenger married a U.S. citizen. Two South American countries offered asylum to two men and ten women.

Conditions for *Golden Venture* passengers who remained in prison were austere. Over time, as many as fifty inmates gave up and returned to China, where they were reportedly held in bondage, beaten, and conscripted into forced labor.[8]

This horrifying result was a potent reminder that filing for asylum is like making a public, international statement, one that a sending country like China, reliant on U.S. trade, does not take lightly. The granting of asylum implies that human rights have not been protected by the sending country.

In 1997, Bill Clinton permitted the release of 52 *Golden Venture* passengers from detention, but they remained on parole and were subject to future deportation.[9]

---

[6] Mary Corey, "From Refugees to Friends," *The Baltimore Sun*, February 21, 1997, https://www.baltimoresun.com/news/bs-xpm-1997-02-21-1997052016-story.html.

[7] Maryalice Yakutchik, "People of the *Golden Venture*: Unlikely Activists Take Up the Cause of Imprisoned Chinese Refugees," *Baltimore Sun*, July 23, 1995, https://www.baltimoresun.com/news/bs-xpm-1995-07-23-1995204040-story.html.

[8] "*Golden Venture* Timeline of Events," May 13, 2013, *York Daily Record*, https://www.ydr.com/story/archives/2013/05/31/golden-venture-timeline-events/74873332/.

[9] In 2017, advocates in York, Pennsylvania, were still fighting to shut down the flow of federal dollars that perpetuated immigration detention even though in 1997, Bill Clinton permitted the release of 52 *Golden Venture* passengers from

In 2003, the whole group of refugees from the *Golden Venture* was protected by pending legislation in the U.S. House of Representatives that Republicans introduced annually even though the bill never came for a vote. Fourteen years later, Representative Chris Smith, Republican from New Jersey, would become the last person to re-introduce special legislation for *Golden Venture* passengers in 2017.[10] The bill never came to the floor.

The advocates for the Reformed Church of Highland Park had modeled their legislative tactic on the very same one that had provided a window of safety for detained passengers of the *Golden Venture*. Lawmakers focused on the strategy of enacting special legislation that was introduced in U.S. Congress even though it was highly unlikely to pass a vote either in committee or on the floor of the House of Representatives.

The Reformed Church hoped that HR-3590, the Indonesian Refugee Family Protection Act, would buy time and protection for undocumented Indonesians. If they were detained after a routine traffic stop, their lawyers could use this ongoing legislative effort as a justification to delay deportation.

However, after obtaining twenty signatures from Democratic members of the House, by October 2011, progress on the legislation stalled. Now that ICE letters of notification of deportation had been received by the Indonesians, church activism stalled, too. ICE had created a ticking time bomb that was about to go off in December.

On Halloween, I was walking back from the New Brunswick train station after a morning meeting in Lower Manhattan when I

---

detention. The former detainees remained on parole and were subject to future deportation, according to Logan Hullinger, "Decades after *Golden Venture*, York County Is an Immigration Detention Hub," *The York Dispatch*, April 26, 2019, https://www.yorkdispatch.com/story/news/politics/2019/04/26/decades-after-golden-venture-york-county-immigration-detention-hub/3586202002/. See also Jamie Noerpel and Jim McClure, "Four Years of Wrongful Incarceration in York County Prison," *Witnessing York*, February 2021, https://www.witnessingyork.com/mapping-meaning/access-to-justice-the-mantra-of-liberty-for-the-golden-venture/. Noerpel and McClure state, "Clinton collected bald eagles. To Clinton, the paper art (Note: To pass time in prison, *Golden Venture* passengers had created sculptures from folded paper.) humanized the detainees. He reportedly was touched by the story and experienced a change of heart. He issued an executive order to parole the remaining 55 in York County Prison in 1997."

[10] For the Relief of Certain Aliens Who Were Aboard the *Golden Venture*, H.R. 616, 115th Cong. (2017), https://www.congress.gov/bill/115th-congress/house-bill/616?s=1&r=31.

texted Seth that I was terrified about what would happen to Georgia's family. Seth texted back, "Come right over."

Arriving at the church, I found Seth, Jean, and Harry seated on armchairs and couches in the parlor. They were talking about what to do next when I blurted out, "I am going to take Rita and baby Georgia and go camp out in the Hamilton, New Jersey, office of Republican Chris Smith. We'll bring diapers and baby food, and we will not budge until Chris Smith champions our Indonesian bill."

U.S. Representative Chris Smith had a reputation for being a conservative Roman Catholic with a conscience.

Ten years earlier, Chris Smith and Carolyn Maloney—our current sponsor for special legislation—had teamed up across the aisle to write the law that provided the T-visas that the men from Kerala, India, were applying for. Chris Smith supported the *Golden Venture* special legislation.

There was a pause in the parlor conversation.

In that moment, the three of us could feel Seth's confidence revive. "You know what we're going to do?" he asked, an idea forming in his mind. "I'll tell you what we'll do..."

Seth devised a plan to ask the children of the church to draw pictures that described how they felt about the federal government taking fathers away. He asked adults to write letters that asked Chris Smith to keep Indonesian families together. When the kids were home from school the next week during the New Jersey teacher's convention, Seth called for a caravan to drive down together to Smith's office in Hamilton and drop off the letters and drawings personally. It was not exactly a strategy, but it was a vital step to reset the Indonesian project before disaster approached.

On a weekday in early November, more than 100 congregants showed up outside Republican congressman Chris Smith's Hamilton office, forty minutes south of Highland Park, in a cul-de-sac of a suburban housing development that included professional offices of doctors and lawyers as well as residences.

Arriving just before the office opened at 8:30 a.m., congregants stepped out of their cars and filled streets and manicured lawns to pray and sing together. It was the first time in a long stretch that Americans and Indonesians had met with a single purpose.

The outing seemed to feed Seth's soul.

Once, in a Wednesday morning Bible study, Seth admitted to the group that he didn't especially find God when he was meditating on his own or contemplating on a quiet walk by the beach. Instead, Seth said, he found God when he saw God working in and among people.

Standing in the parking spaces of a Hamilton subdivision, we joined together to pray and sing and ask God's help to sway a congressman who was physically in Washington, DC, at that very same moment. But it didn't matter where Chris Smith was.

What mattered was that Seth remembered and felt the combined power of God's people, Americans and Indonesians together, imploring God for mercy and ready to help one another face the most terrifying realities.

The adults in the group considered dropping off a pile of mail for the congressman in bulk, but instead Seth asked each child to pick up a letter and deliver it to the congressman's representative personally. The children—Indonesian, Indonesian-American, and American—made a long line on the walkway that ran up to the congressman's office.

One by one, each child approached the reception desk, where Smith's office manager graciously received their letters. Many people videotaped the actions of the children and the reactions of Smith's staff. The videos were posted on Facebook, as an encouragement to everyone who had sent a letter but wasn't able to attend in person.

The next spring, Chris Smith became the only Republican to sign on to the Indonesian Refugee Family Protection Act. Although it has never left committee or even been discussed on the House floor, church advocates felt that Smith's signature was a wonderful and miraculous accomplishment. It certainly demonstrated the proposed legislation's moral worth.

But the most important takeaway from that visit to Chris Smith's office was that Seth felt the encouragement of the Holy Spirit, working through the power of the combined people of the Reformed Church.

The days when Seth could rely on his skillful diplomacy to negotiate with the power brokers in the federal government had come to an end.

A Democratic administration now set its enforcement sights on undocumented immigrants, even though they were parents of U.S. citizen children, and even when they happened to be endangered Christian Indonesians of ethnic Chinese descent.

And Seth had found what he needed to fight back: the combined power of the American and Indonesian churches to condemn the U.S. government for its faithless immorality when it came to destroying families, marriages, and the holy, God-given bond between parents and children.

CHAPTER 22

The Longest Night

In Highland Park, December 2011

On December 5, 2011, the Indonesians and Americans of the Reformed Church, along with hundreds of members of the interfaith and secular communities that supported them, rallied together in an overnight prayer vigil and twenty-four-hour fast. [1]

That night Seth announced, in defiance of the direct orders Indonesians had received from the U.S. government, "Tomorrow, none of our Indonesians will bring airline tickets to their meetings with Newark ICE officers."

The defiance in Seth's announcement made international news.

For a month beforehand, church members had hung a large, hand-painted canvas theater backdrop across the sidewalk in front of the church. Indonesian teenagers painted over the prior year's Vacation Bible School advertisement that, over the summer, had helped to pull

---

[1] New York Times photographer Aaron Houston covered the vigil for an article the next day by Kirk Semple who spoke to Seth by phone, "Canceling Stay, U.S. Orders 72 Indonesians in New Jersey to Leave," Dec. 6, 2011, New York Times, ps://www.nytimes.com/2011/12/07/nyregion/us-tells-72-indonesians-in-new-jersey-to-leave.html.

in more than a hundred children to learn more about the rainforest and Jesus.

Silhouetted shapes of a family filled the new center of the canvas: a mother holding a baby, a father holding the hand of a toddler, in front of a tattered page torn in two.

"70 Indonesians Ordered to Leave US: Keep Indonesian Families Together," the banner proclaimed. To me, the bold-faced letters, in screaming lime and orange, felt as if we had hung up a distress flag on a giant passenger ship.

The banner was arresting. Everyone who passed by the church knew that something terrible was happening in our town.

The Reformed Church had come a long way from the Sunday in the summer of 2006 when Harry's solo appeal broke the ice and brought our country's immigration crisis to the center of our worship of God.

At 8 p.m. on one of the year's longest nights, the church convened an outdoor worship service in front of its square brick bell tower. Hundreds of people gathered in the dark: members, neighbors, and supporters from nearby faith communities. Among them, local, state, and federally elected officials had come prepared to address the crisis. Members of the media mingled with the crowd.

Each family had brought a cloth sheet from their own bed, a sign of the intimacy and vulnerability that hold families together. Princeton Theological Seminarian Karen Jackson led an opening prayer ritual and asked worshippers to offer the corners of their bedsheets to their neighbors. Karen explained the symbolism: that the U.S. government was tearing families apart. Together the crowd rent the sheets into tiny pieces, unleashing powerful emotions that had built up for immigrants and their caring community under pressure from our federal government.

The swishing sound of ripping cotton went on longer than any organizer had imagined.

Then Seth introduced thirteen-year-old Naomi Harahap.

"Throughout the years my family has encountered so many obstacles and we are still doing our best without my father here," Naomi affirmed.

Seth told the crowd about an important clause in the Indonesian Refugee Family Protection Act. The bill, he explained, includes a far-reaching provision that enables Indonesians who were already deported to reapply for asylum from afar, in their home country.

"I'd like to call this the 'Merwan Harahap' clause," Seth said, "because when Naomi spoke back in 2009 about her father's deportation, I felt so broken."[2]

Two years earlier, Naomi had spoken publicly at the Children's Vigil at the church about her father Merwan's deportation in February 2009. Seth reminded us of how eleven-year-old Naomi recounted saying goodbye to her father at the Middlesex County Jail. The younger Naomi shared how upset she was because she could not touch her father. She pressed her hand on one side of the thick Plexiglass that separated them while Merwan pressed his hand on the other side.

As Seventh-day Adventists, Merwan and his wife Riasari had left Indonesia because they had been victims of religious persecution and discrimination. But life in the United States was still very hard.

"There have been so many days I see my mom frozen and unsure about what to do next. As a child, it is very frightening," Naomi explained. After Merwan was deported, the only job Riasari could find paid just $7.35 an hour for working in a warehouse. She paid $25 a week to a driver who brought her to and from work, and she struggled to pay $895 per month in rent.

"It is also frightening to hear about my father over there, struggling and not able to receive a job," Naomi recounted.

As a deported ethnic Chinese Christian, Merwan had been unable to find work in Indonesia. Indonesian ID cards prominently display their owner's religious affiliation. Anti-Christian discrimination was widespread. Riasari sent Merwan money whenever she could.

Two years after Merwan's deportation, their situation had not greatly improved, explained Naomi, "I experience so many nights when all I hear is weeping. This bill can save people from experiencing what families like mine have suffered through."

To energize the crowd, Naomi quoted President Obama saying that change will not come if we wait for some other person or some other time—we are the ones we have been waiting for, we are the change that we seek.

"We can prevent many families from being separated and deported and we can help bring back those who have been deported. I have faith and hope for a brighter tomorrow," Naomi encouraged us.

---

[2] Qtd. in A. Massie, "A letter from US citizen daughter who her father been deported," YouTube video, January 13, 2012, https://www.youtube.com/watch?v=8sdaQQ_GySU.

After speeches by elected officials, a host of activities were scheduled to keep people engaged even though they promised to fast. The sanctuary was transformed into a labyrinth to learn about immigration. The social hall was decorated, a bit earlier than usual, with all the lights and trees of a big family Christmas. The hall became a call center, complete with scripts, where people could leave messages for U.S. senators and representatives to beg for their help in keeping Indonesian families together in New Jersey.

At midnight, participants breathed in freedom through yoga chants and expressed their hopes and dreams in art therapy.

A local sculpture artist, Alan Arp, gathered a team of young men who tied the remnants of the bed sheets that people had torn into long ribbons and then hung them from the top of the bell tower. They spent hours on this task, spreading the ribbons in bands that wrapped throughout the social hall.

In his initial plan, Alan had designed a work of protest art that anticipated each sheet would be torn in two. But the crowd had gone wild. Ripping cotton swaths was such a liberating experience that they tore the sheets to shreds. The draped remnants of torn bed sheets, dripping from the top of the bell tower like some misbegotten garland, bespoke the church's solidarity with families the federal government had ripped apart.

Christmas lights blanketing a giant fir tree outside the parsonage next door twinkled through a rainy mist. All night long, bonfires smoldered under tent canopies. Sitting on lawn chairs around campfires, community members kept watch, singing and praying until dawn.

When the sun rose, and before American volunteer leaders left to accompany Indonesians to their ICE appointments in Newark, the congregation held an Ash Wednesday-type service in the church social hall. Indonesians brought their U.S. citizen children.

Indonesian news media recorded the ritual. On the foreheads of everyone who was reporting to ICE that day, Pastors Seth and Stephanie placed ashes in the form of crosses. The smudged cross was a universal sign.

We have all sinned and yet somehow God forgives us.

By midafternoon, all visits with ICE were complete. No one had been detained. That evening, hungry and exhausted Indonesian families and their American allies returned from ICE in Newark to a giant spaghetti dinner in the church. Then everyone went home, exhausted. But no one was safe.

The next day, Seth sent out an excited but somewhat panicked email.

Camera crews and reporters from CNN and several other national news outlets had finally arrived at the church, following up on the news releases we'd sent out two days earlier.

Now the church was empty, however, except for dusty remnants, leftover posters, and candles from the night before. Indonesians had scurried off to work or were home, sleeping and recovering, emotionally exhausted from the drama and a twenty-four-hour fast. Church members were still working to get the timing right about when to send out press releases. They had offered up a panoply of media opportunities over the last thirty-six hours, yet the national media rallied to Highland Park only after their last energy was spent.

"Any Indonesian who gets this message: Head to the church immediately!" Seth urged in an email.

I rushed to pick up baby Georgia and her mom Rita from their apartment in Edison. Still recovering myself, I vowed never again to combine an overnight vigil with a twenty-four-hour fast. But our all-out effort had worked. National media had come to the rescue.

CNN reporter Mary Snow spent the day with Harry, visiting him in his apartment and in the parsonage living room filled with its traditionally enormous tree trimmed with family decorations. Camera crews captured Harry and Jean Stockdale getting Jocelyn ready and then Harry carrying two instrument cases for her on their daily walk to school.

Harry divulged to Mary that he was 99 percent certain he would be deported, based on what ICE had told him. Nevertheless, Harry's faith told him otherwise.

"Your faith!" Mary exclaimed. Then she highlighted the long saga of Christian persecution in Indonesia, how the Indonesians had complied with NSEERS, and how the church was helping to sponsor legislation to protect them.

Chatting with Mary Snow in the sanctuary, Seth admitted he was deeply angry.

"But more than angry," Seth said, "I am despairing that the politics in Washington would lead to the inability to make compassionate decisions to keep families together."[3]

---

[3] Mary Snow, "NJ Indonesian Immigrants Targeted by the INS," *CNN*, December 11, 2011, https://www.cnn.com/2011/12/11/us/nj-indonesian-immigrants-targeted-by-the-ins/index.html.

Mary's feature aired that Sunday, December 11. Our faith and our prayers had been lifted onto a national platform. The nation was scrutinizing the actions of ICE. We hoped and prayed that ICE and the Obama administration were watching.

Before I left to drive Georgia and Rita home, I stopped by the church office where a member of the Chinese Protestant congregation, which worshiped in the sanctuary at noon on Sundays, had brought Seth a printed copy of *China World News*. The front-page photo featured the New Jersey pastor who stood by undocumented Indonesians. The headline was written in Chinese characters. I could read the number "72."

That is when I learned that this congregation, which joined us at wintertime potluck suppers, was not exactly composed of Chinese people but rather Indonesians of Chinese descent whose families had been granted refugee status in the U.S. The woman I spoke with said her family had directly benefited from intense lobbying by a former Reformed Church pastor who had sponsored them before 1960.

Prior to this, I had no idea that this Chinese Protestant congregation was composed of Indonesians who, decades after immigrating, had become U.S. citizens.

A side-by-side comparison of the two congregations would have been a wonderful study in the long-term difference that a bona fide, government-sponsored, refugee program could make.

My head was in a tailspin. As I learned more about the history of government policy in Indonesia as a source of the origin of animus toward ethnic Chinese in Indonesia, I learned that the Chinese Protestant congregation was an aberration as well. The UN had failed to direct Indonesian refugees to Western countries. That is why the successful migration of the older Chinese Protestant congregation who had worshiped in our sanctuary for decades had required significant intervention from a Reformed minister and his church.[4]

---

[4] Glen Petersen, "The Uneven Development of the International Refugee Regime in Postwar Asia: Evidence from China, Hong Kong and Indonesia," *Journal of Refugee Studies* 25, no. 3 (2012): 326–43, https://academic.oup.com/jrs/article/25/3/326/1554415. Petersen writes, "By the late 1950s, when the post-colonial government of Indonesia decided to launch a series of measures aimed at reducing the economic influence of ethnic Chinese and forcing their assimilation, most Indonesian Chinese were locally born (*peranakan*) third generation descendants of earlier immigrants (Coppel 1983: 1). Under Dutch colonial rule, which lasted for some 350 years until Indonesians declared their independence in 1945, Chinese had enjoyed a privileged economic position as officially sanctioned middlemen between the native population and colonial

It was a stark reminder of the racism and colorism interwoven in American immigration policies.

---

state. But they were frequently resented and targeted by Dutch and natives alike for their wealth and economic prowess. When independence from Dutch rule was finally achieved in 1949, the Chinese minority made up less than two percent of Indonesia's population but their economic role was critical, with ethnic Chinese traders dominating the wholesale and retail sectors in many parts of the country. The anti-Chinese movement in Indonesia thus had deep roots extending back to the colonial period. However, it was reinvigorated in 1956 when one of the country's most prominent native business leaders and former acting President of the Republic, Assaat Datuk Mudo, openly called for the adoption of an official race-based economic policy that would favour ethnic Indonesians over ethnic Chinese. Assaat not only attacked the privileged economic position of the Chinese minority but accused them of chronic disloyalty to the nation: of having sided with the Dutch during the colonial period, with the Chinese Nationalist government during the 1920s and 1930s, and with the People's Republic of China after 1949. The effect of Assaat's widely publicized comments was to unleash what one historian has described as a wave of 'powerful inchoate anti-Sinicism' across the country (Feith 1962: 481–486; also Mackie 1976; Coppel 1983). Matters came to a head in 1959 with the promulgation of Presidential Regulation (Peraturan Presiden) No. 10 (PP10/1959) which banned 'alien' retail traders from rural areas and gave them until 1 January 1960 to close their businesses or relocate to urban areas. Even though the decree was technically aimed at 'aliens' who were not Indonesian citizens, the clearly intended targets were ethnic Chinese regardless of citizenship; the Presidential decree 'applied...to everyone considered "Chinese"' (Mandal 2007: 49). An estimated 500,000 Indonesian Chinese were directly affected by the decree, which led to riots on the main Indonesian island of Java in which several thousand Indonesian Chinese died" (337).

CHAPTER 23

Relentless Pursuit and a Last-Ditch Sanctuary

In Highland Park, 2012

The high-profile media attention from the overnight rally on December 6, 2011, seemed to postpone the execution of deportation orders for many Indonesians.

In a press conference on the steps of the church on December 23, Seth urged immigration advocates not to become complacent. He explained how even the first miracle on the very first Christmas was incomplete: Herod had slaughtered the children of Israel, the Holy Innocents, as he pursued the death of baby Jesus. Yes, the Christ child was born, and yes, like Mary and Joseph's baby, several Indonesian people had been spared. But not all.

Only twenty Indonesians, out of seventy-two, received one-year stays. Among them, Jane Massie and her son, Ryan Sumigar, received one-year extensions to remain. Ryan had graduated high school the previous spring, and Jane was determined to get him through college. Her husband was deported in 2006, but their extensions were good news for him, too. "At least for the time we are here," Jane said, "we will try to give support to my husband."

Fifty more Indonesians were required to report in the first quarter of 2012.[1] Seth was worried. This was no time to let our guard down.[2]

In January 2012, the first Indonesians were picked off the street and swiftly deported.

This time, seven years after the Reformed congregation had been caught off-guard by the raid on the Avenel apartment complex, the leaders of the consistory of the Reformed Church were prepared. After they consulted with their lawyer, the consistory voted unanimously to offer sanctuary.

The church invited Indonesians to live imprisoned within the church walls, relying on the centuries-old traditions of English common law that respected the authority of the church to protect asylum seekers.

The practice of offering sanctuary (or protection) from prosecution dates to antiquity.[3] In the Hebrew Bible's Book of Numbers, God sets aside six sanctuary cities in the land of Cana where a person who accidentally killed another person could take refuge from people trying to avenge the killing (Numbers 35:6).

In the United States, a sanctuary church movement began in the early 1980s in response to thousands of Central American refugees who were fleeing violence from their own governments. Many of those governments had received U.S. military aid to fight their own citizens.[4] Too many refugees died on the route north.

---

[1] Star-Ledger Staff, "More than 80 N.J. Indonesian Christians Receive Temporary Reprieve from Deportation," *The Star-Ledger*, December 23, 2011, https://www.nj.com/news/2011/12/more_than_80_nj_indonesian_chr.html.

[2] Seth talks about an incomplete Christmas miracle in A. Massie, "Press Conference Dec, 22, 2011, at Reformed Church of Highland Park," YouTube video, December 22, 2011, https://youtu.be/0QMEgd6OVX8.

[3] "The concept of sanctuary predates Christianity, going back at least as far as Greek and Roman temples that offered protection to fugitives. Early Christian churches competed with these pagan temples by offering their own protections, and by the end of the 4th century, sanctuary was a part of Roman imperial law. If a person murdered someone and then ran to the church to claim sanctuary, no one could come in and harm, arrest or remove her for punishment" (Becky Little, "Claiming 'Sanctuary' in a Medieval Church Could Save Your Life—But Lead to Exile," *History*, April 18, 2019, https://www.history.com/news/church-sanctuary-asylum-middle-ages).

[4] Because the United States supported the repressive regimes of El Salvador and Guatemala, when U.S. immigration service deported political refugees from these countries, they received almost certain imprisonment or execution. Miriam Davidson describes this in *Convictions of the Hearth: Jim Corbett and the Sanctuary Movement* (Tucson, AZ: University of Arizona Press, 1998).

In southern border states, especially Arizona, concerned citizens and faith leaders, including Jim Corbett, John Fife, and Phillip Conger, began helping refugees from Central America to receive asylum.

Eventually, more than 600 religious organizations signed on to support the "Sanctuary Movement," and some provided aid to congregations that offered sanctuary if they could not offer sanctuary directly in their own buildings.

However, the U.S. government fought the sanctuary movement and went so far as to insert government informants—spies—into congregations and meetings. After a six-month trial in 1985, eleven religious leaders were indicted. Eight were convicted of smuggling and harboring illegal aliens.[5]

Though the advocates of this first Sanctuary Movement lost their case, Americans were appalled by the government's cruelty.

The federal trial helped win public support for more generous aid to asylum seekers, paving the way for the Immigration Act of 1990. Among other provisions, this act established a procedure that enabled the U.S. attorney general to provide temporary protected status, or TPS, to immigrants who are unable to safely return to their home countries because of armed conflict or environmental disasters.[6]

As I learned all this, I became more attuned to the immigration stories around me—especially in places where I had not noticed them before.

Rumor had it that during the 1980s, a Guatemalan family had lived in sanctuary at the Reformed Church of Highland Park. Another group of Latin American asylum seekers was cared for at St. Michael's Episcopal Church in Piscataway, where my youngest daughter attended Pinegrove Nursery School.

Also, I served as a chaplain in 2017-18 with a colleague whose family members arrived in the U.S. in waves during periods of repeated upheaval in Haiti. Several of her relatives received TPS after a massive earthquake devastated Haiti in 2010. Much later, in 2019, I became the pastor of a church where I learned the faithful custodian and the groundskeeper for the last 27 years had fled El Salvador's civil war and received TPS before they became U.S. citizens.

Immigrants fleeing desperate situations surround us.

---

[5] "Sanctuary Trial Papers," University of Arizona Libraries Special Collections, https://speccoll.library.arizona.edu/collections/sanctuary-trial-papers.

[6] John Powell, "Immigration Act (United States) (1990)" in *Encyclopedia of North American Immigration* (Facts on File, 2005), 138.

There is no legal provision for sanctuary in the United States. Immigration officials with a valid warrant signed by a judge can arrest any undocumented immigrant, even in a church, synagogue, or mosque. Anyone convicted of harboring an immigrant risks years in prison because the 1990 Immigration and Nationality Act prohibits anyone from knowingly harboring an undocumented immigrant "in any place, including any building."

Sanctuary, however, is not about hiding people. Sanctuary is a set of practices that a community engages in to protect someone from prosecution.

The legal definition of "harboring" includes knowingly hiding or concealing a person from authorities.[7] This is why, from his very first offer of sanctuary, Seth made it clear that the church would not hide anyone.

To enter sanctuary in the Reformed Church meant agreeing to become a public spokesperson for the public resolution of your case.

Each time someone would request to enter sanctuary at the Reformed Church of Highland Park, the church would hold a press conference. People entering sanctuary needed to agree to tell their stories to the press. Indonesians who chose not to become public spokespeople remained underground until they were caught.

We had friends who complied with orders to deport, rather than endanger or embarrass family members in their home country as public spokespeople in sanctuary.

Sanctuary was not about hiding, as nineteenth-century century abolitionists on the Underground Railroad hid people who had liberated themselves from slavery.

Sanctuary was not about defrauding the government, as the twentieth-century allies of the diarist Anne Frank and her attic

---

[7] According to the ACLU, "in order to secure a conviction under the federal immigration laws, the prosecution must prove that an action taken in aid of an undocumented immigrant has been done with the intent to evade detection by the authorities. If the government knows of that person's location, it would be difficult to say that they are shielding the person from the authorities or that they are intending to violate the law. Some congregations have adopted the approach of informing federal immigration authorities about specific undocumented immigrants offered sanctuary at their place of worship. While this approach may mitigate potential criminal liability for members of the congregation, it may create a greater risk of arrest for the individual immigrant. The individual immigrant and his or her attorney should be part of the decision-making process regarding communication with ICE" ("Sanctuary Congregations and Harboring FAQ," ACLU, April 13, 2017, https://www.sanctuarynotdeportation.org/uploads/7/6/9/1/76912017/sanctuary_faq_4_13_2017.pdf).

household succeeded in tricking the evil Nazi government that was intent upon destroying their Jewish lives for more than two years.

Instead, sanctuary was a tactic to bring about a resolution between individuals and the federal government. The practice of offering public sanctuary aimed to bring about a change in government decisions and policies.

In a sense, sanctuary was a giant dare.

Since the church could not prevent ICE enforcement, the church was daring the government to arrest persecuted Indonesian Christians under the full glare of the national press—instead of in late-night raids.

The Obama administration was on the record as caring about humanitarian values. In June 2011, ICE Director John Morton had established nineteen factors for prosecutorial discretion, which he defined as "the authority of an agency charged with enforcing a law to decide to what degree to enforce the law against a particular individual. ICE, like any other law enforcement agency, has prosecutorial discretion and may exercise it" in the ordinary course of enforcement.

When ICE favorably exercises prosecutorial discretion, essentially it decides not to assert the full scope of the enforcement authority available to the agency in each case.[8]

ICE agents did not have the authority to grant asylum status, but they could settle or dismiss a proceeding, grant deferred action, parole, and even stay a final order of removal—if they so chose.

Among the nineteen factors for discretion was whether the person had a U.S. citizen or permanent resident spouse, child, or parent.

In October 2011, ICE directors and agents in the Newark office had chosen to revoke the discretion that previous directors and agents had extended to Indonesians in Central New Jersey. By offering sanctuary, the church was testing the Obama administration. How willing was the federal government to be seen in the media as contradicting its own core values?

Also in October 2011, John Morton re-established a list of sensitive areas that had been stated many times since 1993: schools, hospitals, houses of worship, weddings and funerals, and rallies and parades were

---

[8] The nineteen factors for exercising prosecutorial discretion are listed in John Morton, "Exercising Prosecutorial Discretion Consistent with the Civil Immigration Enforcement Priorities of the Agency for the Apprehension, Detention, and Removal of Aliens," U.S. Immigrations and Customs Enforcement memo, June 17, 2011, https://www.ice.gov/doclib/secure-communities/pdf/prosecutorial-discretion-memo.pdf

places in which ICE would not engage in arrests, interviews, searches, or surveillance.[9]

None of these memos had the effect of legally binding law.

Thus, sanctuary was a public statement made by our community to wrap Indonesians in our own protection, to say with principled actions—and not just words—that our faith compelled us to protect the sacred bonds between family members and community members to which our government had paid lip service, yet had failed to respect.

Sanctuary was a tactic to call out the Obama administration and its supporters on their failure to follow through with the values they publicly professed.

Yet months passed before any Indonesians responded to the invitation to take sanctuary in the church. Immigration advocates feared that no one would seek the church's protection.

Finally, on March 1, 2012, Saul Timisela became the first Indonesian to accept the church's offer of sanctuary. News media members visited Saul as he publicly imprisoned himself within the church.[10]

Saul's immigration story was dramatic. He and his wife had fled Indonesia when his brother-in-law, a pastor, was attacked by a fundamentalist Muslim mob in 1998.[11] Saul's brother-in-law was beheaded and his body burned, along with his church.

No one reported on Saul without mentioning this, the most abhorrent and relevant component of his story.

Lent had started, and Seth reflected on how appropriate it was for him as a pastor to accompany Saul as he was "walking with Christ into a conflict with power."

Jesus had walked against the powers of Jerusalem that collaborated with Rome, to his own demise.

---

[9] John Morton, "Enforcement Actions at or Focused on Sensitive Locations," U.S. Immigration and Customs Enforcement memo, October 24, 2011, https://www.ice.gov/doclib/ero-outreach/pdf/10029.2-policy.pdf.

[10] Among many reports, NJ.com published a YouTube video of Saul practicing guitar in an otherwise empty sanctuary. See NJ.com, "Indonesian refugee takes deportation fight public, accepts sanctuary at Highland Park church," YouTube video, March 27, 2012, https://www.youtube.com/watch?v=1EhM6T3XZ8Y; Mary Snow, "New Jersey Church 'Safe Haven' for Indonesian Immigrant," March 20, 2012, CNN, https://www.cnn.com/2012/03/20/us/new-jersey-church-safe-haven-for-indonesian-immigrant/index.html.

[11] Bob Braun, "Confined Within Walls of Highland Park Church, a Man Savors His Freedom," NJ.com, March 25, 2012, https://www.nj.com/njv_bob_braun/2012/03/confined_within_walls_of_highl.html

One of John Morton's nineteen factors in favor of prosecutorial discretion was a person's ties and contributions to their community in the U.S., and Saul considered himself a patriot. In 2001, Saul worked for a contractor helping to clean up Ground Zero. Another factor was whether the person suffered from severe mental or physical illness, and Saul believed that his work on Ground Zero had caused liver and heart problems for him.

Later in March, Rovani Wangko joined Saul in sanctuary and, again, this was announced in a media event.[12] ICE had denied Rovani's request for prosecutorial discretion, even though, as a diabetic who would not receive adequate healthcare in Indonesia and as a persecuted Christian, Rovani met multiple factors in ICE Director John Morton's June 17, 2011, memo that promised to refocus ICE on deporting criminals.

Under the scrutiny of national media, ICE provided several Indonesians with stays of deportation. However, nine people with the most dire immigration cases—including Harry and Yana, Saul and Rovani, and four other fathers—were denied stays.

Seth and the Indonesians published their own video, asking President Obama to clarify, "Why am I a deportation priority?"[13]

In the late spring of 2012, a graduate student in documentary media studies at The New School University in New York City named Kelly Ann Bates chose Harry and Yana as the subject of her final project.

Kelly had tagged along for immigration meetings and events, recording footage since the fall of 2011. Kelly edited her footage into a twenty-minute film called *Broken Asylum*, and then she burned 150 DVD copies.[14] Her goal wasn't simply to earn her degree, but to use her degree to do good.

Harry drove Kelly and a team of church advocates, including his daughter Joycelyn, to Washington, DC, to visit with legislators, ask them to sign on to the special legislation for Indonesians, HR-3590, and deliver copies of the film.

Seth did not accompany them, but from New Jersey, Seth called offices ahead of the group's arrival. Throughout the day Seth texted them the times and locations of appointments.

[12] "Highland Park Church to House Second Immigrant Facing Deportation," Associated Press, March 29, 2012, https://www.nj.com/news/2012/03/highland_park_church_to_house.html.
[13] Reformed Church of Highland Park, "Why am I a deportation priority?" YouTube video, March 27, 2012, https://youtu.be/wovdI3NV9Zg.
[14] Kelly Austin Davis, *Broken Asylum,* Vimeo video, accessed August 6, 2022, https://vimeo.com/42500840.

Kelly, Harry, and the advocates were warmly welcomed into U.S. Senator Frank Lautenberg's conference room. Lautenberg had sponsored the Senate version of HR-3590. Staff members watched a screening of *Broken Asylum*.

"You guys have really upped your game," a senior staff member remarked. "We're impressed."

Harry's daughter bravely lobbied for the Indonesian Refugee Family Protection Act, handing out pamphlets and DVDs. One Democratic congressman's chief of staff coached ten-year-old Jocelyn, preparing her to speak to staff members for other U.S. Representatives.

"I am a U.S. citizen and when I grow up, I am going to vote," the aide coached Jocelyn to say. "You are going to need me someday."

On the Saturday before Father's Day, 2012, seven men joined Saul on the steps of the church. They held signs that called out, "President Obama, Honor Your Father Lolo! Keep Indonesian Families Together."

They hoped to remind Barack Obama of his mother's second husband, Lolo Soetoro, the father of his half-sister Malia. Lolo was Obama's Indonesian stepfather who never became an American citizen before he died in 1987.

It was an attempt to make a personal appeal.

These Father's Day signs, personalized to draw the president's attention, reminded me of an art piece that *Golden Venture* refugees, living in prison, constructed of intricately folded paper in the image of an eagle. President Clinton was known to collect artworks depicting American eagles. In 1997, soon after he received a paper eagle from them, Bill Clinton released the remaining *Golden Venture* immigrants from detention.[15]

But the timing was off.

Most members of the media who covered the immigration beat did not cover the church's actions that day. Their news was overshadowed by a major announcement from the Obama administration.

The day before, late on that Friday afternoon, President Obama had announced a sweeping executive order called Deferred Action for Child Arrivals, known from then on as DACA. For young adults who were undocumented but brought to the U.S. while they were minors,

---

[15] Noerpel and McClure, "Four Years of Wrongful Incarceration in York County Prison" states, "Clinton collected bald eagles. To Clinton, the paper art humanized the detainees. He reportedly was touched by the story and experienced a change of heart. He issued an executive order to parole the remaining 55 in York County Prison in 1997."

DACA was very good news. They had become known as Dreamers for the legislation entitled the "Dream Act," which by 2023 still has not become U.S. law.[16]

In the summer of 2012, the church's mission to rescue undocumented immigrants spread to residents of the Highland Park community who did not belong to the church.

The church printed lawn signs that read, "Let Them Stay: Keep PERSECUTED Indonesian Families Together." The lawn signs appeared across the borough and in front of houses of worship around Central New Jersey.

Highland Park's Jewish community, the two minyans that shared space with the church and the conservative Anshe Emeth congregation on South Third Avenue, just a block away from the church, as well as the Reform congregation of Anshe Emeth in New Brunswick, joined demonstrations and called legislators.

The slogan "Let Them Stay" reminded Judy and Steve Richman, who worshiped in Highland Park's conservative Anshe Emeth Congregation, of the "Let Them Go" lawn signs they had posted in the 1980s to urge the release of Soviet Jews to Palestine. As a retired attorney, Judy had helped guide T-visa applications for trafficking victims from Kerala, India, the year before.

Neighbors read about the church's commitments to its Indonesian members in the *New York Times* and on CNN.

An interfaith, nationwide coalition formed to support the undocumented Indonesians now living in sanctuary in Highland Park, New Jersey.

Still, at any moment, federal authorities could have legally entered the church property once brave Indonesian men and women declared publicly that they had sought sanctuary there. However, raiding a church is plain-old bad publicity. When the media asked ICE about Harry and the eight other Indonesians who had imprisoned themselves in the church, ICE told the media that the agency prefers to avoid arrests at "sensitive locations," including houses of worship.

Nevertheless, ICE vans periodically circled the streets nearby.

Sarah MacKinnon, a neighbor and speech therapist in local public schools, had come to consider herself an agnostic before she began

---

[16] Barack Obama, "Remarks by the President on Immigration," June 15, 2012, https://obamawhitehouse.archives.gov/the-press-office/2012/06/15/remarks-president-immigration.

to join the demonstrations for people in sanctuary and began to take turns staying overnight with Harry and the other Indonesians while they lived in the church.

Eventually Sarah, too, joined the church.

CHAPTER 24

Sanctuary Life

In Highland Park, 2012

Over the course of more than 300 days and nights, the Indonesian men, and sometimes their families, lived in the church, celebrating birthdays and doing homework with their children.

Though sanctuary was a public event, the church was not zoned as a residence. Highland Park's fire marshal had to be convinced of the merits of sanctuary. In the end, he agreed not to cite the church for zoning violations, but only if the church was guarded every night from 11 p.m. to 7 a.m. The informal deal allowed people to sleep in the church at night if the church committed that one volunteer would stay awake all night and keep watch in case of fire or intrusion.

Advocates called the night watches "sentry duty" after a snippet of a text from the Book of Isaiah in which God tells the prophet to post a sentry to look for a sign that Babylon, the empire that threatened them, has fallen.[1] Sentries were on the lookout for signs of hope.

---

[1] Isaiah 21:6-9 (NRSV) reads as follows:
For thus the Lord said to me:
"Go, post a lookout;
 let him announce what he sees.

For the people in sanctuary, sentries themselves were a sign of hope.

Church elder Selma Colmant, who had greeted Dora Schriro with a prayer shawl in July 2009, recruited people from many faith communities, ensuring a steady stream of volunteers while broadening the pool of advocates and increasing community awareness.

Since people on sentry duty promised to stay awake, they developed close relationships with the men in sanctuary. Community members like Sarah MacKinnon, who belonged to other faiths or churches, or who had formerly become disillusioned with faith communities, signed on to help.

Ostensibly, sentries were looking out for fire. Instead, when dozens of community members stepped forward, many stayed up all night with the Indonesian men listening to their stories, dining on spicy Chinese Indonesian specialties, and playing unlimited games of badminton.[2]

Though she was in as much danger as Harry, Yana refused to live in sanctuary. She insisted on keeping her job and working the third shift in a factory, which required a forty-minute drive. Yana had worked in the same location for six years and developed seniority that she wasn't about to give up.

In June, hoping to solve some problems with documentation, Yana determined that her best option would be to fly to another state that had a reputation for being especially helpful for people in Yana's situation.

I learned about Yana's plan when first Seth and then Harry asked me to talk with Yana in hopes that I could discourage Yana from

---

When he sees riders, horsemen in pairs,
   riders on donkeys, riders on camels,
let him watch closely,
   very closely."
Then the watcher called out:
"Upon a watchtower I stand, O Lord,
   continually by day,
and at my post I am stationed
   throughout the night.
Look, there they come, riders,
   horsemen in pairs!"
Then he responded,
   "Fallen, fallen is Babylon,
and all the images of her gods
   lie shattered on the ground."

[2] Interview with Sarah McKinnon, March 2017.

traveling out of state. Her plan was very dangerous—Yana could be picked up at the airport or while driving in another state.

One bright June morning, Yana and I stood outside, across from the church, at the corner of South Second Avenue and Magnolia Streets, and Yana read me what I came to think of as an undocumented Indonesian woman's "bill of rights."

Yana explained what it meant to sacrifice everything—her ability to visit her childhood home, to spend time with her aging parents, to nurse them as they aged and died, and even her chance to raise her own son whom she left in Indonesia—in order to work and support them all.

Yana did not make those sacrifices to give up the job she fought hard for, a job that paid for her daughters' swim, dance, and music lessons, a job that paid to build her parents a new home, a job that enabled her son Adrian, the child she might never see in person again, to be the first in his family to go to college.

Since she was a child, Yana had been a hard worker.

Yana's family members still live in the poor farming village in Papua where Yana was born in 1964. From the time that the Japanese military razed their family home during ethnic cleansing in World War II, the family had shared the homes of relatives.

Her mother was illiterate, and her father only reached second grade. Yana and her siblings received charity tuition until they completed Catholic middle school, then Yana sold tickets at a theater to pay her own high school tuition. She worked in a Papua department store until it closed.

To support her parents and siblings, Yana moved two thousand miles away to the capital city of Jakarta, where she worked in a beauty salon and took extension classes. She landed a job managing an office for a logging company. Her son Adrian was born in 1990 but Yana did not marry his Muslim father and feared he would take her son away. She hid Adrian with her parents on their island of Papua. She continued to work in Jakarta to support her extended family back in Papua. When a widespread Asian economic crisis hit in 1996, the logging company went bankrupt.

Yana received an American tourist visa that was good for five years. She moved to Edison, New Jersey. where she worked grueling, eighteen-hour shifts at a twenty-four-hour Burger King managed by a friend she had met in Jakarta. By day, Yana slept on a couch where another Indonesian slept at night.

Tragedy struck when six-year-old Adrian was hit by a car. Yana returned to Indonesia to ensure he received surgery in Jakarta, and then she continued to work there while Adrian recovered in Papua. But in May 1998, when riots swept through Jakarta's Chinese neighborhoods, Yana and a cousin barely escaped on a flight bound for the Netherlands, and then Yana flew back to Newark.

Yana knew she wasn't supposed to re-enter with the same visa, but the customs agent only asked if she had any friends in the U.S. who would help her. When Yana replied, yes, she entered the U.S. and never saw her mother or father or her son Adrian in person again.

In 2012, Yana would not trade the freedom that enabled her daughters to live somewhat normally, to go back and forth to school like their classmates, for Seth and Harry's strategy, which felt to her like imprisonment in the church. Yana feared the enforced passivity of sanctuary could mean the death of her spirit.

Life, as Yana lived it, required her to risk everything, as long as she remained faithful to her unflinching trust that God would provide a way for her.

And Yana was right. Life in sanctuary was not merely gruelingly tedious. For men who could no longer provide for their families by working, sanctuary was downright demoralizing.

Life itself happened outside the walls of the church. During the summer, whenever mothers would go to the beach or pool with children whose fathers were in sanctuary, the fathers could only participate by watching their videos.

Another church had donated a badminton set, and competition on the improvised court was fierce, at least on those nights when the social hall wasn't booked with some community activity or rental event.

Despite efforts to keep up their spirits, families suffered. The loss of the breadwinners' salaries meant that mortgages and apartments were endangered, and wives and children feared becoming homeless. Even when caring American families stepped forward to help cover expenses, but that didn't provide the men with a daily purpose.

Over that summer of 2012, I made individual appointments with each man in sanctuary. Together we created online petitions for them on the change.org internet platform.

Each man dictated his immigration story to me, explaining why he had felt compelled to leave Indonesia and why he felt they could not return.

Each time a member of the public signed a petition, the platform emailed copies of their letter to the stakeholders we identified: U.S. representatives and senators, the field officer at ICE Newark, and the U.S. attorney general.

The men used the petitions to advocate separately for themselves with their own friends, neighbors, and communities.

Saul Timisela had been the first to seek sanctuary at the Reformed Church in March 2012. Saul had arrived legally in the U.S. in 1998 on a visitor's visa during the height of rampant instability and violence that had escalated when the Suharto regime fell. "In Indonesia, I wasn't able to have a steady job, medical benefits, or security for a future life. You cannot live like that for a long time if you want to build a family," explained Saul. "I studied sociology and social practice through the department of politics at university, but most jobs available for my kind of study were government jobs, and the political system started to weaken by then and persecution of ethnic Christians was already happening." Saul became a youth minister at his church, Tanjung Anom Adventist Church, in Surabaya, Indonesia. His church sponsored him to attend international youth conferences.

Muslim extremist groups took to burning motor vehicles near churches like his. "The violence would make it hard to travel to and from Surabaya, so when I received an invitation to travel to America for a Christian youth conference, I accepted," Saul explained. Shortly before he left Indonesia for the conference, however, Saul's family relayed the terrible news about his brother-in-law, the pastor, who was killed during an anti-Christian attack in Ambon.

"My family was worried and told me to accept the invitation from my church to stay indefinitely in the U.S. The violence spread and I was concerned for my safety because I was a minister," explained Saul. After his arrival in the United States and his attendance at the youth conference, Saul was offered a shipping and distribution job, where he worked for over ten years. "God blessed me that I got that job and income," Saul said.

In 2001, following the September 11 terrorist attacks, Saul's company sent him and his colleagues to Ground Zero in Manhattan to participate in clean-up efforts. He worked for four months at Ground Zero, collecting all kinds of debris, bringing loads to New Jersey, and installing new telecommunications hardware at the site. When the Department of Homeland Security implemented the National Security Entry-Exit Registration Service (NSEERS) program in 2003, officials visited his church and explained that congregants like Saul had to register because they were from one of the predominantly Muslim countries listed in the program criteria.

Saul came forward voluntarily and explained why: "The Indonesians in my church, including myself, are all Christians. I felt like I had nothing to hide; we were not terrorists, and I thought that I could only benefit by being honest and coming forward." Saul had always paid his taxes and never committed a crime. Prior to his residing in sanctuary, he was an active member, with his wife Juliana, of the Seventh-day Adventist Church in South Plainfield, New Jersey, ministering in a youth program that planned visits to residents of nursing homes, as well as leading singing and fellowship for the youth there.

Gunawan Liem was born in 1963 in Surabaya, Indonesia, and came to the U.S. on February 27, 1999, entering legally with a B1-B2 visa. He was 36. "I came to the USA seeking refuge from the mistreatment and discrimination that we faced in Indonesia as practicing Christians," he explained. "In Indonesia, violent, fundamentalist Muslims were taking over the town I lived in. It became very difficult for me to practice my religion freely. Extremist Muslims were burning down the Christian churches, and for this I feared for my life if I should have to return to Indonesia." In 2003, Gunawan registered for NSEERS and applied for asylum, thinking that by doing so, he was helping the United States fight terrorism. He served as a deacon in his Seventh-day Adventist congregation, where he worshiped for ten years.

ICE gave Gunawan a deportation order for June 27, 2012, even though his children were U.S. citizens. On June 15, 2012, rather than comply with deportation, Gunawan left his long-time job working in a trucking company and entered sanctuary in the Reformed Church of Highland Park. His children only saw their father when they visited him at the church. But that was better than being 9,000 miles away.

Arino Massie came to the U.S. on July 18, 2001, with a tourist visa. "I overstayed my visa because I feared religious persecution in Indonesia," Arino explained. As a Seventh-day Adventist Christian, Arino and his wife tithed regularly and paid additional offerings through their local church to their church conference and World Headquarters in Maryland. He and his wife actively participated in church activities and programs including, since 2011, serving as head deacon, a prominent ministerial function. He was reelected in 2012. His wife served as head deaconess and usher.

Through his church, Arino actively participated in South Plainfield Clean Communities "Adopt-A-Spot" Program to regularly clean a roadside area, even in winter. "The last time I did it was in the spring. The weather was so nice I took my wife and my son to join together. Two times I participated with an ankle bracelet monitor still on my feet," Arino remembered. The ankle bracelet had been placed by ICE to track Arino. But it didn't stop Arino from serving the country that he felt had rescued him. On June 21, 2012, rather than comply with deportation, Arino left his long-time job working third shift at a refrigerated warehousing company to take sanctuary with nine other Christian Indonesians at our church. His son was a seven-year-old U.S. citizen.

Roby Sanger and his wife came to the U.S. in 1995 because their lives were threatened by an extremist Muslim policeman who had moved in with one of his uncles who lived near Roby. The neighborhood was Muslim-majority. It was close to a large shopping complex. This policeman and his friends always gathered at a crossroads near Roby's home. Every time the Sangers came from church, the men were there, trying to stop them from proceeding. Usually, the Sangers just ignored the men, walking by quickly. "Until one night when my wife and I were on the way home from shopping," explains Roby. "Suddenly this man came and attacked us with a knife in his hand and we ran fast to a neighbor's house. And thank God my neighbor opened the door and let us in until that man went away. Since then, we became afraid and couldn't go out anymore. And we decided to come to America."

In New Jersey, the Sangers became members of the First Presbyterian Church of Metuchen, where they worshiped for sixteen years. Roby's wife became a deaconess and a senior choir member. His girls were also active members in Sunday school, and they joined the choir.

When Roby entered sanctuary in Highland Park, his girls were in fourth grade and first grade. Until that time, Roby had worked as a forklift driver and in a warehouse for seven years. His wife had worked at a beauty product packaging company for sixteen years. They always paid taxes. Roby worked nights so he could bring his U.S. citizen daughters to school and pick them up every day. Their home back in Indonesia remained unsafe for them. A few months into sanctuary, his relatives told Roby that the authorities had found a bomb near their church.

Rovani Wangko came to the U.S. in 1995, entering legally on a visitor's visa. "I overstayed my visa to escape the terrible discrimination against Christians that had taken over Indonesia," explained Rovani. "At various times I had been assaulted when random strangers as members of the public demanded to see my ID and saw on it that I am Christian. It happened when I rode a bus, and another time when I went to the store, and it happened to others in my family and to my friends." In Indonesia, nobody would hire Rovani because he was Christian. "Christians who go to renew a driver's license are put at the back of the line if a Muslim arrives after you. Some Muslim religious leaders incite their followers to commit violence against Christians; mobs feel justified and holy to hurt us," Rovani explained. The discrimination and persecution were government-sanctioned, he felt, because authorities did not step in to prevent the killing of Christians and burning of churches and homes.

After he applied for NSEERS, Rovani filed for asylum, but he was denied because he missed the one-year deadline. He was single but engaged. "Ever since I came to the USA, I worked hard to support myself and help take care of others. I work in restaurant and warehouse industries, and I operate a forklift. I have always paid my taxes, and never committed a crime. I served as an active member of Indonesian Family Church in Elmhurst, New York, for the past seventeen years." Rovani explained why he came forward voluntarily: "I registered for NSEERS when the program was created after 9/11 because I wanted to cooperate with the U.S. government, to live here safely, and to practice my faith freely. My work of charity is assisting people who break down on the road. I carry jumper cables and know how to diagnose car problems. I have rescued stranded motorists on the roadside at least ten times. I love helping people and want to be able to stay here and continue giving my skill as a Good Samaritan." Rovani's sister is a green card holder who became a citizen in 2012. His health was compromised by diabetes, and he could not get sufficient care if he had to return to Indonesia.

The last time Oldy Manopo had seen Indonesia was December 25, 2001, when he and his family were driven in a dump truck to the airport. At the time, Oldy's son was thirteen and his daughter was nine. They left the country while Christian churches were being bombed in Jakarta. Back then, Oldy's wife worked at an Australian coal-mining company. One day a mob of Muslim extremists surrounded the company housing complex. "The police hid the people in a dump truck that drove us to the airport," Oldy explained. When Oldy entered sanctuary, his grandson Sean Manopo was three years old. Oldie's son, daughter-in-law, and daughter were Dream Act young adults from Indonesia who benefited from President Obama's June 15, 2012, executive order for undocumented young adults who came to the U.S. as minor children.

Summer went by—all ninety or so days of it, one at a time.

There were bright moments.

Sometimes when Jocelyn would spend time with her father at the church, they joined a few of the men who would sit around a table in the old Sunday school office and peel sunflower seeds for each other. As the men joked, and when her father wasn't looking, Jocelyn would steal the luscious seeds her dad had peeled.

Considering what was going on at the time, Jocelyn said, that was a pretty good memory.[3]

---

[3] Notes from Jocelyn Pangemanan on a book draft, February 2023.

CHAPTER 25

Slipping through the Cracks

In Highland Park, Fall 2012

In September 2012, when school started again, many Highland Park community supporters of sanctuary gathered on the front steps of the church to donate school supplies and fill and bless the backpacks of students whose fathers remained in sanctuary.[1]

The news media used the backpack event to berate the Obama administration for its heartlessness.

And then, amazingly, ICE spontaneously provided a stay of deportation and work authorization to one of the men in sanctuary. Oldy was free! Church members asked why ICE extended protection to Oldy Manopo. An ICE agent responded that Oldy's young adult daughter received an immigration deferment through President Obama's new DACA policy.

Immigration advocates at the church wondered: was the tide beginning to turn in favor of undocumented immigrants?

---

[1] Eleven years later, as she edited this book from her college dorm room, Jocelyn remembered that she still had the backpack she received that day in her Highland Park home.

165

Meanwhile, Seth and Harry had tried to convince the men who remained to spend every night in sanctuary. Tensions rose as life outside sanctuary became increasingly difficult for their families.

Every few days, beginning in September, I began to check in to the old Sunday school office where I once taught Greek words from the Bible to middle school students who loved books about demigods. For years, the room had served as a storage area for arts and crafts supplies. Now the Indonesians had transformed the office into a kind of living space with a refrigerator and couches.

Elsewhere in the facility, each family had adapted their own private "room," converted from one of many classrooms. Despite the private areas, there was always someone in this common space, and whoever it was, they were always grateful to have visitors. Everyone I met there seemed increasingly sad and tense.

One day, the men in sanctuary gathered on the couches in the common space to meet with a local psychologist, Bruno Oriti, who was a friend of the church and a peace activist. Bruno had connected with a famous artist who offered to work with the men in sanctuary on an art installation that she hoped would focus worldwide attention on their plight.

Decades earlier, this artist, Helen Aylon, had worked with the people of Hiroshima and Nagasaki on a giant display of pillowcases that held their dreams and hopes.[2] The pillowcases art project was appealing to immigration advocates because it echoed the torn-bed-sheet ritual people had found so meaningful in the vigil held the December before.

But Bruno insisted that he would only work directly with the men themselves on the project. Bruno's goal was empowerment. The men, however, were exhausted. They had reached their physical

---

[2] Alex Greenberger, "Helène Aylon, Eco-Feminist Artist Who Pondered Change, Is Dead at 89 of Coronavirus-Related Causes," ARTnews, April 7, 2020, https://www.artnews.com/art-news/news/helene-aylon-dead-coronavirus-1202683365/. As an example of Aylon's work, Greenberger writes, "For 1982's *The Earth Ambulance*, she drove a truck with pillowcases containing dirt from places near nuclear reactors and uranium mines, ultimately carrying them out on stretchers and depositing the earth in a park near the United Nations. For another project called *Bridge of Knots* (1995), she had Japanese women write down their dreams on pillowcases, and she strung her creations around Dag Hammarskjöld Plaza, also near the U.N." See also "Bridge of Knots," installation by Helène Aylon in 1995 at the University of California, Berkeley Art Museum and Pacific Film Archive, https://bampfa.org/program/helene-aylon.

and emotional limits. Ever the trooper, Harry would have soldiered through, but no one else stepped forward to get involved. The public protest art project was tabled.

Then, very early on the morning of October 15, 2012, Saul snuck out of the church building to drive his wife Juliana to her work as a house cleaner. Usually, Juliana was driven to work by another Indonesian who worked in the same place. This morning, however, her ride fell through, and she called her husband.

ICE agents who were monitoring the church before dawn followed Saul and picked him up at the Dunkin Donuts on Route 514, at the border of Highland Park and Edison.

I learned of it through multiple texts, all sent before 7 a.m.

The first was from Harry, the next from Yana, then finally a text from Jean. It was the first time I didn't hear about an immigration emergency directly from Seth. Their unwritten messages suggested that perhaps Seth was the problem.

I was headed to work in Lower Manhattan. On my walk to the New Brunswick train station, I stopped in to find out what was happening at the church.

In the church sanctuary, Jean Stockdale and Harry occupied the front pew. They were comforting Saul's wife Juliana, who sat between them. Sobbing, Juliana repeated the story of how Saul was caught and arrested. She felt terrible. Juliana had pressured Saul to leave the church that morning. Juliana was distraught about her mother who was deathly ill. Not only could Juliana not comfort or visit her mother, but there were funeral and medical expenses Juliana might not be able to pay.

While Juliana spoke, Saul called Jean on the phone. When Jean told him I was there, Saul asked to speak with me. He told me how he was arrested and then he asked me to tell Pastor Seth he was so very sorry.

I told Saul to trust in God and not to worry. I reminded Saul that he was famous and that every article written about him repeated the brutal story of his brother-in-law, the pastor who had been beheaded. "Your brother-in-law will protect you," I told Saul. When Saul hung up, I asked Harry and Jean, "Where is Seth?"

Seth had remained in his house. I left the church building and followed a concrete walkway to the parsonage gate. Knocking on the back door, I found Seth sitting a few feet away at his kitchen counter, drinking coffee and reading the newspaper. He was quiet. I felt he was seething mad. Silently, I sat next to him.

After a few minutes, Seth said, "I told them, I am not chasing ambulances."

"You are angry," I reflected. "And exhausted."

"I am not going to call in any favors for a mess like this," Seth said with conviction. Sanctuary wasn't jail. Indonesians didn't have to stay inside. But the church was saying that they were providing sanctuary for people who weren't leaving. If they did leave, that was their right. But once they were caught outside sanctuary, there was not much Seth could do.

I sat quietly next to Seth for a few minutes. Before I left, I reminded Seth he didn't need to ask anyone from the press for favors. I had read a news article where an immigrant activist in Minnesota had been miraculously released—seemingly just because a reporter published an article about him. The same thing had happened with Karsten, the Princeton seminarian from Germany, when Nina Bernstein threatened to visit him in detention.

"Seth, you don't need to make any excuses. You don't need to comment at all. All you need to do is to hit "reply all" to your last email blast to the media list and type, 'ICE has detained Saul Timisela.'"

That evening after work, I planned to stop by the church as I walked home from the New Brunswick train station. Seth and Steph had organized a vigil to support Saul and Juliana now that Saul was in detention. It was just after 6 p.m., and people had already gathered in a circle on the front lawn when I arrived. I could not believe my ears when I heard amazing news. Saul Timisela had already been released.

Earlier that day, *New York Newsday* reporter Erica Pearson, who received Seth's email about Saul's detention, had visited the ICE office to ask questions about Saul. An hour later, Saul was released with a stay of deportation and work authorization, just like Oldy Manopo earlier that month.

In the press, Seth called their change of heart "glorious." *Newsday* captured a photo of Seth and Saul laughing together: they were so tickled by the completely unexpected reversal of fortune, they looked nearly delirious.[3]

---

[3] Erica Pearson, "Feds Decide Not to Deport Indonesian Christian Who Hid in New Jersey Church for 8 Months," *New York Daily News,* October 15, 2012, https://www.nydailynews.com/new-york/indonesion-christian-arrested-faces-deportation-article-1.1184090.

For the Obama administration, Saul Timisela, brother of a beheaded Christian pastor, was a hot potato.

After Oldy and Saul left sanctuary, even though ICE vans were spotted hovering outside the church, men began to sneak out to help their wives with sick children and work emergencies.

Looking back on this time, Seth remembered taking a phone call from a church member. "Seth, Harry's picking his daughter up from school. Is sanctuary over?" he asked. It didn't look good, the parishioner reminded Seth, for Harry to be walking around our tiny borough where everyone knew just about everybody.

"I knew he was right," Seth wrote later, "But I also knew that from Harry's point of view, picking up his daughter must have outweighed safety that day."

I'd rather have bad optics than kill Harry's soul, Seth told his congregant.[4]

In conversations with the media and the borough leaders, the church had claimed over and over that the men we were protecting stayed put inside our walls. But slowly, it became clear that while sanctuary offered freedom from persecution and deportation, "it was also a kind of jail," as Seth described five years later:

> We were locking up free people—hindering the movement of men who had previously had at least the degree of "freedom" required to make a living, to cover the rent, pay for food, and otherwise contribute to their families' well-being. They had the freedom to embrace—and be embraced—by their wives, to soothe their children, to be comforted by the feeling of family and community. Our friends might have been safe in sanctuary, but they were trapped, dependent on us for pretty much all their material and emotional needs. Sanctuary turned out to be a perfect storm for depression and despair.[5]

When he first noticed that men were sneaking out, Seth had warned them that if ICE captured them outside of sanctuary, all bets were off. Later, Seth explained, "I publicly staked my reputation and the reputation of my congregation on the sanctity of physical sanctuary while privately knowing that those in my care were buckling under the rigidity of the claim."

---

[4] Seth Kaper-Dale, "Keeping Refugees Safe, Without Imprisoning Their Souls," *Zocalo Public Square,* January 30, 2017, https://www.zocalopublicsquare. org/2017/01/30/keeping-refugees-safe-without-imprisoning-souls/ideas/nexus/.

[5] Kaper-Dale, "Keeping Refugees Safe."

Seth admitted about the last months of sanctuary, "I struggled to take things one day at a time. To be honest, it was way too scary to look into the horizon and not be sure how this would all end."

Sanctuary was unraveling.

ICE vans were circling.

Everyone was paranoid.

CHAPTER 26

A Superstorm to Remember

In Highland Park and Keyport, New Jersey, October 2012 to 2016

The entire borough of Highland Park covers only 1.8 square miles. In poor weather or blizzard conditions, many congregants walk to the church, which is just next door to the parsonage where Steph and Seth live with their three daughters. However, in a power outage, the church's nineteenth-century sanctuary, with its densely colored stained-glass windows and its windowless interior hallways and bathrooms, convinced Stephanie that it would be too dangerous to hold services in the dark. Pastor Steph had always said, "We will never cancel a worship service, except during a power outage." Never, that is, until Superstorm Sandy and nine Indonesians in sanctuary proved her wrong.

On Monday evening October 29, 2012, Superstorm Sandy hit landfall on the Jersey Shore, about twenty miles away from Highland Park, obliterating the power grid in much of the tri-state area. For weeks afterwards, darkness subsumed a wide swath of territory from the Manhattan skyline to the Jersey Shore. New Jersey Governor Chris Christie canceled Halloween.[1]

---

[1] Josh Voorhees, "Today is Halloween ... Unless You Live in New Jersey," *Slate*,

Yet, only six days later, on Sunday morning, November 4, the interior of the Reformed Church was glowing brightly. Stephanie hadn't imagined that Harry and the other undocumented Indonesians might be living in the church.

With time on their hands over the past six months, the Indonesian men living in sanctuary had become experts at major and minor building repairs for the church's ancient heating, plumbing, and electrical systems.

After Sandy touched down, Harry called friends who delivered generators and industrial-strength power cables.

First-time visitors Anthony and Renee Grigoli took a seat in a middle pew of the sanctuary and waited for service to begin. They were in the market for a new church experience. Looking around, Anthony saw people from all different nationalities and ethnicities. "Wait a minute," Anthony thought, "this is pretty unusual."[2]

While up front in the sacristy, Pastor Patty Fox conferred with the pianist. She wore a white liturgical vestment known as an alb that was cinched at her waist with a braided rope.

Renee had suggested that she and Anthony try out the church in Highland Park because it was near her job as a social worker. Renee's curiosity got the better of her when she learned that the church had hired Patty, an ordained minister in a same-sex marriage whose spouse was an amazing community advocate. Patty's wife Lisanne Finston-Fox served as the executive director of a beloved New Brunswick nonprofit called Elijah's Promise that she had built from a community soup kitchen.[3]

Anthony was so nervous at his first worship service that later he could not remember exactly what Pastor Seth had preached about. Anthony was listening for a hidden agenda. He could not remember the last time he had heard a sermon that did not have an agenda.

Anthony liked to say that he had searched many a Bible but couldn't find a single verse where Jesus instructed one group of people to tell another group that they were sinners. Primed by his

---

October 31, 2012, https://slate.com/news-and-politics/2012/10/halloween-postponed-gov-christie-postpones-halloween-to-nov-5.html.
[2] Interview with Anthony Grigoli, February 2017.
[3] Jennifer Bradshaw, "Elijah's Promise's Finston Announces New Phase of Journey to Help Those in Need," Patch, New Brunswick, NJ, October 21, 2013, https://patch.com/new-jersey/newbrunswick/elijahs-promises-finston-announces-new-phase-of-journey-to-feed-hungry.

past experiences listening to disturbing, conflict-oriented sermons, Anthony listened primarily to hear some kind of ultimatum.

Anthony waited for Seth to tell the congregation: Who are we against?

At the end of the service, Anthony and Renee stood in a long line of congregants who wanted to greet Pastor Seth before moving toward coffee hour in the Quilt Room, a dining hall whose walls were covered with homemade, glass-enclosed quilts. Coffee hour typically took place in the Social Hall.

The church Social Hall was a gym-like room, large enough for a badminton court. A decade earlier, I had learned contra dancing there, in great long lines below English country dance musicians who stood on a stage while a caller directed us. But the Social Hall was not available that Sunday.

Over the course of the week, cots and tables had transformed the hall into the borough's emergency shelter for Highland Park residents who lacked power and heat.

The hall's back section now served as a town-wide collection depot for Superstorm Sandy supplies that the Community Church of Keyport and its pastor, Rev. Dawn Seaman, had requested.

The year before, Dawn had served the Highland Park congregation as a pastoral intern and went on to be ordained and installed at the Keyport church. Then, in the wake of Superstorm Sandy, Dawn's thirty-five-member church became the supply center and feeding station for people from low-income households in the towns of Keansburg and Union Beach, perhaps the New Jersey area hardest hit by the megastorm.

For the first time in their three-hundred-year history, these impoverished towns, on the shore of the lazy, polluted bay across from New York City, had taken the full brunt of a climate catastrophe that devoured them.

As Anthony shook Pastor Seth's hand, none of these accommodations—the generators lighting the service, the church turned into a shelter, a disorganized pile of brand-new rakes and shovels, cases of bleach and plastic gloves, carton upon carton of drinking water—made any impression on Anthony. He told Seth, "I was waiting for you to attack some group of people in your sermon. You know...'we're the good guys, these other people are dead wrong.' But it didn't happen. And I just want to thank you."

"Well, great!" Seth replied. "Why don't you put your names and address in our visitor's book?" Anthony obliged and then he and Renee planned to head directly home.

But in the hallway of the church's administration building, by the main door that led to South Second Avenue where Anthony's car was parked, Anthony stopped short in front of a bulletin board. Every square inch was dedicated to Sandy relief.

Flyers listed needed food and supplies. One sign warned, "Sorry! Shelters cannot accept clothing donations." Posters announced a benefit concert for storm victims co-sponsored by the church and the American Red Cross. Sign-up sheets listed the names of musicians and poets who would perform. Another sheet collected the names of volunteer cashiers who would be entrusted to manage donations.

In the middle of the board, a sheet announced: "Work Crews Needed to Clear Debris in Union Beach." That sheet was empty. No one had volunteered to clear storm debris.

The day after Sandy struck, Anthony had driven around downed trees in the roadways to the town hall of his home in Hunterdon County, about forty minutes west of Highland Park, to see if anyone needed help. "All good here," a town staff person assured him. Really? Anthony thought uneasily. Someone has got to need help. But as he left the hall, Anthony realized that the non-stop whine that had invaded his ears since Sandy left the scene was the sound of hundreds of generators. People in Hunterdon County were prepared.

Renee reached into her purse and tossed Anthony a pen. He scribbled his name and cell number on the page for clearing debris.

The next Tuesday or Wednesday morning, Anthony was sitting at his desk in his office when he received a call on his cell phone. It was Harry Pangemanan. In his phone's address book, Anthony typed the name, "Harry from church," alongside Harry's number.

For years afterwards, whenever Harry called Anthony, "Harry from church," lit up on Anthony's phone.

Harry told Anthony to be at the church by 9 a.m. the next Saturday morning.

When Anthony arrived, three guys climbed into the church van with him and Harry. The temperature had dropped. The van had scant heat. It was more than a year before Anthony found out that two of his coworkers that day, both Harry and Sammy from Kenya, were undocumented immigrants.

At that point in his life, Anthony had never once thought about undocumented immigrants. He did not know that two weeks earlier, ICE vans had waited outside the church and then captured an Indonesian man named Saul Timisela, who slipped out of sanctuary before 6 a.m. to drive his wife to her housecleaning job.

Harry and Sammy were risking their lives to ferry supplies desperately needed by dozens of unofficial Sandy work crews that had flooded the state. But Anthony had no idea.

Thirty minutes from church, Harry drove the van through the streets of Union Beach, which were inundated by sand and cluttered with tons of debris from flattened homes, until the van could go no farther.

Outside a sand-buried house, they watched twenty people shovel and cart sand. Digging with Harry, Sammy, and Raymond, the third man on their crew, Anthony removed sand from under the porch until the team could pull the home's walkway steps out from where the mud and water had shoved them. The home's residents hadn't been inside once all week. They were renters. The middle-aged wife was crying. She couldn't believe strangers came from faraway towns and even out of state to help her.

Next door, her neighbors were living on their second floor—the only half of their house that had survived. They brought mugs of hot drinks outside for the workers. Groups collected debris along that street, and at the end of the day, residents called for a massive pizza delivery for the volunteers.

Spicy steam arose from dozens of pizza boxes as the sun sank on the devastated street.

In New Jersey, where life circles around New York City, when you go to the beach, you go "down the shore." For the next six months, Anthony spent nearly every Saturday with Harry down the shore. Their work was mostly demolition and clean-up. Anthony felt humbled to be throwing out the appliances, bedding, and craft projects that had composed people's lives.

It was April before emergency services including FEMA started helping to rebuild homes in Union Beach and Keansburg. Until then, residents received temporary rental assistance. Only a few lots were large enough for FEMA trailers.

When Anthony took time out to wonder why he kept returning to the Jersey Shore, he realized that his work on Sandy-damaged homes strangely balanced his day job.

Anthony's employer, A.M. Best Company, supplied industry ratings for the world's top three thousand insurance firms. Anthony loved writing applications that ensured the firm's analysts communicated effectively with their clients. But underneath it all, insurance, as a business, always felt a bit sketchy to him. It troubled Anthony that the multi-billion-dollar insurance industry relies on risk and fear.

"I don't like the endgame, the idea of insurance," Anthony said. Insurance companies gamble on disaster. The buying and selling of fear-based security made Anthony feel a bit uncomfortable.

Few Union Beach and Keansburg residents in Monmouth County, New Jersey, had home or rental insurance. None had flood insurance, a fact that is documented in Rutgers University's Sandy Impact Report, published by its Newark School of Public Affairs.[4]

That report mentions a few FEMA irregularities. Though FEMA clearly states, "Damages to a secondary or vacation home are not eligible under FEMA's disaster assistance program," nevertheless, FEMA received 32,647 registrations for second homes damaged by Superstorm Sandy in New Jersey. An amazing 78 percent received assistance—half were in more affluent Ocean County. "This award rate is much higher than the overall rate of 24 percent," states the report, along with the statement that "FEMA officials have not provided an explanation for this apparent conflict with stated policy."

In Union Beach and Keansburg, FEMA paid each household a total of thirty to forty thousand dollars, a drop in the bucket for houses in newly demarcated flood plains on the Jersey side of New York Bay. New regulations now required them to be lifted on stilts, ten feet above sea level. One resident named Wendy Keilen told Anthony how she had chosen a local contractor whom she personally knew and had paid him her last $30,000 to lift her house.

Wendy deliberately invested her money with a local firm because she strongly felt that, like her, they had lost work and they needed the money. But her contractor was overwhelmed. He left town with her money. His poor job was only half-finished. Wendy Keilen's house was left uninhabitable. She was full of gratitude for all Harry had done for her.

---

[4] Stephanie Hoopes Halpin, PhD, "The Impact of Superstorm Sandy on New Jersey Towns and Households," published by The School of Public Affairs and Administration, Rutgers-Newark, 2013. Accessed on April 2 2022 at https://studylib.net/doc/12542964/the-impact-of-superstorm-sandy-on-new-jersey-towns-and-households

Harry and Anthony did not lift houses like Wendy's. But they worked with groups to waterproof all the new first-story walls and secure new sheet rock ceilings. They installed cabinets and flooring. They provided what homeowners could not pay for.

Working together in a devastated landscape, Anthony and Harry became emotionally attached to one another. Sometimes they worked alone. Other times they were directing a team of unskilled volunteers from churches around New Jersey and out of state. Anthony came to greatly admire Harry. "Sometimes I look over the photos I took from a work trip," says Anthony. "There's Harry, fearlessly up on a roof, showing four teenagers how to take it apart."

Harry had a gift for working with unskilled volunteers. "You have to work with people until they are completely comfortable," Harry coached Anthony. "People won't make as many mistakes if they completely understand what they are doing." Anthony said no one works harder than Harry, because "Harry wants so little. He doesn't do this work for any other reason than that people are desperate for help."

Saturday nights, cold and filthy from a day working on Sandy homes, Harry and Anthony would return the church van to Highland Park. Yana served Anthony many Indonesian dinners. Anthony did not know that six months before Sandy, in June 2012, when Harry first entered sanctuary in the church, he had permanently relinquished his job managing shipping in a warehouse.

Two years after Sandy struck, in June 2014, the church would receive a grant for $100,000 from the New Jersey Fund for Hurricane Sandy Relief to repair forty homes. The church paid Harry as a part-time contractor. Anthony and Harry led work groups from colleges and churches across the country, organized through World Renew, a global crisis organization that coordinates volunteers through the ministry of the Christian Reformed Church in North America. Along the way, World Renew contributed another $70,000.

Using sweat equity supplemented with private donations, the Harry and Anthony duo parlayed those funds into repairs for more than 209 homes, owned by some of New Jersey's poorest families. From that time on, Harry never again worked for a commercial business but instead dedicated his life to the church's ministries.

It was three years after they first met that Anthony first learned about Harry's life as an undocumented immigrant.

On Sunday, January 11, 2016, Harry led an adult education class in the parlor of the church, sandwiched between the 9 a.m. and

11:15 a.m. worship services. Harry told the participants—including Anthony—about the time Pastor Seth miraculously appeared on a plane at Newark Airport after its doors had been shut. At the back of the plane, ICE agents were escorting Harry, handcuffed, to an immense detention center in Tacoma, Washington. Harry explained that before he was taken to the plane from the Elizabeth Detention Center, church members had visited him nightly. They also visited all the detainees in a Bible study Harry ran in Elizabeth. The church had galvanized a public outcry on TV and in newspapers. "ICE wanted to separate me from my church. But that day on the plane, Pastor Seth prayed with me and said, 'Give me two weeks.' Two and a half weeks later, I was on a plane back to Jersey. A taxi drove me home. My family and friends were waiting in the sanctuary. I've been a free man ever since!"

At least that's what Harry told the class of about fifty congregants who had crammed into the couches, armchairs, and folding seats in the church parlor. He was explaining why he had dedicated the last three years to Sandy restoration.

"When God fills our lives with grace, it's up to us to open the gates to pour grace out for others," Harry explained.

Harry left out of his talk the grueling months he spent imprisoned in sanctuary in the church before Sandy.

"For the first few times we went down the shore," Seth explained later, "we 'snuck' Harry and other men there." Church leaders had determined that there was no way on earth that ICE would be prioritizing picking up immigrants who were cleaning up from the storm. And if ICE did, Seth surmised, that would be a media nightmare for them.

Jocelyn remembered sneaking into the disaster area, too. "Me and some other kids tagged along some Saturdays," she said. "Dad gave me a small hammer and I knocked out chunks of concrete foundations and piled the pieces in a mound, while adults handled the big stuff. It was so cold."

For the first six months after Sandy, Harry spent most of his time organizing goods at church, not traveling to work down the shore. Only on Saturdays, when he and Seth imagined ICE agents were home with their families and therefore less likely to be out rounding people up, did Harry travel there with Anthony.

Formally, sanctuary didn't end until February 14, 2013. But that unnecessarily complicated the story. For all practical concerns, Superstorm Sandy had begun to set Harry free.

"God opens the doors with his grace," Harry told church members in the parlor. "Let us receive God's living waters and be a channel into our communities." He was urging church members to sign up to work on job sites or to host dinners and lunches for Sandy volunteers who stayed at the church.

Harry's talk took place on the Sunday of Martin Luther King Jr. Day weekend. The next Monday after Harry led the class, Harry and Anthony had planned a service day with several congregations whose members would help out down the shore.

"No matter what happens at the worksite tomorrow, do not worry," Harry coached his adult ed class. "Somehow the work always gets done. Our job is to make sure everyone leaves happy and safe."

As participants in Harry's adult education class rushed to grab a seat in a sanctuary pew for the next service, the parlor emptied. Harry was smiling, but Anthony felt like his stomach had been turned inside out.

Harry had always made sure Anthony put Renee and his daughter Bethany first before church work. Anthony was shocked to find out that all the time they had worked together, his friend and co-builder was a deportation priority.

"I don't know what to do," Anthony told Harry when the two friends were alone in the parlor. "I didn't know about your status."

Anthony couldn't believe Harry's family was so close to danger. If it came down to it, thought Anthony, Harry and Yana and the girls could move in with Renee and me.

CHAPTER 27

Victory in the Dark

Highland Park and Washington, D.C., 2012 to 1013

By Thanksgiving 2012, Indonesians would show up for photos and press interviews but, except for Harry, no one slept overnight in sanctuary inside the church. Tired and frustrated, men lived mostly at home and only pretended to live in the church for the sake of media interviews. Yana complained to me that her family had celebrated Thanksgiving in the church all alone, except for one other American couple who wandered in and joined them. I felt terrible.

Seth described how sanctuary took its toll, not only on the Indonesians and their families, but on him and the circle of committed volunteers:

> Sanctuary proved psychologically draining for us, too. The hardest part was that there was no obvious end in sight. I felt very guilty about this and struggled with extreme fatigue (I was also trying to keep up with my church responsibilities). When the men started to leave the premises, I had to "unlearn" sanctuary a bit. This could only work, I began to realize, if these men could escape from time-to-time to their true sanctuaries—their homes and

wives and children. I had to learn to accept a possible accusation of fraud, as I publicly staked my reputation and the reputation of my congregation on the sanctity of physical sanctuary while privately knowing that those in my care were buckling under the rigidity of the claim.

As time dragged on, we found ourselves not only supporting the men but also providing major rental assistance to their families, who were on the verge of losing their housing. One church couple renewed their vows to celebrate their 50th wedding anniversary and raised $5,000 to help Sanctuary families with rent. That got us through a particularly difficult month. In all, we put at least $15,000 toward rental assistance. ...

Sanctuary can feel like jail sometimes, for those inside and for those offering protection.[1]

⌘

During the month of December 2012, Seth tried desperately to end sanctuary, devising an advocacy campaign that directly targeted Gary Mead, the Obama administration director in Washington, DC, who managed the five-billion-dollar budget for Enforcement and Removal Operations (ERO). ERO was the division of ICE that detained people in centers and removed them from the country by renting 747 jet airplanes. Seth begged Mead, through the media, through our U.S. representatives and senators, and directly by hounding his office, to have mercy on the Indonesians and the church. Mead did not respond. The pastoral demands of Christmas took precedence, and for a while, a disheartened Seth seemed to step back from the struggle.

Determined to reverse the bad taste left by a dreary and forgotten Thanksgiving, Yana and I planned a community potluck for Christmas Eve. Somehow, Jean Stockdale managed to provide Christmas gifts for every child whose father had lived in sanctuary.

My brother Robby, who had visited Harry while he was imprisoned in Tacoma, flew in for the holiday and encouraged my children and husband to join in with the "Very Merry Sanctuary" holiday spirit.

The social hall tables were laden with an eclectic smorgasbord: Sicilian lasagna, long loaves of garlic bread, and eggplant parmesan (on the one hand) and Chinese Indonesian holiday specialties such as *tinorangsa*, a hot and spicy pork dish that uses a specific spice mix called *bumbu* found in Manado cuisine of North Sulawesi; pork wrapped in

---

[1] Kaper-Dale, "Keeping Refugees Safe."

collard greens seasoned with lemongrass, ginger, and chili peppers; and *kue nastar*, traditional cookies baked with the dough folded over diced pineapple (on the other).

A few days earlier, sensing Seth's exhaustion as Christmas events got underway in the church, I begged a friend, Kevin Kraus, who had produced ABC News for thirty years, if he would cover our Christmas Eve Sanctuary at least on abc.com online. Kevin was a fellow alumnus from my undergraduate college with whom I had reconnected at our thirtieth homecoming weekend that September. He refused to publish a "puff piece." Instead, Kevin pushed me to find progressive voices in the U.S. Congress who might be able to provide real help.

Kevin emboldened me to reach out to a congressman from Chicago named Luis Gutierrez. Not only did U. S. Representative Gutierrez have a reputation for last-minute immigration miracles, but I recognized his name because he had also been one of the early signers of our special legislation to open asylum cases for Indonesians.

Two days before Christmas, I began to contact the staff of Gutierrez's Chicago office. I enlisted the advice of a national immigration activist named Michele Brane who directed the Women's Refugee Commission.[2] Despite the holiday timing, Michele kindly took time out to advise me. She had admired the advocacy work of our church, which she said had been on the radar of immigration advocates like her ever since Nina Bernstein's *New York Times* article in December 2009 about the unorthodox supervision agreement with ICE.

Michele coached me about how to work with Gutierrez. I faxed his Chicago office all the information they needed about the cases of the men in sanctuary. Somehow, Kevin managed to get Gutierrez to speak on the record with him about the cases. And in his resulting story, Kevin made blatant references to Seth's discussions with Gary Mead, including Mead's responses as Seth remembered them.

When *ABC News Online* published Kevin's piece on Christmas Eve, I imagined it must have appeared in Mead's daily briefing of news clips. I wished "a very Merry Christmas gift for Gary Mead" as I prayed that Gary Mead's wife or his children or his pastor might ask him about our story.[3]

---

[2] In March 2021, President Biden named Brane Executive Director, Family Reunification Task Force for DHS.

[3] Kevin Krause, "Christian Indonesians Live in NJ Church's Sanctuary to Avoid Deportation: This Christmas Marks Day 295 for a New Jersey Church Protecting Indonesians," ABC News, December 24, 2012, https://abcnews.go.com/US/christian-indonesians-live-nj-churchs-sanctuary-months-avoid/story?id=18057190.

I don't know that mediation from Gutierrez and Kevin's last-ditch-effort article made any difference in the struggle to bring sanctuary to an end. But for a short time, Seth got to rest while someone else took a shot at advocacy.

Then, suddenly, in mid-January, Seth decided to dial the number that Dora Schriro had given him as her direct line years before. The phone rang and Gary Mead answered this line himself. Mead asked Seth to meet in Mead's ninth-floor conference room on L'Enfant Plaza in Washington, DC.

When the meeting finally took place on Valentine's Day, 2013, the 340th day since sanctuary began at the Reformed Church, Seth asked Jean and me to accompany him. Mead and Seth exchanged pleasantries. Jean and I presented the remaining nine cases again. At one point, Gary Mead left the conference room. Mead's public relations manager explained to us the conditions of a possible deal. If the nine Indonesians were to receive stays, driver's licenses, and work authorizations, under no circumstances could the church issue a press release. "There will be no big parties," he emphasized. "I don't want to hear about any big celebrations," he warned.

He had certainly been reading our news clips. We were a church who loved a good protest party.

When Mead returned to the room, he pulled Seth aside. It seemed to me he was looking for some kind of personal reconciliation with Seth. He had talked nostalgically about driving through New Jersey with his wife on his way to go to New York City for Lincoln Center performances and Broadway shows. It seemed to me that Mead was doing all he could to humanize himself with Seth.

We left Mead's office and retrieved the church van from the L'Enfant Plaza parking lot next door. On the ride back north, Seth called Harry and told him that the meeting sounded promising, and he hoped to receive word later that week or maybe the next.

I had interpreted Mead's PR manager differently. He had given us marching instructions about how we would handle press releases when ERO released our friends. As the van was barreling down DC's New York Avenue. I told Seth and Jean we would hear from the PR manager before we hit the New Jersey Turnpike.

Before we crossed the DC border on U.S. Route 50 heading into Maryland, Seth received a call from Mead's office. All nine Indonesians would receive stays of deportation.

Victory was ours!

In all the research I had done about churches who offered sanctuary to undocumented immigrants, one storyline seemed to hold true. Sanctuary was a series of actions conducted in the court of public opinion. The news media covered sanctuary cases because faith communities were putting themselves, their public standing, and their reputation at risk to protest grave depravity on the part of the government. I had read how government agents were loath to directly engage with a faith community who was making a principled stand. Instead, the government engaged in a counterstrategy of prolonged non-action.

As we had learned the hard way, sanctuary is difficult to maintain both for asylum seekers and church communities. In many cases, after a long period of time with no official resolution, the people in sanctuary would simply slip away unobtrusively, without fanfare, when the media glare died down.

Our case was different.

The federal government had been poised to allow sanctuary in Highland Park to languish until the point of dissolution. But instead, by focusing attention at a national level, Seth and the Reformed Church had achieved a major concession: its asylum seekers had been guaranteed freedom—not with a path to citizenship, but with official orders of supervision that allowed them to work, drive, and live as free people who were not being constantly pursued for deportation.

An international community of advocates and national media had helped achieve a major success. But no one at the Reformed Church could tell anyone.

Before we had left Gary Mead's conference room, Seth had immediately objected. Dozens of news writers were following our story. Gary Mead's public relations manager acknowledged that eventually the story would get out. However, if Mead's office heard of one party, or read one self-congratulatory quote in a news story, all bets were off.

It would take months to arrange for work authorizations, driver's licenses, and temporary stays. While paperwork was processed, anything could happen to waylay the process. Mead's promises could easily dissolve in a trail of smoke.

I crumpled inside as I realized I could not share this news with my classmate Kevin Kraus, who had worked so hard to help us over the holidays. Earlier I had suggested Kevin subscribe to the church newsletter where we would announce the news, but I could tell from the questions he asked me that he probably had not subscribed. Now someone else who was closely monitoring the church newsletter was bound to scoop Kevin.

Seth announced the end of Sanctuary in the church email newsletter. Other media outlets picked up the news. Kevin published just four days later. Four days was forever in the life of national news media.

Kevin was furious with me.

Kevin's lede, or opening, began, "For Harry Pangemanan, just having been able to walk his 10-year-old daughter Jocelyn to school this morning is something extraordinary."

It was half true. While he was supposedly secluded in sanctuary, Harry had walked his daughter to school already plenty of times. For Harry, the difference was that he no longer had to look over his shoulder for unmarked, black ICE vans when he crossed the street.[4]

Soon afterwards, we were shocked when the press reported that Gary Mead announced his early retirement.[5]

Thousands of detainees had been released amid partisan wrangling over a funding remedy called sequestration. To grassroots immigration advocates like us, the Holy Spirit seemed to be using our country's bitter divisions to set the captives free.

Months passed as each person who left the protection of sanctuary waited for individual appointments to secure work authorizations and valid driver's licenses.

One evening, late in the spring of 2013, when everyone's paperwork was finally signed and delivered, Harry and Yana hosted a party in the backyard of their Highland Park home.

Their landlords Rob and Liz Roesner had been committed to immigration advocacy at the church since the Avenel raid in 2006.

---

[4] Kevin Kraus, "Christian Indonesians in New Jersey Leave Church's Sanctuary: They Were Living in the Church Because They Feared Immediate Deportation," ABC News, February 18, 2013, https://abcnews.go.com/US/christian-indonesians-jersey-leave-churchs-sanctuary/story?id=18533493.

[5] Eyda Peralta, "Gary Mead, DHS Official in Charge of Arresting, Deporting Immigrants, Retires," NPR, February 27, 2013, https://www.npr.org/sections/thetwo-way/2013/02/27/173090556/gary-mead-dhs-official-in-charge-of-arresting-deporting-immigrants-retires; Erica Pearson, "Gary Mead, Top Homeland Security Official, Steps Down in Wake of Release of Immigrants, *New York Daily News*, February 27, 2013, https://www.nydailynews.com/news/national/homeland-deportation-czar-resigns-budget-cutst-cuts-article-1.1275230; Elise Foley, "Immigration and Customs Enforcement Frees Detainees as Sequester Looms," *Huffington Post*, February 27, 2013, https://www.huffpost.com/entry/immigration-and-customs-enforcement-sequester_n_2761941.

Outside, Harry and Yana took turns grilling pork and chicken on skewers for satay with tangy peanut sauce. Tantalizing trays of Chinese Indonesian vegetables, rice, noodles, and baked fish filled tables in their walk-out basement.

I sat with my husband Mark on an outdoor porch bench across from Lara Arp, an ordained minister who had taken on the role of executive director of Who Is My Neighbor, Inc., the nonprofit affiliated with the Reformed Church and started by Jean Stockdale that provided educational programs for children and adults.

Lara's daughter Ember was a close friend of Harry's Christa. Lara had coordinated the weekend blitz for the T-visa victims of human trafficking back in October 2009. Lara had organized activities that carried us through a food-deprived, all-night immigration vigil in December 2011 before sanctuary started. We had worked hard together tactically.

That night, it was a joy to sit together in the cool, dark spring air, balancing steaming plates of grilled Indonesian barbecue on our laps, savoring a moment of profound peace. We could finally breathe.

"So, what's next for you?" Lara asked.

The Indonesians had begun calling me Pastor Liz.

"We've been talking about sending me to seminary," I confessed.

CHAPTER 28

Refugees on the Horizon

In Highland Park, Fall 2013 to 2016

In the fall of 2013, the Indonesian community of the Reformed Church of Highland Park seemed finally secure.

A handful of people with complicated cases had received a reprieve directly from Gary Mead. Others qualified for protection from two executive orders signed by President Obama. The first order was called DACA, or Deferred Action for Child Arrivals, a program for people under thirty whom the public called Dreamers.

The "Dreamers" moniker derived from the first version of a bill entitled "The Development, Relief, and Education for Alien Minors (DREAM) Act," which had been introduced in 2001. For the next twenty-one years, some dozen versions of the Dream Act were introduced in Congress. Each would have provided a pathway to legal status for undocumented people who came to this country as children. Despite bipartisan support, none became law. The 2010 bill came closest to full passage when it passed the House but fell just five votes short of the sixty needed to proceed in the Senate.[1]

[1] A fact sheet on the Dream Act can be found on the American Immigration Council

The second order provided a safeguard for parents of U.S. citizen children called DAPA, or Deferred Action for Parental Accountability.

That October, however, Pastor Stephanie gave an alarming sermon about two overloaded refugee boats that had just sunk off the coast of Sicily.[2]

In Naples, Italy, a group of Waldensian missionaries who are our denominational partners published a letter to the churches of our denomination, the Reformed Church in America, explaining how refugees from Africa and Syria had filled their city. The missionaries desperately sought our financial support.[3]

Stephanie preached on a small text in Chapter 17 of the Gospel of Luke. Because it is part of the Revised Common Lectionary, any pastor who followed the lectionary when she chose readings for worship would cover this passage every third year.

I had spent that week at Princeton Theological Seminary, Seth and Steph's alma mater, at a retreat for prospective seminarians. When Stephanie juxtaposed the refugee crisis with that commonly used passage, she changed the course of my life.

After participating in immigration ministry for six years, I had come to realize that not only was the identity of the foreigner key to the Bible as it was preached from and lived by in our Reformed church, but in fact, the critical identity of the foreigner weaves through key passages of Luke's entire gospel.

---

website at https://www.americanimmigrationcouncil.org/research/dream-act-overview.

[2] See Zed Nelson, "Lampedusa Boat Tragedy: A Survivor's story," *The Guardian*, March 22, 2014, https://www.theguardian.com/world/2014/mar/22/lampedusa-boat-tragedy-migrants-africa. In 2022, *The New Yorker* published a comprehensive report on secret Libyan prisons that also explained the growth in the disastrous migrant route between Libya and Italy from 2011 to 2022. See Ian Urbino, "The Secretive Prisons That Keep Migrants Out of Europe," *New Yorker*, November 28, 2021, https://www.newyorker.com/magazine/2021/12/06/the-secretive-libyan-prisons-that-keep-migrants-out-of-europe.

[3] "The Waldensian movement took its name from Valdus or Waldo who, around 1170, following a crisis of conscience, sold his possessions and spent the rest of his life preaching the Gospel to his fellow men. To help the non-clergy understand the New Testament he had it translated into the language which was commonly used at that time, Provencal. His ideas spread all over Europe. Waldo and his disciples, 'the Poor of Lyon', were declared heretics by the Roman Catholic Church, mostly because in their community lay people, including women, were allowed to preach. They were excommunicated by Pope Lucius III in 1184." Waldensians later aligned with the Reformed Protestant movement ("A History of the Waldensians," Musee Protestant, accessed February 23, 2023, https://museeprotestant.org/en/notice/a-history-of-the-waldensians/).

The Good Samaritan, an outsider who acts as a true neighbor when he rescues a robbery victim left to die in a gutter, is a despised foreigner. The risen Christ first appears as a foreigner or stranger on the road to Emmaus. This biblical insight profoundly influenced me as I developed my own Reformed theology.

Earlier that month, in the chapel of Princeton Seminary, I had begun listening to the same passage that Stephanie would preach from in the coming weeks, Luke 17:11-19, on the healing of ten lepers. John White, the Seminary's new dean of student life and vice president for student relations, delivered a spirited sermon that enveloped me in a sense of radical gratitude. Turning back was rare, White said. "I don't even think we do it one in ten times, but when we do, it can change everything."

I paid extra attention because Dean John White's name was identical to the name of one of my undergraduate professors. After the sermon, while sipping coffee in the seminary cafeteria, I was moved to send a thank-you note to the John White from my past. Returning to graduate school had re-awakened my appreciation for my undergraduate experience, where I had learned to love ancient Greek.

The next week, I prepared the same passage for a Sunday school class of kindergartners and first graders.

A sentence in the text struck me speechless. Jesus expressed his consternation that the only leper who returned to give thanks for his healing was a Samaritan, saying, "Was none of them found to return and give praise to God except this foreigner?"

Somehow, both Dean White and I had missed the point entirely.

The one leper who returns and falls upon his face at Jesus's feet in thanksgiving is a Samaritan, someone who was born in the Roman province of Samaria, whose worship did not include the Jerusalem Temple. In the gospels, the Samaritan identity is unclean. To my ears, Jesus's statement sounded damning, even inflammatory.

I am not a foreigner in the country where I reside, so if I put myself in this story, I would locate myself among the lepers who are healed but who do not turn back. In my identity as a U.S. citizen, then, the text implied, I seem to be excluded from the story's moment of grace!

In our primary Sunday school classroom, one of many that had once served as a sanctuary dorm room for an undocumented family between 2012 and 2013, a dozen five- and six-year-olds sat crosslegged on woven placemats, arranged in a circle. I retold Luke's story about how ten lepers had cried out to Jesus for help and then followed

Jesus's instructions and presented themselves to their priests. As they walked, the lepers found themselves healed, but only one foreigner turned back to say thank you. Around our circle, we took turns introducing ourselves and then each of us acted out a gesture to express "thank you" as wordlessly as the one miraculously healed Samaritan who returned to Jesus.

Bedlam ensued when none of us, whether five, six, or fifty-two, could resist falling on our faces, as the thankful Samaritan leper had done at the feet of Jesus.

Parents joined us after their adult education class, and we all rushed into the sanctuary pews for the 11:15 a.m. service. Pastor Stephanie opened her sermon on this Luke passage with a description of boats full of hundreds of refugees that had capsized on October 2 and 11 off the island of Sicily.

Right then and there in my pew, I needed to know the Greek word Luke had used and that our Bibles translated as "foreigner." I dug out my iPhone, opened the free Blue Letter Bible application, and discovered *allogenes*, a compound adjective, where *allo* meant "other" and *gene* meant "born," so the word meant "other-born," or "born elsewhere."

My Greek was rusty from my undergraduate years, but several more familiar and important words stuck out. The lepers cry mercy, or *eleison*, as we had just sung *kyrie eleison,* Lord have mercy, in the opening of service. There was no bread and wine in this story, yet the Samaritan's thankfulness was expressed in the participle that means "eucharistic." There was communion, commonly called the Holy Eucharist—without bread.

Those seven verses contained a fall, healing, saving, communion, and even a kind of resurrection. *Anastas!* Jesus commands the Samaritan at his feet. Arise!

And God was praised.

Like a snow globe, this microcosmic passage seemed to hold the whole story of salvation. Yet one word stood out as not being a part of the typical salvation story—*allogenes*, "other-born,"—and yet it held a central place in this passage. A website I found said that this word is common in Attic Greek and in the Greek of the Septuagint (a well-known Greek version of the Hebrew Bible), however, among all the books of the New Testament, *allogenes* appears this one time only. There is a word linguists use to describe this kind of thing: *hapax legomena*, a word or phrase that only appears once. It was a conundrum that stopped me in my tracks.

The passage seemed to describe a kind of test or experiment.

Could it be that to be radically eucharistic, radically full of thanks and aware of receiving grace, requires being *allogenes*, other-born?

I was astounded because that is quite literally what I had seen in our church, in the mountain-sized faith of persecuted Indonesian refugees, our brothers and sisters in Christ who had packed their suitcases ten and fifteen years ago, put all their faith in God alone, and left their homeland—their jobs, property, parents, even children—forever.

Today they breathed new life into our church and rebuilt houses damaged in Superstorm Sandy. All this, while their political and economic situation in our country was appalling.

This crazy question suffused my thoughts. Was it not possible to be radically, truly eucharistic without being *allogenes*? Can anyone experience the fullness of God's saving and healing power until they truly live as a second-class outsider or foreigner? To me, this passage suggests that, in fact, it might be impossible.

I remembered God's first words to Abram: "Go forth," as Abram left the land of his father and ventured into a strange land (Genesis 12:1). And so, I wondered, if we do not experience life as *allogenes*, if we never go into places where we are unknown and where we have no rights and privileges, do we miss out on experiencing the radical measure of God's grace?

I set my sights on attending seminary in September 2014.

Between 2013 and 2014, Reformed Church members continued to visit New Jersey detention centers. ICE continued to release undocumented people to their care—without any compensation for their food and housing.

There were important wins: Ebenezer, a world-class soccer player from Ghana, had now escaped twice in a shipping container, returning after he was deported because his non-conforming identity was deadly, and on his second trip, he won his asylum case. His children joined him in a house owned by a sister congregation a few miles away.

Our church member named Sonia, an elder-care assistant from the island nation of Dominica, successfully petitioned for citizenship once her daughter married a U.S. citizen and won her own citizenship.

Faith and Grace, sisters from Sierra Leone, taught adult ed classes about their faith practices in Africa. "We had the hardest time at worship services here in the Reformed Church," the sisters explained. "We kept waiting but no one ever seemed to pray in worship."

To Faith and Grace, praying meant hours of boisterous praising, singing, and dancing. Our much more subdued Reformed services never quite satisfied their experience of communal prayer. Grace was ordained as a church deacon. She and Faith coordinated a Sunday-night young adult dinner service. After many years, they, too, finally received grants of asylum.

CHAPTER 29

Interfaith RISE and a Café of Global Grace

In Highland Park, 2015

The year 2015 saw the greatest movement of desperate people leaving their homes around the globe since the end of World War II.

In the wake of the horrific civil war that was destroying Syria, 4.9 million Syrians sought refuge in neighboring countries. Sixteen million more people worldwide had left their countries as refugees. Another 40 million were internally displaced in their own countries because of war, drought, famine, and dire poverty. Three million people sought permanent asylum. Only 1 percent of all refugees were permanently resettled in new countries.[1]

Even when the U.S. does not border nations that are undergoing crises, our country works to generously reduce the burden on countries that are immediate neighbors to warring lands. For example, Turkey, Jordan, and Lebanon received the greatest number of Syrian refugees, but conditions in refugee camps were very poor.

---

[1] Jie Zong and Jeanne Batalova, "Refugees and Asylees in the United States," Migration Policy Institute, June 7, 2017, https://www.migrationpolicy.org/article/refugees-and-asylees-united-states-2015.

For Seth, it was the kids in the church who propelled him to act.

After the children's choir had watched a documentary about Syrian children in refugee camps, they wove quotes from Syrian children through a rendition of the song, "I Want Jesus to Walk with Me."

"This prayer, by the children of the church," Seth said, "led me, as pastor, to know we had to do something more to address the crisis."[2]

In the fall of 2015, Pastor Seth began to meet with residents and leaders in the borough of Highland Park who began to call themselves "Take Ten"—a reference to the suggestion that each town in New Jersey welcome ten refugees.

Unlike the people ICE released in the middle of the night, who had arrived in shipping containers or with questionable tourist visas, people who had few resources and even fewer local contacts, UN refugees came through a system that provided them with work permits, rental grants, Medicaid and public assistance eligibility, all guaranteed by the federal government.

The federal refugee program starts with UN High Commission for Refugees (UNHCR), which prioritizes refugees in its camps who are at extreme risk. Prospective refugees are then cleared by eight U.S. federal agencies. Nine nonprofit organizations receive families cleared by the U.S. State Department and disburse them responsibly in communities across the country. Many of these nine organizations are directly affiliated with faith organizations—many of them Christian. Those faith-based nonprofits rely heavily on the goodwill of local churches to adopt families, mentor them, and help them ease into life in their new locale.

Refugees' greatest needs include language education, affordable housing, jobs, and training. Most importantly, to thrive, refugees need community. Refugees often arrive as families. One church could not work alone. Syrian refugees would need Muslim faith partners.

---

[2] Seth spoke and wrote repeatedly about the power of the children's prayer to focus his efforts toward welcoming refugees through United Nations programs. See Hannan Adely, "'We Should Be Doing More': How the Syria Refugee Crisis Spurred a Volunteer Movement in New Jersey," *USA Today*, December 18, 2021, https://www.usatoday.com/in-depth/news/nation/2021/12/28/syrian-refugees-inspired-americans-help-reshape-resettlement/9024440002/. See also Seth Kaper-Dale, Reformed Church of Highland Park Newsletter, March 2021, https://myemail.constantcontact.com/RCHP-Newsletter--March-2021.html?soid=1103469146412&aid=tf9v0FFoyO; and Mercedes Barba's video project, "The New Americans: Jesus was a Refugee," https://projects.newsdoc.org/thenewamericans/jesus-was-a-refugee/.

The Take Ten group eventually grew into an organization called Interfaith RISE, for Refugee and Immigrant Services and Empowerment. However, just as the brand-new Take Ten group was about to launch its first public fundraising event, the refugee crisis in Europe blew up.

On Friday, November 13, 2015, a series of coordinated terror attacks in Paris killed 130 people, and another 368 people were injured, 100 seriously. Seven attackers died while authorities searched for accomplices.[3] The attacks were the deadliest on France since World War II and the deadliest in the European Union since the Madrid train bombings in 2004. It was 9/11 all over again, but this time for Europe. France had been on high alert since the January 2015 attacks on the Charlie Hebdo offices and an attack on a Jewish supermarket in Paris that killed 17 people and wounded 22.

The Islamic State of Iraq and the Levant (ISIL) claimed responsibility for the attacks on November 13, 2015, in retaliation for the French airstrikes on ISIL targets in Syria and Iraq. French president François Hollande called the attacks, planned in Syria and organized by a terrorist cell based in Belgium, an act of war by ISIL.

All Paris attackers had fought in Syria. Most had French or Belgian citizenship, two were Iraqis. None of the attackers were Syrian, but they had entered Europe among the flow of migrants and refugees.

In the U.S., Republican governors immediately began closing their doors to UN refugees from Syria, deviously conflating ISIL terrorists with Syrian citizens who were victims of persecution by their own government. The Syrian government not only failed to protect its own citizens, but even targeted them for destruction in the civil war that raged against the regime of Bashar al-Assad, who had violently suppressed Arab Spring protestors in 2011.[4]

Two days after the terrorist events in Paris, on Sunday, November 15, Pastor Seth proceeded to lead a public walk-a-thon throughout the borough of Highland Park to raise money to settle Syrian refugees nearby through the work of the coalition of organizations that came to

---

[3] "November 2015 Attacks: A Timeline of the Night that Shook the French Capital," France 24, August 9, 2021, https://www.france24.com/en/france/20210908-paris-november-2015-attacks-a-timeline-of-the-night-that-shook-the-city.

[4] Polly Mosendz, "In Light of Paris Attacks, 26 GOP Governors, One Democrat to Refuse Syrian Refugees," *Newsweek*, November 16, 2015, https://www.newsweek.com/after-paris-attacks-26-republican-governors-one-democrat-refuse-syrian-394859.

compose Interfaith RISE. Stops along the walk included the borough hall, the high school, the public library, synagogues, and churches.

On Tuesday, November 17, New Jersey Governor Chris Christie sent a letter to President Obama informing him that he would not accept any more Syrian refugees into the state because, he said, "The threat posed to New Jersey by ISIS is very real." Christie further stated that he would not accept Syrian orphans, even those under the age of five.[5]

The media sought Seth out because he was more than willing to repeatedly rebuke the New Jersey governor's fearmongering and scapegoating of not only Syrian refugees but all UN refugees.

Through the press, Seth assured the public that UN refugees had submitted to the gold standard of both UN and U.S. vetting. Seth told the press he found Governor Christie's remarks about refugees "small-minded" and "disturbing." He pledged to welcome refugee families to New Jersey regardless.

"We're distraught to think our governor would play into the same political ridiculousness that other governors are playing into, connecting horrific terrorists in Paris to 12 million refugees driven from their homes,"[6] Seth stated.

In January 2016, IRISE settled its first families in Paterson, New Jersey, amid a large Syrian Muslim community. In February, a Congolese family who had spent eight years in an overpopulated refugee camp in Uganda settled in Highland Park. In April, a single mom and daughter from Afghanistan moved into an apartment in nearby Edison. Culture shock was intense for them: one day refugees had been in an immense refugee tent city in Africa or the Middle East, and the next day they were piling on down coats, learning how to use digital thermometers, and experimenting with escalators and elevators for the first time in their lives.

Refugees who are resettled through the agencies that work with the UNHCR have a tight timeframe for becoming financially self-sufficient. Access to entry-level jobs is a key component to successful resettlement.

---

[5] Claude Brodesser-Akner, "Christie: No Syrian Refugees, Not Even 'Orphans Under Age 5,'" NJ.com, November 17, 2015, https://www.nj.com/politics/2015/11/christie_reverses_earlier_call_to_accept_syrian_re_1.html.

[6] Brian Amaral, "Pastor Criticizes Christie, Pledges to Bring Refugees to N.J.," NJ.com, November 17, 2015, //www.nj.com/middlesex/2015/11/syrian_refugees_in_highland_park.html.

For years, the church had hosted a pay-what-you-can café under the auspices of Elijah's Promise, the local nonprofit soup kitchen and culinary school in nearby New Brunswick. But that March, with exponentially growing demand for food services at the main New Brunswick location of Elijah's Promise, the nonprofit was forced to pull out of its Highland Park Café, located in the Quilt Room of the church.[7]

But that got Seth to thinking.

Over the last fifteen years, enticing gifts of new varieties of food shared at gatherings had played a key role in melting hearts and melding together an entirely new multicultural community in the church. Exotic spices and aromas now replaced the tried-and-true roast beef dinners and tuna casseroles of the first years of his ministry, which had driven Seth across the street to the Pad Thai Restaurant, where he could up his spice quotient.

As the congregation diversified, Seth began to imagine that representatives from the global community in the church might be brought together to create a restaurant-style ministry.

That same April, Pastor Seth announced the opening of the Global Grace Café. He told his congregants that there were many reasons for keeping a lunch business going in the church. Its mission was to raise funds to support refugee resettlement, to create small jobs, and to provide job training opportunities for recent arrivals to this country.

Another main goal was to raise positive awareness about refugee resettlement in the state. But the inspiration truly came from years of progressively more delicious church potlucks that featured increasingly diverse and delicious global food selections.

"On a Sunday morning at RCHP, there are 45 countries represented through first generation immigrants," Seth said. "I started thinking, we have the best potlucks of any church in the country, maybe even the world! When you share the table here, you eat food from Korea, Indonesia, Sierra Leone."[8]

---

[7] Charlie Kratovil, "Elijah's Promise Closes 'Better World' Projects Outside Hub City," *New Brunswick Today*, May 4, 2016, https://newbrunswicktoday.com/2016/05/04/elijahs-promise-closes-better-world-projects-outside-hub-city/.

[8] Qtd. in Tammy La Gorce, "Refugees and Immigrants Find Community at Global Grace Café," *New Jersey Monthly*, April 6, 2017, https://njmonthly.com/articles/eat-drink/fleeing-bad-bringing-good/.

It was a bold plan for a church to provide a lunch spot in town, five days a week, fifty or so weeks a year. But Seth had a ringer, and he bet she could handle the heat.

He asked Emily Randall-Goodwin, a recent Rutgers graduate and a student from Johnson and Wales Culinary School to manage the café. As head chef and café manager, Emily took pride in exposing people in Central Jersey to new ideas through their palates.

"It's great to see people enjoying foods from different cultures that they would have never tried otherwise," Emily said.

Together, Seth and Emily identified chefs who were excellent cooks, represented a wide array of culinary expertise, and who felt good about highlighting food from their homelands.[9]

Some countries had become known to the public because of the death and destruction that was covered in the news media. Focusing on cuisine instead enabled immigrants to showcase the beautiful parts of their prior lives and their pride in their homelands.

Each day the café featured a particular country or region with chefs who arrived as refugees or asylum seekers.

On Mondays, Francis Fernandes from India cooked paneer tikka masala and coconut curry. Tuesdays, Najla prepared creamy Syrian hummus. Wednesday featured Guyanese stews. Thursdays, elder Patrick Beckford's son Darnelle recreated his family's Jamaican jerk chicken. Friday was Yana's day to treat everyone to Chinese Indonesian staples and specialties. Vegan soups were prepared by sisters Faith and Grace Kamanda from Sierra Leone. Yvonne Mukayisenga from Congo became known for her greens and chapati flatbread.

Yvonne explained how the café served as a haven for her. A war in Congo had killed most of her family and separated her from her eldest son, whom she still could not locate, and caused her to flee to a refugee camp in Uganda.

"Here we are all learning from each other's cultures," Yvonne said. "When I think about things that have happened, I feel bad. But in the café, I feel good. This is a nice family to have."[10]

Seth wasn't sure if the new café would catch on. "We hope and pray that this effort becomes financially sustainable, but the positive

---

[9] Susan Loyer, "Global Grace Café Crosses International Borders," My Central Jersey, June 10, 2016, https://www.mycentraljersey.com/story/life/faith/2016/06/10/global-grace-cafe-crosses-international-borders/85562708/.

[10] Lindsay Tuen et al., "A Café for the Community," Aim2Flourish, Rutgers Business School, accessed April 2, 2022, https://aim2flourish.com/innovations/a-caf%C3%A9-for-the-community.

energy it is creating in our town and region, and the way that it is building up refugees and asylees, means that it is already a success," he said. It also brought in enough revenue to assist new arrivals in small ways.

One of the steepest barriers to successful resettlement is the difficulty in building community connections across cultures and languages. The café helped flip the typical script, the one in which Americans dig deep into their pockets to support needy strangers who can offer them little in return.

At the Global Grace Café, Highland Park and New Brunswick residents received hospitality *from* refugees and learned to appreciate their culinary and cultural gifts, while helping and encouraging them.

As the Highland Park community enjoyed and supported refugees in the neighborhood, the State of New Jersey withdrew its official support.

On April 7, 2016, a letter from acting New Jersey Human Services Commissioner Elizabeth Connolly gave 120 days' notice to the U.S. Office of Resettlement Services of the state's intent to withdraw its involvement.[11] In June 2016, the state's Office of Refugee Resettlement that coordinated with federal agencies closed.

However, because UN refugee resettlement programs are federally mandated, Governor Christie could not interfere with nationwide resettlement efforts—with one exception.

Without state participation, individuals who are refugees do not qualify for county-run public assistance. That state money had to be made up by NGOs and federal agencies. Luckily, all other benefits remained: Medicaid, food stamps, jobs, and childcare assistance. At the same time, Interfaith RISE continued to grow in its programs, number of staff members, volunteers, and donors.

By 2017, Interfaith RISE facilitated a coalition of 300 people from 38 faith and community organizations in Central New Jersey, led by the Reformed Church. It was one of three agencies in New Jersey officially recognized by the U.S. State Department and the only New Jersey partner of the United States Committee for Refugees and Immigrants (USCRI)—one of four NGOs designated to disburse State Department funding locally.

---

[11] Susan K. Livio and Jonathan D. Salant, "Christie Administration: N.J. Won't Help Resettle Refugees," NJ.com, April 20, 2016, https://www.nj.com/politics/2016/04/nj_withdraws_from_refugee_resettlement_program.html.

CHAPTER 30

The Nightmare Returns

In Highland Park and Red Bank, New Jersey, 2017

On Friday night, February 10, 2017, Harry and Yana Pangemanan were relaxing in their basement family room, eating dinner with their daughters, now 16 and 11. Their employment situation had changed dramatically.

For the first time since her children were born, Yana now worked only during the day. This gave her more time to spend with her daughters, but she had far less freedom. After so many years of flexible daytime hours, working days was an adjustment too.

Harry continued to work only for the church, despite periodic requests from his last employer to return to work after sanctuary ended in 2013. Harry served as the main repairman for the church and its affordable housing properties and as the leader of Sandy reconstruction projects on the Jersey Shore.

When anyone asked why he didn't return to his previous job, Harry only spoke of all the church had done for him and his family.

The next week, the Pangemanan parents planned to go to their regularly scheduled, biannual visit to ICE. These meetings had been pro-forma affairs for the past four years, ever since Gary Mead, as the head of Enforcement and Removal Operations, had arranged for their stays of removal in February 2013. No ICE officer had raised any concerns about the Pangemanans continuing to receive stays of removal.

With the new Trump administration, I was concerned once again about their immigration status, and so I visited the family's home that evening with a homemade lasagna, a favorite dish of Harry and Jocelyn. Yana, no fan of Italian food, smothered her portion with sweet Chinese hot pepper sauce. She and the girls had just finished their round of cooking Chinese Indonesian food for the Global Grace Café. Jocelyn was grateful for a change.

In the middle of our visit, Harry received two texts from Pastor Seth. The first said that an elderly Indonesian couple from the next county over had knocked on the parsonage door: they were desperate for help, but they spoke no English. Harry texted back he would be right there.

The second text included a *Washington Post* article with the headline, "Federal agents conduct immigration enforcement raids in at least six states."[1]

Harry left to meet Seth so he could interpret for the Indonesian couple. Old fears crept back. Yana stayed on the couch with her girls and asked them what they remembered about the time when their father lived in sanctuary in the church.

Jocelyn moved across the room to an area with a daybed where Jean Stockdale had once slept. Instead of revisiting a traumatic period of her childhood that had been filled with pain and uncertainty, Jocelyn downloaded a Netflix movie.

Yana told her younger daughter Christa about the miraculous moment, four years earlier, when she heard that sanctuary had ended.

"I was in the middle of T. J. Maxx, shopping for Valentine's Day," Yana recounted, remembering her surprise at the phone call she received from Jean Stockdale. That was in 2013, when Jean had called from the church van as it left Washington, DC, to tell Yana that everyone in sanctuary would receive stays of deportation, driver's licenses, and work authorizations, and that meant that sanctuary was over.

---

[1] Lisa Rein, Abigail Hauslohner, and Sandhya Somashekhar, "Federal Agents Conduct Immigration Enforcement Raids in at Least Six States," *Washington Post*, February 11, 2017, https://www.washingtonpost.com/national/federal-agents-conduct-sweeping-immigration-enforcement-raids-in-at-least-6-states/2017/02/10/4b9f443a-efc8-11e6-b4ff-ac2cf509efe5_story.html.

"I screamed right there, in the middle of the store, Thank you, Jesus! Thank you, Jesus! I was crying, in public," Yana emoted. "People ran to me. Women surrounded me. Some of them were praising God, too!" Yana laughed so hard; she wiped tears from her eyes. "They were praising God. They didn't even know why!" Yana recalled.

An hour later, Harry returned from the Reformed Church of Highland Park and kissed his daughters goodnight.

Back in 2013, thanks to Pastor Seth and the advocacy of the church and its wider community, as well as the media, Harry and Yana and many Indonesians had received stays that had kept them safe from deportation and enabled them to work for the last four years.

Now, Harry, Seth, and the whole church were on edge because of an executive order President Trump had signed on January 25: "Enhancing Public Safety in the Interior of the United States."[2]

Under the Trump administration, all bets were off. Anyone who had a final order to deport the country became a deportation priority—even if they had previously negotiated a stay with the U.S. government. Some 750,000 young adults who had already registered for Deferred Action for Childhood Arrivals (DACA), called Dreamers, were terrified.

The same was true for anyone, like Harry and Yana, who may have been eligible for Deferred Action for Parents of Americans and Lawful Permanent Residents (DAPA), a program President Obama had hoped to implement but had failed to enact.

A particularly concerning element of the January 25 executive order was a clause that threatened to permit no exemptions.

"We cannot faithfully execute the immigration laws of the United States if we exempt classes or categories of removable aliens from potential enforcement," Trump's executive order stated. It directed departments and agencies to employ all lawful means to enforce the immigration laws of the United States. The order authorized the hiring of 10,000 new enforcement and removal officers.

President Trump had wasted no time.

He issued that first order on his sixth day in office. Any doubt about the resolve and resources that the new administration would invest to enact it dissolved two days later, when a second order, which became known as the notorious "Muslim Ban," or "Trump Travel Ban,"

---

[2] Donald J. Trump, "Executive Order: Enhancing Public Safety in the Interior of the United States," January 25, 2017, https://trumpwhitehouse.archives.gov/presidential-actions/executive-order-enhancing-public-safety-interior-united-states/.

suspended visas from Iran, Iraq, Libya, Somalia, Sudan, and Syria, and provoked widespread protests in airports when travelers were detained.

The second order also drastically restricted the number of refugees admitted into the U.S., suspended the U.S. Refugee Admission Program for 120 days, and sought to permanently close U.S. borders to all Syrian refugees.[3]

By the time a federal judge stayed this second order, DHS agents had mobilized to detain 700 travelers and revoke up to 60,000 visas.[4]

While all that chaos was taking place, amazingly, Harry and Yana were granted a six-month stay the next week at their February 2017 check-in at ICE headquarters in the federal Rodino building in Newark. There was one big change, however. The front of Harry's new driver's license was emblazoned with the words "Temporary Immigration Status."

Since a driver's license is a universal form of identification, the new label functioned as a kind of digitally stamped yellow star.

The couple tried to remain hopeful, but Harry admitted that it was hard to keep up their spirits while waiting for the next shoe to drop.

Later that spring, ICE began to act locally. On the evening of April 19, 2017, ICE agents from Newark informed the New Brunswick police that the next morning they would process a warrant for the arrest of a criminal who was also undocumented. Failing to find the man named in the warrant, the next morning a van full of agents conducted a wide-sweeping raid of homes in the area and vans driving people to work. Agents detained ten people, eight of them parents. The spouses and children of those who were detained arrived at the Reformed Church, where a new group was meeting in the sanctuary.[5]

An interfaith community surrounding Highland Park had formed a new network called DIRE—Deportation and Immigration

---

[3] Donald J. Trump, "Executive Order 13769: Protecting the Nation from Foreign Terrorist Entry into the United States," January 27, 2017, https://www.federalregister.gov/documents/2017/02/01/2017-02281/protecting-the-nation-from-foreign-terrorist-entry-into-the-united-states.

[4] Rebecca Hersher, "Federal Judge Stays Trump Travel Order, But Many Visas Already Revoked," NPR, February 3, 2017, https://www.npr.org/sections/thetwo-way/2017/02/03/513306413/state-department-says-fewer-than-60-000-visas-revoked-under-travel-order.

[5] Susan Loyer, "ICE Conducts 'Targeted Enforcement Action' in New Brunswick," My Central Jersey, April 20, 2017, https://www.mycentraljersey.com/story/news/local/people/2017/04/20/ice-conducts-targeted-enforcement-action-new-brunswick/100705100/.

Response Equipo (Team). A month earlier, DIRE had its genesis in an emergency vigil Seth had called in response to President Trump's executive orders. More than four hundred people showed up for the vigil, so many that they carried their candles outside.

People were incensed.

"We closed shop on the immigration committee of the Reformed Church that night," Seth said, "and we put all our eggs into the basket of interfaith people working under DIRE, part of a nonprofit related to but independent from the church."

An 800 number, the brainchild of Joel Watcherli, who became the DIRE leader, enabled immigrants to call for immediate assistance.

Two hundred volunteers signed up to receive alerts and training to respond to emergency calls. During an ongoing ICE raid, the goal for volunteers was to show up in neon-yellow T-shirts that said, "Supporting Immigrant Rights," and which listed the 800 number and the website to sign up for DIRE alerts. The hope was for DIRE volunteers to act as witnesses, record ICE actions, and track the people whom ICE apprehended. Follow-up would happen later, as DIRE leaders worked with partners across other agencies to ensure families not only had legal representation, but food, childcare, and rent money while a wage earner was detained.

Unfortunately, at the time of the first raid in April 2017, the Spanish and English brochures for DIRE, the ones that would spell out how our country's Fourth and Fifth Amendments protect undocumented immigrants, had not yet been distributed to New Brunswick neighborhoods.

DIRE volunteers had not been able to capture ICE in the act, so men were detained in the sweep. Families then needed follow-up support, and at that time, much of that assistance was coordinated through a nonprofit called Lazos America Unida, led by its fearless director Teresa Vivar, in New Brunswick.

After that raid, volunteers from DIRE, wearing their screaming yellow T-shirts with the 800 hotline number, began patrolling the area around the entrances to the county court building in New Brunswick. Courthouses were vulnerable places because ICE agents were able to cross-check the names of people who appeared for proceedings with those who had open cases and deportation orders in the immigration system.

ICE detained people while they were in fact complying with the courts and law enforcement—paying traffic fines and appearing for court orders. Immigrants feared coming forward, even for help. This practice endangered vulnerable people and the rule of law on city and town streets.

Even though I had studied our country's core documents in high school, and had spent years as an immigration advocate, it wasn't until this moment that I finally realized that certain provisions of the U.S. Constitution pertain to all people—and not solely to U.S. citizens.

The constitution's Fourth Amendment protects the right of everyone "to be secure in their persons, houses, papers, and effects, against unreasonable searches and seizures," and this right "shall not be violated, and no warrants shall issue, but upon probable cause, supported by oath or affirmation, and particularly describing the place to be searched, and the persons or things to be seized."

This check in the Fourth Amendment limits the federal government's power when it comes to the personhood of our bodies, our belongings, and our homes.

The Fifth Amendment goes on to ensure that no person "be deprived of life, liberty, or property, without due process of law."[6]

High-school social studies had taught me that the Fourteenth Amendment to the U.S. Constitution ensured that the states also extend the protections of the Bill of Rights to their residents. This amendment nullified the Supreme Court's Dred Scott decision that descendants of people from Africa could not be citizens,[7] and it ensured that everyone has equal protection under government entities. The Department of Justice was created in 1870 to enforce these protections within the states.

But I was not taught that the language of the Fourteenth Amendment extends beyond citizens to all persons: "nor shall any State deprive any *person* of life, liberty, or property, without due process of law; nor deny to any *person* within its jurisdiction the equal protection of the laws."[8]

---

[6] "Fourth Amendment: Searches and Seizures," Constitution Annotated, accessed March 2, 2022, https://constitution.congress.gov/browse/amendment-4/.

[7] In his dissent, U.S. Supreme Court Justice McLean appealed to the theological principle of *imago Dei* along Lockean lines: "A slave is not a mere chattel. He bears the impress of his Maker and is amenable to the laws of God and man; and he is destined to an endless existence" (see "A Dred Scott Dissent," Northwestern Pritzker School of Law, February 23, 2017, https://libraryblog.law.northwestern.edu/2017/02/23/a-dred-scott-dissent/).

[8] "Fourteenth Amendment: Equal Protection and Other Rights," Constitution Annotated, https://constitution.congress.gov/browse/amendment-14/.

These constitutional protections extend to people even when they cannot produce evidence that the federal government has authorized their presence within our borders.

Slowly, too slowly, I came to understand that the struggle to keep families together centered around the core question: Who is a person?

Clearly, our government failed time and again to treat some people as full persons. Why did it take so long for these lessons to sink into my brain?

For more than a decade, my Reformed church had witnessed agents of the U.S. government routinely strip basic human rights from undocumented neighbors, families, and friends with brutal, dehumanizing tactics.

Yet the full extent of these legal protections only became firmly embedded in my consciousness in April of 2017, in Red Bank, New Jersey, in a Monmouth Street diner.

I was eating breakfast with Marc Kline, a Southern-educated rabbi who had earned his Juris Doctor from the University of Arkansas at Little Rock and practiced law prior to enrolling in rabbinical school. Together we were drafting an early version of a "Know Your Rights" pamphlet for people from Latin America who lived and died in our New Jersey neighborhoods even though they did not have formal authorization from the federal government to do so.

I think of Marc back then as "Jersey-fresh," because he had just been installed at Monmouth Reform Temple after first serving congregations in Lexington, Kentucky, and Florence, South Carolina.[9]

As a Southern rabbi, Marc's love of freedom, equality, and the rule of law had led him to serve as chair of the Lexington Fayette County Urban Government Human Rights Commission, where he uncovered and remedied racially motivated disparate lending practices at local banks. Back in 2000, Rabbi Marc had co-led a march on Columbia, South Carolina, where forty-six thousand people had protested to bring the Confederate battle flag down from atop the statehouse dome. "Your heritage is my slavery," statehouse protest placards proclaimed.[10]

---

[9] "Rabbi Kline Welcomes YOU!" Monmouth Reform Temple, accessed April 8, 2022, https://monmouthreformtemple.org/welcome-rabbi-kline/; John Burton, "Marc Kine, The Responsible Rabbi," *The Two River Times*, September 28, 2017, https://tworivertimes.com/marc-kine-the-responsible-rabbi/.

[10] David Firestone, "46,000 March on South Carolina Capitol to Bring Down Confederate Flag," *New York Times*, January 18, 2000, https://www.nytimes.com/2000/01/18/us/46000-march-on-south-carolina-capitol-to-bring-down-confederate-flag.html. The confederate flag was permanently removed in 2018.

Rabbi Marc and I met for breakfast because the week before Marc had attended a lunch meeting of interfaith leaders at the Global Grace Café. Somehow Marc had been cajoled into crossing the hallway from the interfaith meeting on folding chairs in the Quilt Room to the more comfortable parlor, where the new DIRE group was meeting that day.

At the meeting of the fledgling group, Marc and I volunteered to write a pamphlet to advise undocumented people of their rights when federal agents challenged them.

We followed up at the classic Jersey diner near Marc's new home.

Over crispy slices of French toast, I pushed Marc to interpret the Fourth and Fifth Amendments. Really, are you sure, Rabbi? I pressed. These rights belong to everyone?

"Absolutely everyone," Marc responded resolutely.

¡*No Abras la Puerta!* Don't open the door! our pamphlet warned when it was finally printed in the summer of 2017, with Marc Kline's principled insistence. Only law enforcement officials with a warrant, signed by a judge, with your name and your address on it, have a right to enter your private domicile without your permission.

Even if you can't prove you have been provided with authorization to live in the United States of America, don't open the door!

After that diner breakfast, and sporadically over the next few years, along with hundreds of other volunteers, I walked door-to-door in Central New Jersey neighborhoods where high concentrations of vulnerable immigrants lived, handing out Know-Your-Rights brochures and wrapping them around the knobs of closed doors.

I couldn't help but travel back to 2006 in my mind. If only we could have distributed an Indonesian-language version of that pamphlet before the events of May 24 in preparation for that tragic early morning raid of that year.

Maybe we could have saved thirty-five families.

I didn't know the law then, but the officers of Immigration and Customs Enforcement (ICE) knew. ICE officers knew the letter of the law and, for the most part, at least in the raid that people who became my friends had lived through, ICE agents abided by the letter, if not the spirit, of the law.

See Lynn Riddle, "And the Children Watched: The Day the Confederate Flag was Lowered from South Carolina's Statehouse Dome," *The Greenville News*, December 16, 2018, https://www.greenvilleonline.com/story/news/local/2018/12/16/when-confederate-flag-lowered-south-carolina-statehouse-dome/2296443002/.

Back in May 2006, ICE agents knew better than to enter the homes of non-citizens without an invitation. But they didn't need to overcomplicate matters. All they needed was to induce the terror of assault rifles in a show of overwhelming force, the fear of family separation, the dread of returning to a country where your people were subject to persecution and discrimination, the sense of humiliation for not speaking much English, and the shame of not having complied with the rules.

All these factors would ensure that when ICE agents knocked, doors would simply open for them. And families would be torn apart.

CHAPTER 31

The End of Humanitarian Discretion

In Highland Park, 2017

In the wake of President Trump's presidency, the civic landscape around Highland Park and New Brunswick changed.

Politics became even more personal at the Reformed Church when Seth decided to run for governor of the State of New Jersey as the Green Party candidate. His campaign theme centered around Jesus's injunction that, in the kingdom of heaven, the last will be first.

The kingdom of heaven starts here on earth, so when we serve the last first, Seth explained, conditions improve for everyone.

This slogan is an ingenious way to counteract our innate bias to favor people and forces whom we perceive to be most powerful, and thereby to restore a true sense of equality among human beings.

Seth had announced his campaign two weeks before the presidential election of November 2016. "I ran for governor as a Green Party candidate because I was so disappointed with serious flaws in the Democratic primary process, which would end in the spring," Seth said, as he explained further:

I wanted to ensure that there would be someone still speaking a progressive word after the Primary ended. This would encourage the Democrat in the race for governor of New Jersey to go full-on 'pro immigrant and refugee' without wavering, instead of sliding to some strange 'middle' on that issue.

Seth canvassed the streets of Newark and Camden with teams of staff members whom he paid a living wage of $15 per hour. He and his canvassers learned just how many of New Jersey's poorest people could not vote, either because they could not register—in cases where people had been incarcerated—or because they simply had not registered.

Meanwhile, the City of New Brunswick voted down a declaration to become a sanctuary city, and Highland Park approved a statement that enabled its police officers to withhold immigration status information from federal agencies when people were involved in minor infractions.

"When ICE is trying to meet their quotas, they go for low-hanging fruit," Seth said, explaining how the borough statement could be helpful. And, he said, if you are ICE, "you don't want to go to a place where you think local government is going to get in your way."[1]

The Reformed Church of Highland Park joined five hundred Jersey congregations in a movement run by an organization called Faith in New Jersey that promised to offer sanctuary to people who were suddenly the target of deportation quotas.

Finally, on Monday, May 8, 2017, disaster struck home for the Reformed Church community. Four Indonesian men, long-time U.S. residents and husbands, fathers, and grandfathers who had participated in sanctuary at the Reformed Church between 2012 and 2013, reported for a visit to ICE headquarters in Newark's Rodino building.

The men went willingly, hoping to renew the stays of deportation they had received when sanctuary ended in February 2013, as directed by Gary Mead, head of Enforcement and Removal Operations.

---

[1] Spencer Kent, "Highland Park Considering Becoming a 'Sanctuary City,'" NJ.com, February 13, 2017, https://www.nj.com/middlesex/2017/02/highland_park_to_consider_declaring_itself_sanctua.html; "Highland Park, NJ Borough Council 2/21/17 Meeting," YouTube video, February 23, 2017, https://www.youtube.com/watch?v=uDqTVYRQyOQ (the discussion on safety for immigrants begins around 49 minutes in). The Borough's final policy did not declare the borough to be an immigrant sanctuary. See "Highland Park Adopts Immigrant Inclusivity Policy," My Central Jersey, June 15, 2017, https://www.mycentraljersey.com/story/news/local/how-we-live/at-risk/2017/06/15/highland-park-adopts-immigrant-inclusivity-policy/399932001/.

However, instead of renewing the stays as ICE had done for the last four years, ICE agents immediately detained all four: Arino Massie, Oldy Manopo, Rovani Wangko, and even Saul Timisela, the first person to entrust himself to the protection of sanctuary within the Reformed Church back in March 2012.[2]

The fact that these same four men had been the focus of national media attention and had been released from sanctuary from the highest level of ICE leadership emboldened New Jersey reporters to ask ICE for an accounting.

To explain why ICE detained these four Indonesians, ICE spokesman Luis Martinez issued a statement for the press that echoed the language of President Trump's January 25th order. That order prioritized enforcement (that is, deportation) for people in the following seven situations:

a) Have been convicted of any criminal offense;
(b) Have been charged with any criminal offense, where such charge has not been resolved;
(c) Have committed acts that constitute a chargeable criminal offense;
(d) Have engaged in fraud or willful misrepresentation in connection with any official matter or application before a governmental agency;
(e) Have abused any program related to receipt of public benefits;
(f) Are subject to a final order of removal, but who have not complied with their legal obligation to depart the United States; or
(g) In the judgment of an immigration officer, otherwise pose a risk to public safety or national security.[3]

In his answer, Martinez dangerously conflated all seven immigration situations into one single reason when he said that, although ICE focuses on individuals "who pose a threat to national security," the agency will "no longer exempt classes or categories" of unauthorized immigrants from enforcement. He emphasized that "aliens who illegally enter the United States and those who overstay or otherwise

---

[2] Spencer Kent, "ICE Detains Indonesian Immigrants Who Now Face Deportation," NJ.com, https://www.nj.com/middlesex/2017/05/ice_detains_christian_immigrants_who_now_face_depo.html.
[3] Trump, "Enhancing Public Safety in the Interior of the United States."

violate the terms of their visas have violated our nation's laws and can pose a threat to national security and public safety."[4]

In the chilling logic of Martinez's statement, humanitarian exemptions themselves threatened the rule of law in the United States.

How lawful is a rule of law that does not permit humanitarian exemptions?

Especially in the case of immigration where no coherent legal system exists. And when the only action governmental actors consider is to place the whole weight of the country's immigration debacle on the backs of people whom they refuse to recognize as persons worthy of rights.

On a weekday morning, a few days later, DIRE advocates met at dawn in the roadway and parking lot outside the Elizabeth Detention Center. They were hoping to delay any vehicles that might transport their friends to Newark Airport for flights that would land somewhere in Asia and then ultimately in Indonesia. They sang songs of hope and protest and broke golden loaves of braided challah bread, much as the first immigration advocates at the Reformed Church had broken bread the day in 2009 that ICE shipped Harry Pangemanan to Tacoma, Washington.

This time, however, they did not celebrate the Christian sacrament of Holy Communion.

This time, the leaders who gathered to lead the hastily organized outdoor prayer service were Reform Jewish, Unitarian Universalist, Episcopalian, Muslim, Buddhist, and Catholic.

Seth and DIRE advocates knew time was short, so to try to slow down deportations of the four men who had previously been spared by Gary Mead, they demonstrated outside the detention center daily, including on Thursday, May 18, when they learned Arino Massie had been deported.

Arino was the breadwinner for his family, having worked in a refrigeration factory. While he was detained, his church was beginning to figure out how to support the family financially. His attorney had filed a stay of deportation and the hearing had been set for that morning, May 18. The protest was a last-ditch effort to prevent his deportation.

Seth announced the terrible news to thirty or more advocates gathered in the afternoon sunshine, holding signs in the roadway alongside Elizabeth Detention Center.

---

[4] Qtd. in Spencer Kent, "ICE Details Indonesian Immigrants."

"Arino's attorney got a call at 10 a.m. that his stay of removal was denied," Seth explained. An hour later, Seth received another call, this time from Arino himself. "Arino called to say, 'Pastor, I'm already on the plane. I'm headed for Japan. Thanks for all the efforts of the community. Tell the community I love them. Tell my son I love him.'"[5]

ICE had not permitted Arino to say goodbye to his teenage son.

Arino, as a longtime elder in the First Indonesian Seventh-day Adventist Church in South Plainfield, New Jersey, had just helped raise funds for a new building. "I'm crying, very sad," one of Arino's fellow church members told reporters at the protest. "This is the dream land; we came here to have a better future."

Frederick, a friend of Arino's, told reporters at the detention center protest that he worried what would happen to Arino once he returned to his home country. Harry Pangemanan had previously reported to immigration advocates that in Indonesia, there were laws on the books that anyone who was deported after filing for asylum from the country could be detained in Indonesia for five years. An asylum claim, after all, charges that a person will not be treated with justice in their home country. Claims of religious persecution are not conducive to international business.

"Can you imagine someone applying for asylum and then going back to Indonesia? How are they going to treat him?" wondered Fredrick Rattu, who himself came to the U.S. from Indonesia in 1994 with a tourist visa yet had found a pathway to become a legal resident during the Clinton administration.[6]

Over the years, at immigration protests, I had met many other people like Arino's friend Frederick who, by some lucky chance, had been spared Arino's fate. For me, they were a constant reminder of the unequal and random enforcement of the immigration policies of the United States.

While advocates learned about Arino, the other three men, Oldy Monopo, Rovani Wangko, and Saul Timisela, remained in custody a few hundred feet away, locked behind the detention center walls. Unlike Arino, they did not have current passports from Indonesia.

---

[5] Morgan Lee, "ICE Deports Christian Who Fled Persecution Back to Indonesia," May 19, 2017, https://www.christianitytoday.com/news/2017/may/ice-deports-christian-persecution-indonesia-new-jersey-100.html.

[6] Hannan Adely, "Indonesian Christian Man Deported after Long and Public Battle to Stay in the U.S.," NorthJersey.com, May 18, 2017, https://www.northjersey.com/story/news/nation/2017/05/18/indonesian-christian-man-deported-after-long-and-public-battle-stay-u-s/331272001/.

Seth surmised that their lack of passports had delayed Indonesia from accepting their deportations.

The reporter to whom Frederick spoke noted that Arino was one of 41,000 suspected undocumented immigrants who were arrested during President Donald Trump's first hundred days—a 40 percent increase from the same period in 2016.[7]

U.S. Representative Frank Pallone dispatched staff members to the protest and then tweeted out photos of the protest along with an update about Arino's deportation, which he called tragic. That morning, Pallone had petitioned the director of ICE Newark to exercise prosecutorial discretion on behalf of all four Indonesians,[8] but his efforts came to naught.

Frank tweeted, "These refugees have suffered enough, they shouldn't be collateral damage of #Trump administration's extreme & discriminatory policies on immigration." The next week, Pallone joined U.S. Representative Carolyn B. Maloney (D-NY) to reintroduce the Indonesian Refugee Family Protection Act. Maloney explained, "These individuals came to this country to escape extreme violence born out of hate and intolerance for their religious beliefs. We must not force them to return to that brutality due to a paperwork error. This bill does not, in itself, grant asylum, but does prevent families from being ripped apart by removing a procedural barrier."

Quick action on the bill was crucial, Pallone explained, now that "recently in my congressional district we have seen four men who fled religious persecution in Indonesia face detainment, with one already being deported. These individuals have become valuable members of their community and it is a tragedy for them and their families to be split apart."[9]

---

[7] Adely, "Indonesian Christian Man Deported"; Dave Moye, "Boy Comes Home from School and Finds Dad Has Been Deported," *Huffington Post*, May 24, 2017, https://www.huffingtonpost.ca/entry/arino-massie-deported-son-school_n_5924b2a8e4b0650cc01fe4e9.

[8] On May 18, Pallone first tweeted, "I have sent a letter to #ICE & am calling #ICE today to again express my strong opposition to their detainment & possible deportation," and then updated, "Tragic update to this story:ArinoMassie,1 of 4men detained,is currently on plane to Indonesia.The other 3 men remain at the Detention Center" (Frank Pallone, Twitter post, May 18, 2017, 2:29 p.m., https://twitter.com/FrankPallone/status/865273220131409923, typos in original).

[9] Frank Pallone and Carolyn Maloney, "Press Release: Reps. Pallone, Maloney Reintroduce Bill to Help Indonesian Refugees Seeking Asylum," May 26, 2017, https://pallone.house.gov/press-release/reps-pallone-maloney-reintroduce-bill-help-indonesian-refugees-seeking-asylum.

In the early years of advocacy, Seth had coached the church immigration team to focus its efforts on the unique story and fact patterns of this singular community of Indonesians who were Christian.

Challenging the Trump administration, however, required a wider span of support.

A new voice, Archange Antoine, encouraged the protesters at the detention center on May 18 to not despair in the face of this shocking deportation: "We have to stay aggressive; we have to stay ebullient; we have to stay unapologetic to the forces that are standing against our families." Archange led Faith in New Jersey, a statewide coalition of religious groups that was organizing large rallies to support immigrants facing deportation and encouraging houses of worship to offer sanctuary.

With Arino gone, with another three other men hovering on the cusp of deportation in detention a few miles from Newark Airport, and with dozens more people with final orders at risk, Seth took a first step in a new direction: putting a full media spotlight on a single child who had just lost his father to deportation.

Seth distributed pages from the diary of Arino Massie's thirteen-year-old son Joel to the press. The diary had helped Joel process some of his strong emotions during a terribly complicated crisis in his life.

A week before his father's deportation, Joel described his foreboding: "Thinking about this makes me cry because it makes me think about the 13 years that I've spent with my dad who is about to disappear from my life," Joel wrote. "Please don't deport him."[10]

The day after Arino was deported, the *Star-Ledger* editorial board published the diary pages, asking its readers in a headline, "Who threatens national security: Trump, or this N.J. dad?"

While noting that the president claimed to be a protector of Americans and a defender of persecuted Christians, the board concluded, "Is tearing these families apart, and a father away from his American son, really an example of either?"[11]

---

[10] Karen Yi, "N.J. Indonesian Man Deported by ICE Leaves Behind Young Citizen Son," NJ.com, May 18, 2017, https://www.nj.com/essex/2017/05/nj_indonesian_man_deported_by_ice_leaves_behind_yo.html.

[11] *Star-Ledger* Editorial Board, "Who Threatens National Security: Trump, or This N.J. Dad?" NJ.com, May 19, 2017, https://www.nj.com/opinion/2017/05/who_threatens_national_security_trump_or_this_nj_d.html.

CHAPTER 32

Questions with No Answers

In New York City, New York, May 2017

I vividly remember the day Arino was deported because I was one of many advocates whom Seth had called to join him in the protest in Elizabeth.

Reporters asked me, as an elder at the Highland Park church, why I protested at the detention center. I spoke in general terms:

> Arino has a child who needs him to bring home food every night and pay for his health care. What's going to happen to the children when we take the breadwinners away?[1]

Since losing thirty-five parents in our community to the 2006 deportation raid, I could answer this question anecdotally for families in our community.

Talking about hardship is always challenging, but a group of women who had been left behind to care for children in 2006 later met to explain how their lives had become so much more complicated. Everyone's situation was unique, but there were important com-

---

[1] Adely, "Indonesian Christian Man Deported."

monalities. They left the Woodbine apartments because they could no longer afford them, forfeiting the social solidarity that helped them manage work problems, illnesses, childcare, and friendship. Their spouses who were deported to Indonesia now depended on their wives in the U.S. for support, yet these wives with minimal English were working at jobs that at best offered minimum wage. Often a mother shared a single bed with all her children, unofficially subletting a single room in the apartment of an acquaintance. Children missed out on school when their mother's unofficial renting arrangements ended, and the family had to find another room in another district.

The protest took place on a sunny spring afternoon, one day before my graduation from Union Theological Seminary in New York City. I remember the feel of the red cotton button-down shirt on my shoulders. I wore red and black frames on my glasses, choosing the colors to prepare myself for the red and black festivities about to take place the next morning on the other side of the Hudson River.

For the past three years, I had commuted on NJ Transit trains and buses, drilling myself on Greek and Hebrew flashcards on the red subway line from Penn Station to Columbia University, far removed from the ups and downs of Highland Park's immigration roller coaster and the ongoing suffering of Indonesian families.

When I enrolled at Union, I imagined that working on the master of divinity degree would give me some perspective on the vitriol Americans harbored against 11 million people who are part of our communities even though they are out of status with the federal government.

Instead, I discovered that New York City was awash in thousands of similar stories. Each story belonged to a pattern that was as irreducibly unique as the story of persecuted Indonesian Christians in Central New Jersey.

When I spoke about undocumented Indonesians in Central New Jersey in my seminary classes, people nodded along empathetically, but I found no foothold to merge this story with my studies.

Yet training at Union Theological Seminary had helped me to understand the drive to destroy immigrant families in more absolute terms of good and evil.

The day after ICE deported Arino, I was invited to speak at the baccalaureate service before graduation. My time at Union had shown me that the cross at the center of my faith tradition stood at a crossroads of deeply conflicted meaning.

A giant sign or direction marker overshadows the path to justice and wholeness, I explained, recalling our teacher James Cone's words to my classmates, "It has been called a cross and a lynching tree."

And each night, for four hundred families who made their home in America, the way of the cross begins at the Elizabeth Detention Center, I told my classmates, where parents go when their families are about to be torn apart.

I told them this had happened the day before our baccalaureate service took place, when our government deported my friend Arino, father of thirteen-year-old Joel. In the James Chapel audience at Union Theological Seminary, friends, family members, and teachers gasped audibly when I told them my friend, Joel's father, had just been deported.

The problem is that some people don't read signs very well, I warned fellow graduates. When they see a cross and a lynching tree, they don't see a divine stop sign, I explained. Instead, they see a green light.

Some people interpret the cross as an unmistakable signal to go forward, to proceed full speed ahead. They believe the "go" signal they receive to be divinely inspired. They imagine that their persecution of "lawbreakers" is a sign of their faith. If we tell them to stop, they just may feel justified to go harder, and faster, and tear more families apart.

For our dear teacher Dr. Cone, who would die of cancer the next year in April 2018, the proof lay in the account Cone related about the astonishing response of a woman named Mamie Till Bradley to the murder of her fourteen-year-old son Emmett Louis "Bo" Till in August 1954.

"If lynching was intended to instill silence and passivity," declared Cone, "this event had the opposite effect, inspiring blacks to rise in defiance, to cast off centuries of paralyzing fear."[2]

At the center of Dr. Cone's best-selling book, *The Cross and the Lynching Tree,* is the hushed blanket that had fallen over some five thousand public lynchings committed at the end of the nineteenth century and into the twentieth century. Hundreds of years of intense and pervasive trauma had rendered many Black Americans speechless. White Americans were so ashamed of the truth of the history of our hatred of and dis-valuing of Black personhood that we had blotted decades of lynchings from both our personal and institutional memories.

[2] James Cone, *The Cross and the Lynching Tree* (Maryknoll, NY: Orbis Books, 2011), 66.

All this subterfuge changed because of one Black woman. Mamie Till Bradley shocked the country by making a public spectacle out of her son Emmett's "battered and bloated corpse." She risked her own life and exposed her gaping wound of motherly desolation for all to see. In the simple act of unsealing his casket, Bradley sacrificed her private grief to create an undeniable public tableau that laid bare the irrational brutality of white racism.

This is activism on the same order of magnitude as Jesus's willing death on the cross and Martin Luther King's daring presence during the Atlanta sanitation workers' strike.

Calling out the callous evil of Emmett's lynchers and the pernicious complacency of white America, Mamie Till Bradley explained: "This is not for Emmett, but to make it safe for other boys."

Six hundred thousand people viewed Emmett's body and attended his funeral. Millions more followed news reporting. Three months later, Rosa Parks refused to give up her bus seat, and the civil rights movement finally caught fire. As Cone said, the timing was no coincidence. Mamie Till Bradley understood how to employ the saving power of the crucifixion as few others since Jesus.

In the fight for civil rights, it was not incidental that Americans were finally able to acknowledge the evil in our society and our own lives by seeing through the eyes of a mother who unveiled her deepest and most intimate wound.

Bradley's actions clearly revealed the pervasive, persistent, impenetrable evil of white racism so that both Black and white Americans could acknowledge it and respond.

Emmett Till would have been just one more statistic except that his mother became a willing surrogate for us. She represented multiple archetypes at once: Hagar whose son Ishmael had been disinherited from any future; Jochebed sacrificing her infant son Moses in a Nile basket; Mary who bore and raised a child destined to save through his own murder.

The resurrection of a vibrant civil rights movement resulted from Bradley's actions. That movement wasn't perfect, and it didn't completely repair the world. But it connected communities and advanced significant improvements.

I wondered then and I wonder still: What horrific, transformative moment would be required to stop the destruction of immigrant families and U.S. citizens who are woven into the heart of America?

For me, the cross had become a bright red stop sign, a direction marker for those times when you see a person beat and hurting, such as the robbery victim on the Jericho Road in the Good Samaritan story in the tenth chapter of the Gospel of Luke (Luke 10:25-37).

And when I wonder, as the lawyer asked Jesus, "What must I do to inherit eternal life?" I, too, am led to follow the Samaritan, whose actions were guided by a gut-wrenching feeling of solidarity that was so overwhelming he seemed to feel the pain of the man who needed help as if it were his own pain.

The Good Samaritan was an excluded foreigner, like the sole leper who turned back to give God glory in Luke 17, and his status as someone who was excluded seemed to enable him to feel the pain of another more deeply.

The gospel of Luke calls this feeling *splangnizomai,* for the place where we share the pain of others, deep in our intestines, our *splangnon*. Two thousand years later, we tame this ugly, gut-wrenching feeling with the smoothness of its traditional translation as "compassion."

The next Sunday, I preached at a local Reformed church in New Brunswick, relying on the text suggested by the lectionary.

Jesus's farewell to his disciples in Chapter 14 of the Gospel of John helped me imagine what my friend Arino Massie might have said if he had been given a chance to say goodbye to his thirteen-year-old son before he was deported.

"I am going away but I will not leave you orphaned," Arino would have promised Joel. "I will always be in God my Father and you, Joel, will always be in me, as I will be always in you."

If you saw a picture of Joel and Arino, you would say that it's true, the father is in the son and the son is in the father, I promised the congregation. The younger and older men were spitting images of each other.

For Jesus, though, being one in this way was not good enough.

For a son like Joel to be at one with his father, when his father is a condemned man whom society deems to be a criminal and deserving of a punishment so severe that it humiliates him and tries to wash him off the face of the earth, *that* would be an abomination—because then there would be little hope for either life.

So, Jesus promised something more—to send an *Advocate,* a new name for the Holy Spirit. This "advocate" is a Greek word that means a defense lawyer.

The Holy Spirit will come to your defense, Jesus told his disciples.

The Holy Spirit is not just any lawyer, but the very Spirit of Truth.

The very Spirit of Truth would come because when Jesus was tried, convicted, and executed as a lawbreaker, humanity itself was on trial.

CHAPTER 33

What about the Children?

In Highland Park and Washington, D.C., 2017

On May 24, Seth convened a press conference at the Highland Park church.[1] Camera crews and reporters packed the church parlor. A reporter asked Arino's son Joel, who may never again live with his father in the United States, "What was your favorite moment with your father?"

The thirteen-year-old eighth-grader put his head down on his arms, folded on the table in front of him, and responded through his tears, "All of them!"

Putting the spotlight on a U.S. citizen child whose life had been torn apart by the U.S. government was a move of desperation.

Joel, with Seth's backing, bravely bared his agony and vulnerability for everyone to see. Was it healthier for Joel to bear witness publicly to what the government had done to his family or to bear his suffering alone and unheard?

---

[1] Jay Dow, "N.J. Boy Comes Home from School to Learn His Dad's Been Deported," PIX11 News, May 23, 2017, https://pix11.com/news/n-j-teen-comes-home-from-school-to-learn-his-dads-been-deported/.

Joel bravely stepped forward.

In Central New Jersey, the media began to respond.[2] In front of the cameras, Seth, now a state gubernatorial candidate, apologized to Joel on behalf of the country.

"It is the worst thing I can think of for our government to take your dad away from you," he said to Joel. "I'm sorry on behalf of this country and I'm hopeful maybe we can find some compassion in leaders who I hope had no idea of the damage they are doing to you, Joel."

Seth hoped that our national leaders had no idea of the damage they were causing for children. But the question remained: if they knew, would they care? Could the suffering of a child like Joel move the public and awaken curiosity about thousands of private dramas, just like Joel's, taking place every day, all over the county?

Across the country, 4.4 million U.S. citizen children under the age of 18 lived with at least one undocumented parent in 2018. Detention and deportation threatened the well-being of children by increasing poverty, food insecurity, homelessness, and absence of health insurance.

A child's risk of experiencing mental health problems like depression, anxiety, and severe psychological distress increased in hostile immigration environments. Children exhibit stress- and anxiety-related behavioral changes, including symptoms of toxic stress, when they are suddenly separated from their parents, which negatively impacts brain development. They are also at greater risk of developing chronic mental health conditions that include depression and post-traumatic stress disorder (PTSD), as well as physical conditions such as cancer, stroke, diabetes, and heart disease.[3]

In New Jersey in 2021, about 218,000 children—most of whom were U.S. citizens—had an undocumented parent. Twenty-nine percent of them lived in poverty, nearly double the 16-percent national rate for child poverty.[4]

---

[2] Suzanne Russell, "Edison Boy, 13: Why Was Dad Deported?" *Courier News and Home News Tribune*, May 19, 2017, https://www.mycentraljersey.com/story/news/local/middlesex-county/2017/05/19/tearful-boy-13-why-dad-deported/332645001/.

[3] "Fact Sheet: U.S. citizen Children Impacted by Immigration Enforcement," American Immigration Council, June 24, 2021, https://www.americanimmigrationcouncil.org/research/us-citizen-children-impacted-immigration-enforcement.

[4] Data from Children Thrive Action Network, cited in "Number of the Day: 218,000," *NJ Spotlight News*, October 4, 2021, https://www.njspotlightnews.org/2021/10/218000-nj-kids-undocumented-parent-poverty-path-to-citizenship/.

On a Tuesday in June, just before Father's Day, Seth and Joel traveled to Washington, DC, for a press conference held in the U.S. Capitol Building.[5] The goal was to send up a warning signal about the escalation of pain and suffering that U.S. citizen children were experiencing because of the radical change in ICE enforcement policies and the withdrawal of prosecutorial discretion for the sake of children.

A nonprofit advocacy organization called America's Voice sponsored the event. This DC group was formed in 2008 by lifetime immigration advocate Frank Sharry after he had led the National Immigration Forum, where he worked with U.S. senators on comprehensive immigration reform for eighteen years.

Senator Bob Menendez and Representatives Frank Pallone and Luis Gutierrez devoted time to speak in person during the hour-long event. New Jersey media and their audiences focused their attention on riveting stories like Joel's that showed the Trump administration's destructive impact on our local communities. This press conference highlighted two heart-breaking stories: Joel and his father Arino, who had already been deported, and an Ohio family of six whose father Jesus was in imminent danger of deportation.

Sadly, neither story made a dent in the international media explosion that surrounded the Trump administration that day.

Senator Menendez spoke first, and as an elected official from New Jersey, he focused on Arino's situation. "Arino isn't a 'bad hombre'[6] but a good father. He is not a criminal but a casualty of a mass deportation agenda," Menendez said before adding, "If no one is prioritized, everyone is a target."

Though the senator regretted the lack of film crews in the conference room, he acknowledged the media had bigger fish to fry.

---

[5] "Ahead of Father's Day, Sen. Menendez, Rep. Pallone, Rep. Gutiérrez, Immigrant Families, and Faith Leaders Urge Trump and Sec. Kelly to Stop Destroying Families," *America's Voice,* June 13, 2017, https://americasvoice.org/press_releases/fathers-day-advocates-say-stop-destroying-families/; see also a video of the press conference at https://www.facebook.com/americasvoice/videos/10155299204813614/?pnref=story.

[6] "At the third and final presidential debate, Trump upheld his idea to build a wall on the U.S.-Mexico border, citing illegal immigration and the influx of drugs to the United States as national security issues. 'We're going to secure the border, and once the border is secured at a later date, we'll make a determination as to the rest,' Trump said. 'But we have some bad hombres here and we're going to get them out'" (Lizzy Gurdus "Trump: 'We Have Some Bad Hombres and We're Going to Get Them Out,'" CNBC, October 19, 2016, https://www.cnbc.com/2016/10/19/trump-we-have-some-bad-hombres-and-were-going-to-get-them-out.html).

Then he himself shuttled off to the Senate chamber where the showcase event of the day was taking place.

There, Attorney General Jeff Sessions was testifying before the Senate Intelligence Committee on Russian interference in the 2016 U.S. election.[7] As CNN put it, "all eyes were on [Sessions] on Tuesday as he testified before the Senate intelligence committee less than a week after ousted FBI Director James Comey's testimony. Lawmakers grilled Sessions about his role in Comey's firing, his own involvement in the Trump campaign, and his meetings with Sergey Kislyak, the Russian ambassador to the US."[8]

Such spectacular events always had a way of preempting our work to spotlight the destruction of families that the U.S. government undertakes in our own hometowns.

The church's U.S. representative, Frank Pallone, described two smokescreens that contributed to what he called "the big lie" when it comes to destroying families in the name of homeland security.

First was the impression that the Trump administration detained and deported only people who had criminal records, which is simply not true. Anyone undocumented is in danger of detention and deportation, including young adults called Dreamers, insisted Pallone, since there is still no legal basis for Dreamers to stay here.

The second smokescreen was the claim that the U.S. government is not going after Christians. This was a myth, Pallone said, because clearly Christians were being targeted and sent back to countries that could arrest and punish them for their faith.

"This room should be lit up!" Representative Gutierrez exclaimed. "This should be a story that America is hearing!" Then he apologized, "Excuse me if I seem to be belittling the few members of the media who showed up here today."

To Gutierrez, the unfilled seats in the conference room that Tuesday before Father's Day meant that Trump's agenda was working. Americans were coming to believe that peaceful people were indeed dangerous to our society and needed to be eliminated. Though he represented Illinois, Gutierrez had a close relationship with the children and their father Jesus from Willard, Ohio, and he pushed for

---

[7] "Attorney General Testimony on Russia Investigation," C-SPAN, June 13, 2017, https://www.c-span.org/video/?429875-1/attorney-general-calls-collusion-accusations-detestable-lie.

[8] Saba Hamedy, "Top 8 Lines from Jeff Sessions' Hearing," CNN, June 13, 2017, https://www.cnn.com/2017/06/13/politics/jeff-sessions-hearing-top-lines/index.html.

more of us to demonstrate about the plight of this family and others like them.[9]

"We need to put ourselves in a position not only to talk, but also to walk," Representative Gutierrez urged. "If I don't do everything I can possibly do to stop the deportations, then I think I failed in my mission." America's Voice executive director Frank had introduced Gutierrez as a deal-maker on the inside and a movement-maker on the outside. The press conference via Facebook Live was the first time I had observed Gutierrez in action, and I couldn't help but remember how kind his office had been to help our church on Christmas Eve back in 2012, when we were trying to resolve sanctuary for two handfuls of Indonesians.

"When are they going to put the faces of these children on what they are doing?" Gutierrez asked. While listening in, I despaired about the difference that focusing on children's perspectives would make.

Gutierrez said his job was to keep the smiles on the faces of children like the ones who were acting silly just off camera. He asked if we wanted these children to become orphans. I thought of how we count on the suffering of children to tug on our heartstrings. Child spokespeople talk us through appeals for donations to highly funded organizations like St. Jude's Children's Hospital, March of Dimes, Care, and Save the Children.

Yet the plight of U.S. citizen children forced by their own government to live without the support of a parent has yet to capture our national attention. Nevertheless, there is a lot of data to support the fact that the United States is destroying its own child citizens through the detention and deportation of long-term residents.

The citizenship clause of the Fourteenth Amendment to the United States Constitution states, "All persons born or naturalized in the United States, and subject to the jurisdiction thereof, are citizens of the United States and of the State wherein they reside."

However, since the 1980s, support for children born to undocumented parents has been tainted by critics who apply to them the term "anchor babies."[10] True, when these children become adults,

---

[9] The Willard, Ohio, family of Jesus Lara, who was deported soon after this press conference, was featured in a campaign run by America's Voice, #DontDeportMyDad, as seen in a June 17, 2017, Facebook post: https://www.facebook.com/groups/689881901164135/search/?q=jesus%20willard%20ohio.

[10] One of the first uses of the term, "anchor babies" dates back to 1987, when San Diego State University sociology professor Kenji Ima and psychologist Jeanne Nidorf interviewed dozens of troubled Southeast Asian teens and examined the

they can apply for their parents' residency and citizenship, but only if their parents haven't been undocumented residents for ten years. Thus, for U.S. citizen children to apply for green cards for their parents, their parents would need to return to their home countries for ten years. And then, it is not at all clear that this request would be granted. Most undocumented people reside here, not so that their children can apply on their behalf in ten years, but because living conditions in their home countries are untenable.[11]

Most undocumented parents have no intention of leaving the U.S. for ten years.

Thus, when people use this derogatory term, "anchor baby," they imply that children who are born to parents who are not authorized to live here are somehow lesser people, not full citizens, contrary to the Fourteenth Amendment, ratified in 1868, which not only grants citizenship to everyone born in the United States but also guarantees them freedom, due process, and equal protection under the law. This derogatory term discredits the birthright of our young citizens and diminishes our sense of responsibility to care for this vulnerable group of young people who are a vital part of the backbone of American society.

We live in a country where people advocate for an unborn child's right to life, even when the person whose body supports that unborn child chooses to withdraw her support.

By the same argument, why do we allow the federal government to irrevocably withdraw parental support of a U.S. citizen child by deporting that child's parents—especially when the government has many other means of restricting that parent's authorization?

Why doesn't the Fourteenth Amendment's equal protection clause, which guarantees the rights of all people who fall under the jurisdiction of the United States, also empower the cause of U.S. citizen children who need their parents to survive and thrive?

---

criminal and probation records of one hundred more and delivered the following profile: "They are 'anchor children,' saddled with the extra burden of having to attain a financial foothold in America to sponsor family members who remain in Vietnam" ("A Profile of a Lost Generation," *Los Angeles Times*, December 13, 1987, https://www.latimes.com/archives/la-xpm-1987-12-13-tm-28306-story.html).

[11] "The Typical Unauthorized Immigrant Adult Has Lived in the U.S. for 15 Years," Pew Research Center, June 12, 2019, https://www.pewresearch.org/fact-tank/2019/06/12/us-unauthorized-immigrant-population-2017/ft_19-06-12_unauthorizedimmigration_typical-unauthorized-immigrant-adult-lived-us-15-years_3/.

Why aren't the rights of U.S. citizen children who need their parents to survive weighed against the harm done to the country when a parent resides in the U.S. without authorization?

Each year, about 6 percent of all children born in the United States, some 250,000 children, are born to unauthorized parents. That is down from a high of 390,000 in 2008, yet far above 30,000 in 1980.[12]

There is a lot of concern and consternation about "birth tourism," a practice in which wealthy pregnant people who are not U.S. citizens check in to a private clinic just before birth to provide their child with a U.S. passport. This takes place about 30,000 times a year, and it is certainly concerning.

However, promoting birth tourism is not the concern of immigration advocates who care about deportations and how they destroy communities, families, and harm children whose lives are woven into the fabric of American society.

"Look at these children!" Representative Gutierrez focused the attention in the June 13 press conference on the three boys and one girl of Jesus Lara, who had been handcuffed and detained after dropping off his nine-year-old child at school. "If he follows the law, and complies with deportation, then he abandons his children. Or what do we do, [do we] send them back to a country they never knew? So that they can return when they are eighteen to the country that turned its back on them?"

Despite all the attention drawn to dramatize the flow of new immigrants on the southern U.S. border, the typical unauthorized immigrant adult is a long-term resident like Jesus, a vital member of his family and community, and one who has lived in the U.S. for fifteen years.[13]

In the late spring of 2017, DIRE and the Reformed Church joined a host of advocates who together cried out for help, looking for someone or something that could reverse the persecution and destruction that the newly installed Trump administration worked so industriously to cement into policy, budgets, organizations, leadership, public rallies, and legal strategies.

But this time no form of advocacy proved effective. Despite hundreds of phone calls to ICE and government leaders, and numerous visits, protests, and early morning interfaith rituals at the Elizabeth Detention Center, no one at ICE engaged with our church.

---

[12] "The Typical Unauthorized Immigrant."
[13] "The Typical Unauthorized Immigrant."

By June 2, all four men who had been liberated from sanctuary in the Reformed Church of Highland Park had been deported. That one was grieved by his wife and American citizen son, another by his brand-new bride, and a third by his wife and his adult children who remained in the U.S. under DACA protection, raising his grandchildren—all these factors were irrelevant to an administration impervious to mercy and grace. Not even the martyrdom of his brother-in-law, a pastor beheaded in the middle of a worship service, could save Saul Timisela. Seth, immigration advocates, the press, and a whole host of elected U.S. representatives and congressmen found no avenue to shock or shame ICE leadership, who remained intent on persecuting immigrants as rule breakers by tearing their families apart.

The devastation of four Indonesian families put the Reformed church community on edge about what was in store for others.

"We have forty-three people who are going to have to check in over the next ten months," Pastor Seth told the press. "Every week is an excruciating decision over what do we do."

In New Jersey, 50,000 people shared their uncertainty. Across the country, there were 900,000 more with final deportation orders.

For the first time since Gary Mead's intervention in 2013, the Pangemanans did not appear in July for their pre-scheduled, six-month visit. They weren't alone.

CHAPTER 34

A Global Community Celebrates Anyway

In Highland Park, 2017

After graduating from seminary, I prepared to work the next fall as a resident chaplain at a local hospital across the river from Highland Park in New Brunswick. I hoped to learn how to care for people of all faiths and no faiths who were experiencing health crises, while I completed requirements for ordination in my denomination, the Reformed Church in America. That summer, I began pitching an article about how to counter our country's hatred of immigrants to *America: The Jesuit Review.*

In July 2017, I grew concerned when *America* published an interview with Antonio Spadaro, SJ, one of the Jesuit co-authors of a Vatican-reviewed paper titled "Evangelical Fundamentalism and Catholic Integralism," in which Spadaro stated, "We have expressed our opinion on…a strange form of ecumenism" uniting "fringe groups of Catholic integralists and some groups of evangelical fundamentalists in the political field." Spadaro continued:

Often this fundamentalism is born from the perception of a threat, of a world that is threatened, a world that is collapsing, and so it responds with a religion from a reading of the Bible transformed into an ideological message of fear. It's a manipulation of anxiety and insecurity. And the church is therefore transformed into a kind of sect, a sect of the pure, the *option* of the pure, even though numerically small, which then seeks to impose its vision on society, prescinding any form of dialogue. It's a way of dropping out of what is perceived as a "barbaric" mainstream culture. Some call this "authentic Christianity." Intolerance thus becomes the mark of purism, while evangelical values like mercy do not form part of this vision—which is very conflictive, belligerent [and] seeks to impose itself in political ways.[1]

In a barrage of pitch emails to the editors of *America*, I argued that the only solution to counteract deadly messages of murderous fear was to highlight interfaith efforts. An ecumenism of love, I proposed, was needed to counteract ideological messages of fear that have enabled, as Spadaro argued, "intolerance [which] thus becomes the mark of purism," where "evangelical values like mercy" are rejected, and the faithful become a sect of the pure, "numerically small, which then seeks to impose its vision on society, prescinding any form of dialogue."

I hoped to write an article that would show how multiple faith communities supported refugees through Interfaith RISE and how together they had changed those dynamics in my corner of Central New Jersey.

Then, in August 2017, attorneys and advocates in El Paso, Texas, began to hear increasing numbers of immigrants who had been detained after they crossed the U.S. border talk about how their children were taken away and that they had no idea where their kids were being held.

Not until almost a year later, on May 15, 2018, did the Trump administration finally announce the official policy they termed "zero tolerance," known through the media moniker "family separation." As the media sought to understand exactly how many children had been separated already, they discovered that in July 2017, the Trump

---

[1] Gerard O'Connell, "Exclusive Interview: Antonio Spadaro on His Article about 'The Ecumenism of Hate' in the U.S.," *America: The Jesuit Review*, July 14, 2017, https://www.americamagazine.org/faith/2017/07/14/exclusive-interview-antonio-spadaro-his-article-about-ecumenism-hate-us.

administration surreptitiously had begun a pilot program for immigrant families in El Paso. Federal prosecutors charged all adults who crossed the border unlawfully from New Mexico to West Texas, including parents arriving with young children from Honduras, El Salvador, and Guatemala and claiming asylum.[2]

Though seeking asylum is not a crime, the Department of Homeland Security jailed adults, including those who sought asylum, on charges of misdemeanor illegal entry or felony re-entry. Reclassifying children as "unaccompanied," DHS sent children into a network of shelters located across the country that were run by the U.S. Department of Health and Human Services.

Later, it became clear that no effort was made to keep a database with the names of children and the contact information for their parents to enable family members to reconnect.

The impact on children and families was enormous. Efforts to reunite families torn apart from 2017 on continued through 2023, despite the change in administrations.

Next, in September 2017, President Trump announced the end of deportation protections for 800,000 undocumented young adults (called Dreamers) who had come to the United States as unwitting children.[3] Protests erupted across the country. Top business leaders, including Facebook founder Mark Zuckerberg, vehemently objected. This step was almost too much even for President Trump, who claimed to reporters that he had "great love" for the beneficiaries of the Deferred Action for Child Arrivals (DACA) program he had just ended. Attorney General Jeff Sessions focused on the legal necessity of eliminating the program in response to the nine Republican state attorneys general who threatened to sue to halt the program if Mr. Trump did not dissolve it.[4]

---

[2] Lisa Riordan Seville and Hannah Rappleye, "Trump Admin Ran "Pilot Program' for Separating Migrant Families in 2017," NBC News, June 29, 2018, https://www.nbcnews.com/storyline/immigration-border-crisis/trump-admin-ran-pilot-program-separating-migrant-families-2017-n887616.

[3] "Nearly 800,000 immigrants who have lived illegally in the United States since they were children would be subject to removal once their government-issued work permits expire under the Deferred Action for Childhood Arrivals program" (David Nakamura, "Trump Administration Announces End of Immigration Protection Program for 'Dreamers,'" *The Washington Post*, September 5, 2017, https://www.washingtonpost.com/news/post-politics/wp/2017/09/05/trump-administration-announces-end-of-immigration-protection-program-for-dreamers/).

[4] Nakamura, "Trump Administration Announces End of Immigration Protection Program."

In November, *America* finally accepted my pitch for an article about interfaith efforts to welcome and resettle refugees in and around Highland Park, New Jersey.

Meanwhile, the campaigns Americans waged against undocumented people grew increasingly hostile. As the Trump administration separated children from parents at the southern border, the Reformed Church of Highland Park began caring for migrating children who arrived on their own and for parents who were still looking to be united with their kids.

To prepare for the *America* story, I shadowed IRISE volunteers to learn how they made time to care for immigrants and refugees. I wanted to understand why so many people were committing to welcoming strangers in Central New Jersey.

I tagged along while a father who had been a translator for American forces in Iraq went shopping at Target and Walmart, guided by U.S. citizens who had adopted his family.

Then an American family invited me to lunch with a young married couple who had escaped violence in their home country in sub-Saharan Africa. The couple had obtained a visa to attend a wedding. The wedding was canceled. But when their household was attacked, the couple boarded the flight they had previously for Newark, New Jersey, anyway. As they debarked the plane, they were detained. They hadn't understood that their visa was invalidated when the event was canceled. They spent months at Elizabeth Detention Center—held separately because men and women were not permitted to visit.

The husband described three instances when DHS agents handcuffed him, roughly placed him in a van, and tried to force him to agree to "self-deport" as they drove him to Newark Airport. Somehow, he found the willpower to refuse. He could not leave his wife—who was held separately from him, while kind guards ferried secret notes between the two spouses. In their home country, they had been victims of terrorism. Eventually an immigration judge found their asylum case convincing, and they won permanent asylum.

To complete the story, on a crisp November Sunday, I joined two hundred people in a procession through the Borough of Highland Park as part of the annual fundraising walk for Interfaith Refugee and Immigrant Services and Empowerment.[5] IRISE had grown into

---

[5] Most of this chapter is adapted from Elizabeth Colmant Estes, "To Save America's Soul, We Need an Ecumenism of Love," *America: The Jesuit Review*, February 23, 2018, https://www.americamagazine.org/faith/2018/02/23/save-americas-soul-we-need-ecumenism-love.

a coalition of sixty organizations dedicated to resettling refugees and assisting asylum seekers in Central New Jersey. Walking among the crowd, I recognized only a few familiar faces. I was curious about the powerful force that brought these strangers together to invest their time, energy, and money to help immigrants whom more and more Americans viewed with suspicion, anger, and hatred.

In the golden afternoon sunshine, a tall gentleman with a graying ponytail towered over the procession. Amid a sea of posters bearing messages of welcome ("Refugees Make Our Country Great") and warning ("Will Trade Racists for Refugees"), the man declared, "Jews, Christians, Muslims, pagans, and atheists, all working together. Makes you think. Maybe God...exists."

His remark was somewhat tongue-in-cheek. John Fischer was a retired Lutheran pastor and explained that in forty years of ordained ministry, he had rarely attended a meeting like the monthly Interfaith RISE gatherings at the Reformed Church of Highland Park led by the church's co-pastor, Seth Kaper-Dale.

"Seth comes in with a long list of tasks that need to get done, and people just raise their hands. By the end of the meeting, every need is cared for," he exclaimed. "It lifts your spirit."

Back in 2014, when Lutheran Disaster Response, a ministry of the Evangelical Lutheran Church in America, asked congregations to provide shelter for people who lost their homes in Hurricane Sandy, the parsonage of Our Savior's Lutheran Church, where Rev. Fischer worshiped, stood empty and in need of repair. The tiny congregation dedicated $35,000 to renovate the four-bedroom house for a New Jersey family until their own storm-damaged home was once again livable. That family then found new housing and the parsonage became vacant just as Interfaith RISE was desperately searching for a place large enough for an Afghan refugee family.

After a decade in Iran, all six family members moved in.

Nearby, at St. Luke's Episcopal Church, an interfaith group wanted to support a refugee family but needed a house. Nancy Zerbe and her husband Pete Materna, who are Catholic, were introduced to Interfaith RISE by neighbors who started the group at St. Luke's and who had then assisted the Afghan family now residing in the Lutheran parsonage.

After the Catholic couple participated in the 2016 annual Interfaith RISE Walk-a-Thon, they joined as representatives of their own congregation, St. Peter the Apostle University and Community

Parish in New Brunswick. As IRISE volunteers, they shuttled refugees and asylum seekers to medical appointments and grocery stores.

"Imagine taking an Iraqi family to an American supermarket for the first time and trying to explain—via Google Translate on a cell phone—the difference between organic and nonorganic produce!" Nancy exclaimed. She and Pete connected Interfaith RISE clients and coordinators with a local office of Catholic Charities. They introduced St. Peter's congregants, including a tutor trained in English as a second language, to Interfaith RISE.

Changes to federal immigration policies under the Trump administration made their immigration ministry feel like a call from God. According to Nancy, "Helping refugees and asylees assimilate and feel welcome in a new home provides a powerful way to live out Christ's teaching that 'as you did to one of the least of these my brethren, you did it to me' (Matthew 25:40, RSV)."

The previous spring, this Catholic couple had joined Deportation and Immigration Response Equipo (DIRE) for weekly trips to the Elizabeth Detention Center, the converted warehouse on the outskirts of Newark Liberty Airport. Every Monday evening, a van shuttled volunteers from Highland Park to the center for visits with some of the three hundred men held in detention by the U.S. Department of Homeland Security.

On Wednesdays, another group visited a few of the center's thirty detained women. They met asylum seekers confined there from four to eighteen months. Some said they had been pressed by Department of Homeland Security agents to return to the dangerous countries they had fled.

Over the course of their visits, Nancy and Pete came to know a young Nigerian woman who was being held separately from her husband. In May 2017, an immigration judge granted the Nigerian couple legal asylum status. Late on the night when DHS released the couple, Nancy and Pete returned to the center, took the Nigerians to a cheeseburger dinner, and then brought them home, where the two couples lived together temporarily.

The Nigerian woman said that for the rest of her life she would never forget how that night's warm breeze felt on her skin.

The Nigerians took to calling Nancy and Pete "Mum and Dad." The Americans coached them through their initial job interviews and then through the trials and pitfalls of the couple's first paid employment.

Although the Reformed Church of Highland Park–Affordable Housing Corporation originally formed to shelter homeless people in the local area, the corporation began to broker leases for Interfaith RISE refugees and asylees, including a New Brunswick apartment for the Nigerian couple.

To prepare a new home for an arriving family, Sarah Hymowitz, a Highland Park resident, and an Interfaith RISE liaison to Anshe Emeth Reformed Temple in New Brunswick, published an online registry—just like the gift registries we use for bridal showers—for household items that refugees desperately needed, from rugs to lamps, detergent to toothpaste.

"If I send an email on Monday," Sarah said, "often by Wednesday, one hundred items are spoken for." At first, she had asked for gently used household items. But the response was overwhelming. Instead of providing one pot, a volunteer bought a brand-new set she found on sale. "I get a nice glimpse of how generous people are. It's a very concrete way to help. You see someone wearing the coat you bought. You know someone is sleeping beneath the bedspread you donated."

Other volunteers painted walls, cleaned kitchens and bathrooms, and delivered furniture to prepare homes for families who sometimes arrive straight from rugged refugee camps in countries like Uganda and Jordan. A Jewish woman who keeps kosher learned how to cook halal dishes to greet families with a warm meal on the night they arrive. Several men were devoted to picking up refugees at area airports.

Community networks cannot be paid for or measured, but they make lives work.

Abrupt immersion in American culture can be challenging. Louise Sandburg from the Jewish Center Interfaith Resettlement Committee in Princeton directed cultural orientation for Interfaith RISE in 2017. One of the first things Louise taught refugees was how to dial 911.

The previous spring, when a child spilled hot tea on himself, an Arabic-speaking Highland Park police officer accompanied the family for hours in a hospital emergency room. One night, a Congolese baby spiked a fever. Pastor Seth dispatched a neighbor to demonstrate how to use a digital thermometer and call a health clinic doctor.

Interfaith RISE's director Paola Stevens also served as the social worker who coordinated services for refugees in 2017. She explained that as an affliate site of the U.S. Committee for Refugees and Immigrants, Interfaith RISE was mandated to coordinate services for each refugee's first ninety days in the country, including health screenings, shelter, Medicaid, job training, and ESL lessons.

Connecting people to faith and ethnic communities was also critical. Sunni families flourished in the community of a Sunni mosque. Syrian interpreters were affliated with the Islamic Society of Central New Jersey on U.S. Route 1 in Monmouth Junction.

"The goal is self-sufficiency and independence," Paola explained. "We want to be here for them, for as long as it takes." With forty-six refugee arrivals to Interfaith RISE from January to November 2017, resettlement operations would have ground to a halt without volunteers. Broadcasting urgent and specific calls for help was key to Interfaith RISE's success. It was also key to Pastor Seth's pastoral philosophy.

"Early on, a church leader told me she was terrified because she used to know everything that went on, but now she no longer did," Seth recounted. Then Seth assured her, "We don't need to know. We don't need to control everything in the body of Christ—that's where many churches fail." He called his approach "creating intentional, compassionate community."

As participants in the 2017 Interfaith RISE Walk-a-Thon paused outside houses of worship, the borough hall, and schools, community leaders spoke words of welcome, and refugees who arrived in the past year from Afghanistan, Iraq, and Syria introduced themselves.

One father told walkers that he called his parents to say how his Jersey neighbors had shown him great kindness. "When I see one of you, you are my loved ones," he said in newly learned English.

Late-season leaves crackled underfoot as walkers shuffled onto the lawn of Highland Park's public library. There, Sami Catovic, the director of the New Brunswick Islamic Center, explained how the tradition of welcoming refugees is deeply inscribed in Islam's holy texts: "Fourteen hundred years ago, Prophet Mohammed, peace be upon him, was suffering in his home of Mecca and fled with his community to Medina, as migrants and refugees, where he received help from a new community."

In Medina, Sami explained, the Prophet declared an end to the divisions of tribe and ethnicity. From then on, there would be only migrants and helpers. Sami gave thanks for the most beautiful gathering on that Sunday afternoon. It is simple, he said: "We are either immigrants trying to establish ourselves or helpers assisting those trying to establish themselves."

Judy Richman, who helped refugees with English conversation and took families on trips to the local Stop & Shop, taught me the meaning of the Hebrew phrase *tikkun olam*, which means repairing our shattered world. "*Tikkun olam* is the obligation to take actions that increase dignity, equality, justice, and healing," explained Judy. Thanks to her work with Interfaith RISE, she now knows where to find the best halal butcher and the most excellent Southeast Asian supermarket.

"Every act of loving kindness brings us closer to God's vision for the world," Judy said. "Torah repeatedly commands us to protect the widow, the orphan, and the stranger."

For me, the defining moment of the 2017 walk came in the form of a question. A young woman from Princeton University's Office of Religious Life asked the crowd, "Who are we without welcome?"

The woman, Maya Wahrman, told how her great-grandfather arranged for his family's escape from Frankfurt to Palestine in 1933 and paid for a visa for a woman, a stranger, who could not afford to migrate legally. Years later, when the woman visited with her new family and offered to repay her debt, Ms. Wahrman's family gained friends who, years before, might not have survived the Holocaust had they been unable to flee Germany.

Many Jews use the Hebrew word for "cataclysm," *Shoah*, instead of the word most Americans use, "Holocaust"—an ancient Greek word meaning "burnt offering." Cataclysm is one experience that many Interfaith RISE volunteers and immigrants share. Ms. Wahrman then told us how immigrants changed her life.

A Pakistani asylum seeker was the first person Maya visited in Elizabeth Detention Center—and Maya was the first Jewish person the Pakistani man had ever met. After he had been released, Maya visited him late one night in his new home after she had said goodbye to another detainee in Elizabeth who was about to be deported. Despite the hour, her friend surprised her with a full Pakistani dinner.

Because Maya's family remains in Jerusalem, another asylee, a Palestinian, called himself Maya's Israeli uncle. "We have to care for you," he told her, "because we are your American family."

"I want to thank you for who I am because of this community," Ms. Wahrman told us.

At the end of the 2017 walk, refugee chefs provided the walkers with refreshments. In the spring of 2016, this tradition had helped inspire the opening of the lunchtime café called Global Grace in the dining hall of the Reformed Church, where Monday through Friday, a chef from Indonesia, Syria, Congo, Sierra Leone, or India cooked favorite recipes from his or her homeland, earned income and met neighbors. In 2017, the café contributed hundreds of dollars a week to Interfaith RISE. Thanks to national media coverage of the café in outlets like National Public Radio, customers drove for miles to support the café.

As my friends had taught me through their Muslim, Jewish, and Christian traditions, radical hospitality is a positive form of resistance to powers and principalities that viciously consume human lives at an increasingly horrific rate.

Fida Ayoubi from the New Brunswick Islamic Center volunteered at the café and also served as an Arabic translator for Interfaith RISE. Her family was saved by Christian neighbors during their harrowing escape from Lebanon's civil war during the 1970s.

"Helping refugees with the Interfaith RISE community has been very good for my soul," Fida said. "It's taught me the humbleness, generosity, and goodness of selfless people who help just to help." Fida is supported by many of Central Jersey's Islamic communities. "When I am looking for donations and friendship for refugees, I send out a message, and those needs are met."

As the Interfaith RISE walk ended, I retraced my steps and returned for my own family dinner. A slowly setting sun cast long shadows on the pavement outside buildings where we had paused earlier. Over the course of the afternoon, I had come to share Maya Wahrman's gratitude. Lingering in the fresh November air was the unmistakable sense that I had received an ineffable gift, an intuition of greater wholeness, a pervasive thankfulness that I could not have experienced had I stayed inside.

As Christians, our goal in life, as Nancy Zerbe reminded me, is to stop living like the security-minded goats we find in Matthew 25 and instead become ever more like the extravagant sheep who give food to hungry people, water to anyone who thirsts, and, of course, welcome to strangers. We cannot do it alone. Good Samaritans everywhere know that when someone asks for help, they are inviting us to become full-fledged children of the one, true God of all faiths and traditions.

By joining with neighbors who were opening their doors and lives to immigrants, the part of me that had been sickened by my country's anti-immigrant tactics felt as if it had begun to heal.

CHAPTER 35

Some Who Are Vile and More Who Are Splendid

In Highland Park, Winter to Spring, 2018

On the morning of January 25, 2018, ICE agents staked out the suburban New Jersey neighborhoods where Roby Sanger and Gunawan Liem lived with their wives and U.S. citizen children. Both men were authorized to work and reside in their New Jersey homes under official Form I-247 stays of deportation that they had been receiving annually ever since they spent 340 or so days in sanctuary at the Reformed Church of Highland Park from 2012 until February 14, 2013.

Their most recent stays were still in effect.

As both fathers dropped off their children for school, agents followed along in unmarked vehicles with darkened windows.

After Roby Sanger delivered his daughters to their middle and high schools in Metuchen, New Jersey, ICE agents arrested him.

After Gunawan's daughter boarded her school bus in Franklin Township, agents arrested Gunawan as well.

Roby and Gunawan entered immigration detention at Essex County Jail. Meanwhile, another set of ICE agents entered the streets of Highland Park looking for Harry Pangemanan.

That Thursday morning was especially cold, so even though their schools were only a few blocks away, Harry's daughters had gotten ready for school and waited in his car in his backyard driveway, with the heat on, so that Harry could drop them off.

Somehow, however, before he opened the screen door to step into his backyard, Harry had the presence of mind to look around outside. On the street where his driveway emptied out, Harry spotted an unmarked Ford Explorer with telltale darkened windows. Peering out from his enclosed back porch, Harry called fifteen-year-old Jocelyn on her mobile phone.

"You'll have to walk to school today, honey."

Harry didn't have to say anything more. The girls got out of the car and walked to their schools.

Then Harry called Seth, who drove four blocks to Harry's home. Harry jumped into Seth's car. It was a very close call. Seth drove Harry to the church where he joined other Indonesian friends who had already taken sanctuary in the church: Arthur Jemmy and his wife Silfia Tobing, who had formerly participated in the first round of sanctuary in 2012–13, and Yohannes Tasik, a warehouse worker and father of a three-year-old U.S. citizen daughter.

Next, Seth drove to Highland Park High School, where Jocelyn's teacher told her to go to the principal's office. When she arrived, she found Pastor Seth and Principal Lassiter, who explained that her father was safe for now at the church and that Seth was letting Yana and Christa know what was happening.[1]

On his way back to the church, Seth passed the Pangemanans' house on the corner of their street and spotted two ICE agents knocking at Harry's back door. Seth parked his car and, for three minutes, filmed ICE agents as they knocked and called out to people in the empty house, while Seth broadcast live on Facebook.

"This is what is happening right now in Highland Park, New Jersey," Seth narrated. "Just one week after the borough honored Harry with its Martin Luther King Jr. award for rebuilding 209 homes damaged in Superstorm Sandy…ICE is coming for a man who has lived here peaceably since 1993."[2]

This time, however, Seth was sounding the alarm on a news platform he had created himself the previous fall, along with the team

---

[1] Notes from Jocelyn Pangemanan on a preliminary draft, January 2023.
[2] On January 25, 2018, Seth broadcasted ICE agents at Harry's door via Facebook Live; see video available at https://www.facebook.com/watch/?v=2000056440248984.

he had built to support his Green Party bid for New Jersey governor. Together Seth's team had won thousands of followers across New Jersey for his Facebook page.

Exactly one year had passed since President Trump issued his executive order of January 25, 2017, "Enhancing Public Safety in the Interior of the United States," which removed any exemptions of classes and categories of removable aliens.[3] In New Jersey, ICE actions were targeting the same Indonesians who had been spared in 2013 by the head of Enforcement and Removal Operations, Gary Mead.

In May 2018, Newark ICE Field Director John Tsoukaris had ordered the detention and eventual deportation of the first four men who had been previously spared: Arino Massie, Rovani Wangko, Oldy Manopo, and Saul Timisela. Now the same Newark field office, led by the same director, pursued the remaining three fathers who also had previously taken sanctuary in the church.

Seth called out the Newark director John Tsoukaris by name, a man who seemingly nursed a grudge against the Indonesians whom Gary Mead had graciously released with stays and work authorizations in 2013.

To me, the vindictive pursuit conducted by ICE Director John Tsoukaris was reminiscent of the Javert character in Victor Hugo's *Les Misérables*. All three men that ICE stalked that morning—Roby, Gunawan, and Harry—were covered under legitimate stays of removal.

America's immigration system was full of contradictions and inequalities, but Field Director John Tsoukaris's ability to make exceptions, to extend prosecutorial discretion as his predecessor had, to consider the needs of U.S. citizen children—none of this would get in the way of executing his own view of law and order now that the U.S. president championed indiscriminate deportations.

"John Tsoukaris—Field Office Director of ICE in Newark—was not keen on the precedent set by his predecessor Scott Weber," Seth said. "He came to power and felt that people with final deportation orders should be deported even though the spirit of the Obama administration at the time was that prosecutorial discretion should be utilized. He was going after them even though his predecessor agreed with us that these folks would have won their asylum claims if it were not for the one-year time bar that was put in place in the late 90s that they didn't know about when they arrived here."[4]

---

[3] Trump, "Enhancing Public Safety in the Interior of the United States."
[4] Mary Ann Koruth, "Sanctuary Saga Leads to Temporary Immunity

I was struck by Seth's speaking about an ICE director as "coming to power." What kind of power does an ICE field director wield? Is he more than a cog in a giant immigration detention and deportation system, following orders in a hierarchy with clear commands, implementing laws that permit little wiggle room?

But Tsoukaris himself described his position of power in a post he wrote for a U.S. government website called *Homeland Security Today*. He wrote that for the last eight or more years, he had personally controlled a forty-million-dollar budget, directed 250 employees plus contract staff, and most importantly, he had been empowered with enough prosecutorial discretion to destroy lives and break up families at will, or save them.[5]

Seth called Highland Park mayor Gayle Brill-Mittler, who in turn called New Jersey governor Phil Murphy, sworn into office only nine days earlier. Gayle traveled to the church along with Metuchen mayor Jonathan Busch, where they met New Jersey's brand-new governor. While they spoke with families reeling from the most recent ICE actions, U.S. Representative Frank Pallone joined them in a sanctuary already filled with local neighbors and immigration advocates.

Across New Jersey, headlines described New Jersey governor Phil Murphy speeding to the church to denounce ICE actions.[6] At a

---

from Deportation," *New Brunswick Today*, February 20, 2018, https://newbrunswicktoday.com/2018/02/20/sanctuary-saga-leads-to-temporary-immunity-from-deportation/.

[5] "I manage over 250 employees and a budget of over $40 million, as well as a facility with contract security staff. I oversee all immigration enforcement programs and activities in New Jersey, including identifying criminal noncitizens incarcerated with federal, state, and local facilities. I also manage the Fugitive Operation Program, which locates and apprehends noncitizens ordered removed from the U.S. and those wanted overseas. I oversee cases of noncitizens going through removal proceedings, both detained in ICE custody and those required to report to ICE, and coordinate removals of individuals to their country of citizenship. I collaborate on activities within my field office with the highest level of federal, state, and local government officials, with intelligence organizations and international law enforcement entities such as Interpol, and I exercise final authority in the grant or denial of prosecutorial discretion related to deportation or removal" (John Tsoukaris, "Perspective: A Day in the Life of a DHS/ICE Field Office Director," *Homeland Security Today*, February 16, 2022, https://www.hstoday.us/featured/perspective-a-day-in-the-life-of-a-dhs-ice-field-office-director/).

[6] Sophie Nieto-Munoz, "Gov. Murphy Races to Sanctuary Church after ICE Detains 2 in N.J. (VIDEO)," NJ.com, January 25, 2018, https://www.nj.com/middlesex/2018/01/hold_murphy_shows_up_at_church_that_houses_immigra.html.

campaign rally the previous October, Murphy had spoken in support of undocumented immigrants: "We will stand up to this president," Murphy said. "If need be, we will be a sanctuary—not just city—but state. This is America. The America I know is the poem at the base of the Statue of Liberty."[7]

While advocates, elected officials, and family members met and prayed in the sanctuary of the Reformed Church, Mayor Busch from Metuchen told the governor he was concerned that Roby Sanger's children still did not know that their father had been arrested after they had left his side to go to school that morning.

As he said this, the Metuchen mayor looked at the children's mother, who nodded to confirm this, but Seth asked all cameras to be directed away from the women. The mothers shared the same immigration situation as their husbands, though so far ICE had not targeted them. Yana explained how Gunawan's wife, her dear friend, was in trouble because she did not drive, did not work, and did not speak English, so how was she going to take care of two U.S. citizen children by herself?

Then, through tears, Yana described her own fears to the governor. "My children have dreams," Yana cried. One hoped to become an engineer, the other a pediatrician. "I don't want to kill their dreams!" Yana implored.[8]

All six children whose futures were threatened that day were U.S. citizens, all had been guaranteed the ability to follow their dreams by the U.S. Constitution, yet those dreams depended on the presence of their fathers in their lives.

Governor Murphy told the crowd he considered himself a "newbie"—it was only his second week on the job, but in his words and by his actions, he made it clear that safeguarding immigrant families of people who faced religious persecution back home was core to his mission.

Addressing Yana, who had described the rapes, murder, and chaos she had left behind in Indonesia in 1998, Murphy said, "This is not our country, not our values, it's not the place you came to escape

---

[7] Qtd. in Samantha Marcus and Brent Johnson, "11 Fiery Moments and Fact Checks from Guadagno-Murphy Debate in Race to Replace Christie," NJ.com, October 11, 2017, https://www.nj.com/politics/2017/10/fiery_moments_and_fact_checks_from_1st_guadagno-mu.html.

[8] See the video posted by NJ.com reporter Steph Solis, accessed March 5, 2022: https://www.pscp.tv/w/1gqGvYNOjrwKB.

persecution! I lived in Asia in the late 90s; I visited Indonesia a lot and I saw it with my own eyes."[9]

Seth added that a thousand churches had burned from 1998 to 2012 in Indonesia. He lamented that although U.S. domestic policy might change through the burning of one church, no amount of persecution seemed to change the status of the Christian Indonesians.

Murphy's presence was due in part to the fact that Seth had run an innovative campaign for governor, backed by the Green Party. Though the rules prevented Seth from qualifying to participate in most televised gubernatorial debates, nevertheless, Murphy said, "We got to know one another on the campaign trail, and I think people would say we were born under the right star [perhaps he meant 'the same star']. We understand the notion of America, our values and constitution, open doors, the beacon of immigration around the world. That's the America I know, and that you know, Frank [Pallone], Seth, and others here..."

Harry Pangemanan looked up squarely in the face of the governor and piped in, "And we Indonesians, we know that America, too!"[10]

On January 25, 2018, Harry was the fourth Indonesian to enter the second round of sanctuary in the church. He joined Arthur Jemmy and Silfia Tobing, who had first entered Sanctuary in 2012–2013 along with Harry and then, on October 10, 2017, re-entered sanctuary when Arthur decided not to report to ICE.[11]

Arthur had his own immigration nightmare to tell. In 2000, Arthur and his parents sat in their Indonesian church when a mob, wielding machetes, disrupted the service. His pastor told everyone to stay calm. Arthur explained how his pastor walked down the aisle. As he approached the hoodlums, before he could say anything, his head was already on the floor. They chopped off his head (reminiscent of Saul Timisela's story). The interlopers set the church on fire. The Jemmy family fled with the rest of their congregation. Arthur remembered looking back and seeing plumes of smoke rise in the distance. Less

---

[9] Qtd. in Steph Solis video.
[10] "Gov. Murphy and Congressman Pallone at The Reformed Church of Highland Park in reaction to ICE raids," YouTube video, NJ.com, January 25, 2018, https://youtu.be/pLwNR-mTfnM.
[11] Hannan Adely, "Fearing deportation, Indonesian Christians seek shelter in N.J. church," NorthJersey.com, October 10, 2017, https://www.northjersey.com/story/news/nation/2017/10/10/fearing-deportation-indonesian-couple-takes-sanctuary-church/749597001/.

than a year later, Arthur's parents emptied their savings account to send Arthur to Jakarta and then to the U.S.[12]

In mid-January, Yohanes Tasik entered sanctuary after ICE came knocking on doors in an early morning raid in Avenel. They were pursuing Indonesians for detention, including Yohanes, even though he wore an ankle bracelet and had been reporting regularly.[13]

In the sanctuary, by the time that photographer Aristide Economopoulos captured Governor Murphy warmly embracing Yohanes and his three-year-old daughter surrounded by a crowd that morning, the terror in the faces in the room around them had dissolved into smiles.

The meeting transformed into a press conference in the parlor, where Seth used a wire cutter to remove the ankle bracelet from Yohanes.[14] Following his ministerial vows, Seth was setting the captives free.

That Thursday, there was a hope and a prayer that for now, four extremely vulnerable Indonesians were safe from ICE agents, and that New Jersey mayors, the state governor, and a high-profile U.S. congressman had committed to find a solution for those in sanctuary as well as the fathers whom ICE now held in detention.

Yet events that took place the very next night rattled everyone, especially the Pangemanan family.

After visiting with Harry in sanctuary, Yana and Christa walked the four blocks back to their family home. Amos Caley, the associate pastor of the Reformed Church, accompanied them.[15] Among Amos's

[12] Koruth, "Sanctuary Saga Leads to Temporary Immunity." See also Ted Sherman, "Meet the Controversial Pastor Fighting to Protect N.J.'s Undocumented Immigrants," *NJ.com*, February 8, 2018, https://www.nj.com/news/2018/02/hes_invoked_god_and_enlisted_a_governor_but_can_he.html.

[13] On January 12, 2018, Seth broadcasted live as he sped to rescue Yohanis Tasik and his three-year-old daughter, who were being pursued by ICE agents back at the Woodbine apartments in Avenel, site of the 2006 ICE raid. In a raid at dawn, agents had been knocking on doors, terrorizing families. See the following Facebook video, accessed March 4, 2022: https://www.facebook.com/kaperdaleforgovernor/videos/1993819377539357/.

[14] Facebook video cited above.

[15] In writing this book, I often find that memories fail in times of the highest trauma. Amos remembers being one of the first people onsite in the discovery of the break-in but not who was with him. Yana remembers being present with Christa and a third person. Jocelyn is certain she remained at the Reformed Church and only heard about the break-in. So, I surmise that reporter Steph Solis incorrectly reported that the break-in was discovered by Amos, Jocelyn, and Christa and that Jocelyn stayed with her father at the church.

many duties as the leader of the church's advocacy against torture, solitary confinement, and the abuses of the New Jersey prison system, and as music minister and youth leader, Amos had developed close ties with the Pangemanan girls, who knew him also as their confirmation guru. The three of them arrived at the Pangemanan home around 7:30 p.m. on Friday night, January 26, and they noticed that the outside door was ajar.

Amos had spotted significant damage to the front door and frame. The living room was left mostly intact, Amos said, but two bedrooms in the back of the house were "trashed." Local reporter Steph Solis tweeted photos of the busted door and Yana's ransacked bedroom.[16]

The bedrooms were completely turned upside down, Amos reported. "The closet in the hallway where all of the coats are was torn up. To me it felt like [someone was] sending a message of some sort or like they were looking for something non-money wise."

Theft happened. Thieves stole hundreds of dollars in cash that eleven-year-old Christa had saved. They stole Yana's precious gold jewelry.

Yet Amos felt the intentional plundering of the bedrooms appeared not so much to be a robbery but rather an attempt to terrorize the family psychologically.

"Imagine walking into your home and your bedroom, the place where you sleep, where you dress, where you keep valuable objects—essentially the one place in the world you ought to feel most safe, and it is completely upended," Amos recollected. "It's one of the greatest personal violations someone can commit against you without touching your physical body." Looking back in 2023, Amos said he had no doubt whatsoever that it was done by ICE, anonymously yet deliberately.[17]

The next morning, a Saturday, Seth heard from a neighbor that the Edison home of Arthur Jemmy and Silfia Tobing was damaged as well and their air conditioner was kicked in. Edison and Highland Park

---

[16] Steph Solis, Twitter post, January 27, 2018, 12:30 p.m., https://twitter.com/stephmsolis/status/957304749799469056/photo/2; see also Steph Solis, "Homes of Indonesian Immigrants in Highland Park Sanctuary Vandalized, Advocate Says," *Courier News and Home News Tribune*, January 27, 2018, https://www.mycentraljersey.com/story/news/local/middlesex-county/2018/01/27/homes-indonesian-immigrants-highland-park-sanctuary-vandalized-advocate-says/1072119001/.

[17] Amos Caley in an email, February 27, 2023.

police departments were notified. The personal nature of the violence terrified Seth, and in a moment of extreme anxiety, he blamed ICE agents in a Facebook post:

> "So, friends. I wrote this am to tell you about Harry and Yana's house being vandalized. I am writing now to tell you that Arthur and Silfia's house, in another town, also was trashed. I believe that this is coordinated attacks by ICE—the abusive arm of our out-of-control Administration. Please share this news. Two of the families in Sanctuary have had their homes broken into and ransacked while they have been in Sanctuary. Abuse, abuse, abuse... Trump, get your filthy hands off our people. peace, seth"

Seth readily admitted to reporters that he did not know for sure who the perpetrators were. His accusations were rash, but still, it wasn't clear that ICE agents had not been involved. In any case, his accusations served as a warning to ICE, who responded to media inquiries with consternation.

"ICE law enforcement officers carry out their sworn duties daily with the utmost professionalism, in accordance with their training," ICE spokeswoman Jennifer Elzea wrote in an email in which she admitted the break-ins were unfortunate. "To suggest that they would cause intentional harm to property is irresponsible and spreads undue fear in the community which this individual [i. e., Seth] claims to support."

Unpublicized to the media, church members discovered that the interior of the church also had been vandalized. Spaces including public restrooms suffered from damage and graffiti. Hatred felt like it had penetrated to the very core of the faith community.

A bit of respite arrived on Sunday morning in the form of a few dozen neighbors and members of local faith communities: a minyan, a Buddhist prayer group, and a team from the congregation of Anshe Emeth Memorial Temple, sheltering from the rain beneath umbrellas in front of the church to express their solidarity and to safeguard the building and its vulnerable occupants. Together, these interfaith friends surrounded the entire exterior of the Reformed Church during its two worship services at 9 and 11:15 a.m.

Judy and Steve Richman said, "everyone should feel safe when they worship" and that they were commanded by Scripture to be there as people who worshiped with their Jewish minyan in the church. They carried a sign that quoted Deuteronomy 10:19 in Hebrew and English: "You shall love the immigrant."[18]

Five miles away on that same Sunday afternoon, a standing-room-only vigil for Roby and his family took place at 1 p.m. in the sanctuary of the First Presbyterian Church of Metuchen, where one Sanger daughter had been confirmed and the other participated in the current confirmation class.

"Roby Sanger sits in a detention center alone, but he is not alone," Rev. Justin Karmann said as he urged participants to contact top ICE officials and handed out their email and phone numbers. A local mom said she kept up on these kinds of injustices, "but then it just became more personal. These are our neighbors and it's our community and we are here to support. We are here to let them know they have support."

After the vigil, some five hundred supporters marched through the streets of Metuchen before gathering in front of the borough hall to hear from a new set of elected officials who pledged their support.[19] The movement to support undocumented Indonesians spread well past Highland Park.

Things became murkier the next week when Harry and Arthur discovered that among other random belongings, the vandals in Highland Park and Edison had taken valid Indonesian passports and left behind passports that were no longer valid.

"This does not make sense," Arthur exclaimed after learning how his Edison apartment had been ransacked.

Harry reported that the most current Indonesian passports of his wife and U.S. citizen daughter were also taken.

"It seems way more sinister, at least to me," Seth said during the next Thursday afternoon's press conference, doubling down on his claim that federal immigration officials had conducted the break-ins as some type of warrantless raid.

"Unless the criminals who went in knew exactly to go for unexpired travel documents, the people who went in that house, they were trained to look for unexpired travel documents, and I would

---

[18] Daniel J. Munoz, "Local Residents Rally for Immigrants Seeking Sanctuary in Highland Park Church," January 29, 2018, *TAPintoNew Brunswick*, https://www.tapinto.net/towns/new-brunswick/articles/local-residents-rally-for-immigrants-seeking-sanc.

[19] Cheryl Makin, "Justice Sought at Rally for Detained Indonesians," January 28, 2018, *Courier News and Home News Tribune*, https://www.mycentraljersey.com/story/news/local/outreach/caring-communities/2018/01/28/justice-sought-rally-detained-indonesians/1072962001/.

suspect that those are people who are somehow connected with the knowledge that such a thing would be helpful in the hands of ICE," Seth said.

He suggested that if the passports managed to find their way to ICE, it would massively speed up removing Arthur and Harry from the country.

"In order for ICE to send someone away, they need a travel document, so when they detain someone, they request that document from the consulate and then once they get that document, [ICE] can send that person away," Seth explained. "But it's a lot faster if you break into the house and steal the valid travel document so that once you detain someone, you can send them away immediately."[20]

The press conference on Thursday, February 1, 2018, took place during a meeting of sixty or so people who had volunteered with Detention and Immigration Response Equipo (DIRE), the grassroots group organized to defend and alert the community of potential ICE action in their neighborhoods.

At the meeting, Seth was not optimistic about the duration of this second round of sanctuary in the church when he told everyone, "It is not known if Sanctuary will last six days or six months." Volunteers came forward anyway, offering to cook and provide childcare for what looked like a growing number of families.[21] Seth told the group, "We are not aiding and abetting, we are highlighting but not hiding people. We are making sure people see the atrocious nature of Trump immigration policies. He is the hate-crimes president who is carrying out racial and ethnic cleansing under the guise of immigration reform."[22]

Four years later, Yana and I looked back and discussed this very bleak period. We met at my mother's assisted living facility. Yana had purchased an elegant green tea cake, filled with luscious white chocolate, to celebrate my mother's birthday. It was February 1, 2022, and the darkness of that time of year still hung heavy in Yana's heart.

Together, we remembered how, four years earlier, texts from Harry had led me to find Yana in a sub-acute, temporary ward of the

---

[20] Daniel J. Munoz, "Edison, Highland Park Immigrants Say Their Passports Were Stolen During Weekend Break-In," *TAPintoPiscataway*, February 2, 2018, https://www.tapinto.net/towns/piscataway/sections/middlesex-county-news/articles/edison-highland-park-immigrants-say-their-passpo-3.
[21] Koruth, "Sanctuary Saga Leads to Temporary Immunity."
[22] Andre Malok, "Undocumented immigrants avoiding ICE find sanctuary at N.J. church," YouTube video, NJ.com, February 20, 2018, https://www.youtube.com/watch?v=DCmm7U384EQ&t=145s.

hospital where I was working as a resident chaplain. Yana had been crippled with abdominal pain that no doctor could pinpoint.

"Stress," we said together.

Four years later, Yana told me and my mother over Chinese take-out and cake that she considered the break-in of her home, the violation of her personal space, the theft of her youngest daughter's childhood savings, the burglary of special pieces of jewelry that her parents and Harry had given her, to be the lowest point of her life.

That was saying a great deal, after everything that Yana had been through—leaving Indonesia as Jakarta burned, being unable to visit her parents and nurse them through illness, supporting her own children while Harry was in Elizabeth Detention Center and then Tacoma, enduring 340 days of her husband living in sanctuary.

None of these monumental challenges seemed as hopeless to Yana as the stark reality of being a victim of a despicable hate crime, targeted at the heart of her home where she raised her daughters. In all those other trials, Yana linked her survival to her agency. She had exercised tremendous willpower and made difficult decisions. But there was no agency in being a crime victim, especially for a mother who could not protect her daughters.

In early 2018, Jocelyn and Christa were at the center of Harry's biggest worries as well. Whoever ransacked his house didn't just hurt him, but they terrified his daughters. He felt heartsick, he said, because of his girls, who are "thinking they don't have any more safer space for them except my church."[23] After their home was broken into and vandalized and their name was included in news reports, the entire Pangemanan family moved back into the room that doubles as a children's library at the Reformed Church.

The Pangemanans were terrified. The day of the break-in, Jocelyn took out her frustrations on her father, yelling at him and crying. So, during the week, it was important that the girls continued to go to school. One of Jocelyn's classes watched a documentary where her father was mentioned. A student talked about "an immigrant whose house got robbed," and Jocelyn lowered her head. She didn't want to look in the eyes of anyone who might have known what was happening

---

[23] Steph Solis, "Homes of Indonesian Immigrants in Highland Park Sanctuary Vandalized, Advocate says," *Courier News and Home News Tribune*, January 27, 2018, https://www.mycentraljersey.com/story/news/local/middlesex-county/2018/01/27/homes-indonesian-immigrants-highland-park-sanctuary-vandalized-advocate-says/1072119001/.

to her family. After class, she was relieved when a teacher pulled her over and offered some comfort. She said, "It was a really nice moment."[24]

Yana barely slept for a whole week. She would stay up, crying, as she watched Jocelyn and Christa sleep on the air mattress they shared in the Sunday school library. When the girls couldn't bear to spend another night in that room, Seth found other spaces on the grounds where they'd be safe. For years, Jocelyn held onto the plushie toy she was gifted in sanctuary.[25]

"We are trying to stay strong as a family, take one day at a time," Harry told the Associated Press. "You do your best today, do something useful, and tomorrow is in God's hands."[26]

The move back into sanctuary seemed a desperate step backwards. And yet, in telling this story as it reaches the point that seemed to be the most hopeless of all, I find myself wondering: Is it only a trite saying that it is always darkest before dawn? Logically, the very moment that our faces are turned furthest from the sun is, in fact, just before the moment rays of sunlight come back into view.

Certainly, on Friday, February 2, 2018, just one day after Seth and the Indonesians complained to the press about stolen passports, no one expected that everything was about to turn around, not just for Harry and Yana, Arthur and Silfia, Yohannes and his daughter, but also for the men in detention and their young families at home.

Even the Indonesians languishing in detention—Gunawan, Roby, and another Indonesian father from Avenel, Parlin Sinaga—all of them, astonishingly, were about to be saved.

---

[24] Notes from Jocelyn Pangemanan on a preliminary draft, January 2023.
[25] Notes from Jocelyn Pangemanan on a preliminary draft, January 2023.
[26] David Porter, "Judge Temporarily Halts Deportation of Indonesian Christians," NBC New York, February 3, 2018, https://www.nbcnewyork.com/news/local/judge-temporarily-halts-deportation-of-indonesian-christians-in-nj-highland-park/1598663/.

CHAPTER 36

Aiding the Advocate

In Highland Park and Newark, New Jersey, 2018

"I told Arthur when he moved in," Pastor Seth Kaper-Dale later told a reporter from the local paper *New Brunswick Today*, "This time we're going to get someone to help us with a lawsuit."[1]

Seth had made that promise back on October 17, 2017, when an important legal precedent had not yet been set. But Seth spoke with a deep conviction that the undeniable truth of the government's relentless and unwarranted persecution of Christian Indonesians was about to be revealed in the full light of day.

"I will no longer talk much with you," Jesus told his disciples before he led them out into the garden where he willingly gave his life up in exchange for their freedom. "For the ruler of this world is coming. He has no power over me, but I do as the Father has commanded me, so that the world may know that I love the Father" (John 14:30, NRSV).

For me, these words from the fourteenth chapter of John's Gospel are the most difficult of all of Jesus's statements. It is challenging

---

[1] Koruth, "Sanctuary Saga Leads to Temporary Immunity."

to believe that the brutal rulers of this world have no power over people who love God. Even as I witness people destroyed and families torn apart, I want to believe that the perpetrators have no real power!

But Jesus also promised his disciples something more when he said, "Very truly, I tell you, the one who believes in me will also do the works that I do and, in fact, will do greater works than these, because I am going to the Father. I will do whatever you ask in my name, so that the Father may be glorified in the Son. If in my name you ask me for anything, I will do it" (John 14:11-14, NRSV).

Jesus put all his faith, all his trust, in loving, mutually dependent relationships. He performed every one of the signs and wonders, he said, only with God's help. His power was in God, as his disciples could see. Yet somehow his disciples who remained on earth would do greater works than Jesus. Was that perhaps because the pendulum would swing in their direction as more forces for good lined up together? God, Jesus, and us—all tied together, mutually supporting one another in the power of the Holy Spirit?

"If you love me, you will keep my commandments," Jesus instructed his disciples. "And I will ask the Father, and he will give you another Advocate, to be with you forever. This is the spirit of truth, whom the world cannot receive, because the world neither sees it nor knows it. You know this spirit, because it abides with you, and it will be in you" (John 14:15-18, NRSV).

In the Gospel of John, the Advocate, the spirit of truth, is a "paraclete"—literally, "one who is called alongside." One who stands by you, who holds you up, who advocates on your behalf when you call out to God because you are being persecuted and crushed. This Advocate is not able to argue both sides of any case, as a secular attorney is trained to do, because this Advocate sees with God's eyes and speaks on God's behalf. This Advocate is the spirit of truth itself.

Twenty years after all hell broke out in Indonesia against ethnic Chinese Christians, the spirit of truth was about to come to rest among them and those who loved them in Central New Jersey. Yet the spirit's movement had begun the summer before, among Indonesians in New England.

In August 2017, some two dozen Indonesians residing for the last ten years or so in New Hampshire had been shocked when they checked in for their routine visits with ICE in Manchester, a sub-office under the direction of the main ICE field office in Boston. ICE ordered every one of them to book plane tickets back to Indonesia and return to ICE in the next thirty to forty-five days with their tickets.[2]

These New Hampshire Indonesians had been part of an order of a supervision program inspired by the 2009 program that the Reformed Church of Highland Park had announced in the *New York Times* that December.[3] In fact, Seth had spent much of 2010 setting up that program with ICE in New Hampshire. He helped set up a similar program with ICE in New York City. He even flew to California to try to set up the same kind of program in Los Angeles. "I was not successful in LA," Seth said.[4]

Back in 2009, the Boston field office audaciously named its order of supervision program "Operation Indonesian Surrender." ICE worked with churches across New England to identify law-abiding, productive immigrants from Indonesia who were residing under a final order of removal. As a similar program had accomplished in New Jersey, the supervision program in New England allowed Indonesians to step out of hiding in the shadows and identify themselves to ICE in exchange for the ability to remain and work in the United States legitimately, under an order of supervision.[5]

In New England, ICE limited the program to individuals who had had U.S. citizen children or spouses since 2012. By 2017, about seventy people in the Boston area participated.[6]

Just as ICE had worked with churches in Central New Jersey, ICE in New England traded on the trust and the faith that vulnerable immigrants held in their American churches and offered what seemed to be a reprieve in the guise of a humanitarian effort.

Perhaps ICE leaders between 2009 and 2016 were well-meaning. But under the Trump administration, the organization's orientation to harmless residents completely reversed. Because these Indonesian immigrants had removal orders, the government already had the

---

[2] Zack Huffman, "Judge Rankled by US Policy Pivot on Christian Indonesians," Courthouse News Service, October 23, 2017, https://www.courthousenews.com/judge-rankled-us-policy-pivot-christian-indonesians/.

[3] Nina Bernstein, "Church Works with U.S. to Spare Detention," *New York Times*, December 12, 2009, https://www.nytimes.com/2009/12/13/nyregion/13indonesians.html

[4] Seth Kaper-Dale, comments on a preliminary draft, February 2023.

[5] Amrit Cheng, "ICE Is Trying to Deport Families Who Fear Religious Persecution Without Due Process," October 30, 2017, https://www.aclu.org/blog/immigrants-rights/ice-and-border-patrol-abuses/ice-trying-deport-families-who-fear-religious.

[6] Huffman, "Judge Rankled by US Policy Pivot."

authority to remove them at will. Then, President Trump's fateful executive order of January 25, 2017, prioritized these harmless and productive people for removal.

It may take decades before there is a full picture of the administrative incentives and pressures that were applied to turn ICE offices against people who were exemplary for their peacefulness. While we await researchers to process Freedom of Information Act requests, one can see the effect of these quota systems in the HBO series *Immigration Nation*, where a film crew embedded in various ICE offices documented the actions of agents competing to meet arrest quotas. This series showed how compliant immigrants who follow the rules are much easier targets for detention and removal than typical criminals.[7]

Then something happened that seemed miraculous, though an uncountable number of steps by untold numbers of people paved the way.

In Boston, the American Civil Liberties Union (ACLU) filed a suit against the U.S. government on behalf of Indonesians in New Hampshire.

A hundred years earlier, this nonprofit organization had formed to protect people rounded up between 1919 and 1920, in what became known as the notorious "Palmer Raids." These were the early days of irrational fear about the growth of communism. Attorney General Mitchell Palmer led a campaign to arrest thousands of people without warrants and without observing constitutional protections against unlawful search and seizure. Detainees were brutally treated and held in horrible conditions, and many were summarily deported.[8]

In 2021, the ACLU called itself "the nation's largest public interest law firm." With a caseload of some two thousand lawsuits managed by one hundred staff attorneys who worked with two thousand volunteer attorneys, the ACLU could not defend every worthy cause. So, instead, it selected lawsuits that would have "the greatest impact, cases that have the potential for breaking new ground and establishing new precedents that will strengthen American freedoms."[9]

In the New Hampshire case, the ACLU was building on its success with one hundred undocumented Iraqi Christians in Michigan, whose

---

[7] Sonia Saraiya, "*Immigration Nation* Is a Must-See Window Into an American Horror Story," *Vanity Fair*, August 3, 2020, https://www.vanityfair.com/hollywood/2020/08/immigration-nation-review.
[8] "ACLU History," ACLU, https://www.aclu.org/about/aclu-history.
[9] "ACLU History."

deportations were stayed after federal judges agreed that country conditions for them endangered their lives. In the Michigan case, the ACLU argued that if returned to Iraq, Iraqi Christians would face persecution, torture, or death, and that they therefore could not be deported before they had a chance to present their claims to an immigration judge.[10]

The Immigration and Nationality Act enables a judge to prohibit the federal government from removing a noncitizen to a country where that person's life or freedom would be in danger because of race, religion, nationality, membership in a particular social group, or political opinion.[11] This federal law supersedes all other considerations. For Iraqis and Indonesians supported by the ACLU, this federal law became a saving grace.

In Boston, the ACLU complained that the government failed to account for changed circumstances in Indonesia that should have allowed its clients' protection. "The U.S. Commission on International Religious Freedom included Indonesia in its 2017 list of countries of particular concern," the ACLU complaint stated. Such countries are less repressive than an extreme case such as North Korea, but the group "includes Iraq, a nation to which deportations of Christians has been halted by another federal court."[12]

---

[10] The title of the case of the Iraqi Christians is *Hamama v. Adducci*. For an overview and the case documents, see "Hamama v. Adducci," ACLU, November 20, 2018, https://www.aclu.org/cases/hamama-v-adducci.

[11] The Immigration and Nationality Act was first enacted in 1952 by collecting many provisions and reorganizing the structure of immigration law. Since then, this law has been amended numerous times. It contains many but not all the important provisions of immigration law in the United States Code, or U.S.C., a collection of all the laws of the United States. Title 8 of the U.S. Code covers "Aliens and Nationality." The entire law in its current state is available on the U.S. Citizenship and Immigration Services site at https://www.uscis.gov/laws-and-policy/legislation/immigration-and-nationality-act. Three discrete areas in the Immigration and Nationality Act and its regulations contain asylum eligibility provisions related to changed circumstances or to changed country conditions. The first is an exception to the requirement that an asylum applicant file an application within one year of entry. (Note: this is the one-year time bar, added to the U.S. Code in 1997, effective in 1998, that prevented Indonesian asylum cases from being heard.) This exception applies if the applicant establishes "changed circumstances which materially affect the applicant's eligibility for asylum," as explained in Dina Sewell Finkel, "Changed Circumstances and Country Conditions with Respect to Asylum," *Immigration Law Advisor* 3, no. 8 (2009): 1–5, 13–15, https://www.justice.gov/sites/default/files/eoir/legacy/2009/09/01/vol3no8.pdf.

[12] Amrit Cheng, "ICE Is Trying to Deport Families"; Huffman, "Judge Rankled by US Policy Pivot."

"In its rush to deport as many immigrants as possible," stated Lee Gelernt, deputy director of the ACLU's Immigrants' Rights Project. "ICE is putting families who have lived in the United States peaceably for decades in grave danger of being persecuted or killed. This must be stopped."[13]

Conditions had grown steadily more deadly for Christians in Indonesia. But the moral character of the petitioners and the gratuitous cruelty of withdrawing federal support seemed to particularly rankle the federal judge.

"This is a hard case," U.S. District Judge Patty Saris told the court. "These are good and decent people that stayed here with our blessing. I understand that administrations change and policies change, but all these circuits say that there were changed circumstances in Indonesia."[14]

On November 27, the federal court in Boston blocked the deportation of the Indonesians in New Hampshire because they were at risk of persecution, torture, or death in Indonesia due to their faith. Changed country conditions gave the New Hampshire Indonesians a chance to reopen their asylum cases.[15]

For more than a decade, Pastor Seth had followed the predicament of the New Hampshire Indonesians. Indonesians across the United States maintained a constant web of supportive communication. Many who settled in New Hampshire had fled New Jersey when "Operation Return to Sender" raids began in May 2006.

With New Jersey's governor appearing in his church sanctuary, and U.S. Representative Frank Pallone petitioning ICE in Newark on behalf of fathers with orders of supervision detained after dropping their kids off at school, Seth's call to the ACLU in New Jersey resulted in an immediate response.

On Friday, February 2, Alexander Shalom, the senior supervising attorney for the ACLU of New Jersey, filed a class-action suit on behalf of the Indonesians in Central New Jersey, with Harry Pangemanan as the lead complainant, against John Tsoukouris, ICE field office director

---

[13] Lee Gelernt, "ACLU in Federal Court Friday to Stop Deportation of NH's Indonesian Nationals," InDepthNH.org, October 19, 2017, https://indepthnh.org/2017/10/19/aclu-in-federal-court-in-boston-friday-to-stop-deportation-of-nhs-indonesian-nationals/.

[14] Huffman, "Judge Rankled by US Policy Pivot."

[15] "Federal Court Halts Deportation of Indonesian Nationals," ACLU, November 27, 2017, https://www.aclu.org/press-releases/federal-court-halts-deportation-indonesian-nationals.

in Newark, and his superiors in the Department of Homeland Security and the U.S. Department of Justice.

Mr. Shalom made an urgent plea for immediate stays of removal to prevent imminent deportation and transfer, in order that they may reopen their cases for asylum. He was aided by the firepower of attorneys from the firm of Paul, Weiss.[16]

On the very same Friday afternoon, U.S. District Judge Esther Salas issued a temporary restraining order stopping ICE in Newark from deporting Indonesian immigrants while she reviewed the class-action lawsuit.

It's worth noting that Esther Salas was the first Latina on the U.S. District Court in New Jersey, appointed by President Obama in 2011. Salas was born in California, a first-generation Cuban/Mexican American, and she remembered translating for her Cuban mother to receive welfare benefits.[17]

Judge Salas's order applied very broadly to all the plaintiffs listed and extended to all members of the proposed class, defined as, "All Indonesian nationals within the jurisdiction of the Newark ICE Field Office, with administratively final orders of removal predating 2009 and were subject to an order of supervision."[18]

Suddenly, an enormous blanket of protection covered not just the people in sanctuary but everyone who had participated in the 2009 program for immigration supervision in New Jersey. It shined a spotlight on the actions of all the relevant players in the federal government, from the Newark Field Office to the detention centers in Elizabeth and Essex County Jail, all the way to Attorney General Jeffrey Sessions.

All these authorities were "temporarily enjoined and prohibited from removing or causing the removal—or transferring or causing the transfer—from the United States of all named Petitioners/Plaintiffs in

---

[16] "Paul, Weiss Obtains Temporary Restraining Order Preventing Deportation of Indonesian Christians in New Jersey," Paul, Weiss, February 2, 2018, https://www.paulweiss.com/practices/pro-bono/news/paul-weiss-obtains-temporary-restraining-order-preventing-deportation-of-indonesian-christians-in-new-jersey?id=25940.

[17] Chris Sagona, "Immigration Stories: Esther Salas," *New Jersey Monthly,* February 6, 2018, https://njmonthly.com/articles/politics-public-affairs/immigration-stories-esther-salas/.

[18] Qtd. in Bill Bowman, "Updated: Federal Judge Temporarily Stays Deportation of Indonesian Men Arrested by ICE," *Franklin Reporter & Advocate,* November 16, 2018, http://franklinreporter.com/22116-2/.

this action who have final orders of removal, who have been, or will be, arrested, detained or removed by ICE."[19]

The ruling halted the imminent deportation of the three Indonesian Christian detainees, Gunawan Liem of the Franklin Park section of Franklin Township, Roby Sanger of Metuchen, and Parlindungan (Parlin) Sinaga of the Avenel section of Woodbridge. Gunawan, Roby, and Parlin remained in detention—Judge Salas did not release them—but at every level of leadership, their captors were expressly forbidden to transfer them, as Harry had been transferred to Tacoma, Washington, in 2009, or to deport them, as Arino, Rovani, Saul, and Oldy were deported in May and June, 2017.

The federal action was such a complete reversal in fortune for communities of people in Central New Jersey that it took a few days for the enormity of Judge Salas's order to sink in. That Saturday in Metuchen, advocates gathered again to support the fathers who remained in detention. To respond to the judge's actions, Congressman Frank Pallone (D-District 6), State Senator Patrick Diegnan (D-District 18), Metuchen mayor Jonathan Busch, and other borough officials and attorneys met with Seth and Harry Pangemanan at Cai's Café to talk about the next steps to come in the legal battle that would decide the fate of the immigrants.[20]

"There is a tremendous sense of relief," Seth said. At regular Sunday services on February 3, Pastor Seth announced the official end of sanctuary for the families who had been living in the church. As reporters watched and photographers clicked, the Pangemanan family stood in front of the congregation. Worshippers formed a chain around them and prayed.

Harry and Yana had already packed their sanctuary belongings and headed home, even though it was a home that had been violated.

"I'm going to stay positive," Harry told reporters. "I feel safe about going out and doing my work, mainly because of the community. They have been very, very supportive. My first plan is to make my daughters feel comfortable in our home again—make them feel safe, and not worry, after this trauma."[21]

[19] "Paul, Weiss Obtains Temporary Restraining Order."
[20] Nick Muscavage, "Metuchen Event Supports Indonesian Immigrants Caught in Legal Limbo," *Courier News and Home News Tribune*, February 3, 2018, https://www.mycentraljersey.com/story/news/history/new-jersey/2018/02/03/metuchen-holds-event-indonesian-immigrants-legal-limbo/303548002/.
[21] Koruth, "Sanctuary Saga Leads to Temporary Immunity."

Joyce Phipps, an immigration lawyer from Bound Brook who had provided legal counsel to the Indonesians from the time they first began filing for asylum in 2002 (because they had voluntarily registered for the NSEERS program), told reporters that the local legal community had recently undergone a major change. In 2018, Joyce, as the director of a nonprofit group serving immigrants and refugees called Casa de Esperanza, credited Seth and Harry with raising awareness of the illegal immigration debate. To reporters, Joyce recounted her recent experience at a legal workshop on asylum, where several lawyers who had heard about what was going on in the church in Highland Park had approached her.

"People who had never done immigration law wanted to do something. And it all came out of the Indonesians," Joyce said. "I think Seth's actions have spoken to people of faith who are particularly concerned about our nation's moral direction and see the issues of faith as those of social justice."[22]

On February 8, Congressman Pallone called on John Tsoukaris to release the three Indonesian fathers from ICE custody while their immigration cases were pending.

For his part, Mr. Tsoukaris held on to his detainees, unmoved by the broad support for the Indonesians from the community, the numerous pleas from elected officials, the compassion and alarm expressed by a U.S. District Judge's unconditional support, widespread reports in the media and now the country's top-level public interest legal advocates.

On Valentine's Day, 2018, I left the hospital where I had been distributing Ash Wednesday ashes as a resident chaplain, picked up my mother, and headed to Elizabeth Detention Center, where an Ash Wednesday evening vigil took place annually.

A few hundred people, religious groups, and immigration activists thronged the parking lot. We listened to speakers and prayed for God to release the captives inside. Participating in this annual vigil was important for me.

In my earliest public action in 2010, a year after Harry's detention, I had joined a twelve-mile Ash Wednesday protest march from Jersey City's Liberty State Park, overlooking the Statue of Liberty, to Elizabeth Detention Center, and it had terminated with this same vigil. Marchers like me tied posters around our necks with the names of people who

---

[22] Sherman, "Meet the Controversial Pastor Fighting to Protect N.J.'s Undocumented Immigrants."

had died while in immigration detention. That long, bitterly frigid day enabled me to reorient myself to my new reality as part of a growing community of immigration activists. Making our way through Jersey City's icy streets, I struck up a conversation with Princeton seminarian Karen Jackson, who later would lead our bedsheet ritual in December 2011. I officially joined Facebook on that Ash Wednesday, February 19, 2010, so that I could share photos of the march. In one, a new friend from Ghana posed with a sign that read "Asylum Is Not a Crime."

On that combination Valentine's Day/Ash Wednesday, 2018, in the Elizabeth Detention Center parking lot, I wore a handmade stole I had purchased during my seminary senior year trip in January 2017 to a Salvadoran village twenty-five years after the end of that country's civil war. On the stole's deep-green fabric, waves of corn, *huaraches*, mountains, and sunshine were topped by the face of Monsignor Oscar Romero, whom many villagers had met before he was martyred for speaking up for them. The women-run cooperative that stitched, farmed, and taught there explained how they desperately sought to keep their young people from migrating. Street murals painted death on the other side of the U.S. border. We seminarians had participated in an all-night funeral mass for a young adult son whose body had been returned from Plainfield, New Jersey, to the village home his money had helped build. Along with the stole, I carried one of the containers of ashes from my chaplaincy visits in the hospital.

I wouldn't be allowed to take the container inside the detention center, but I felt compelled to see if there was a chance I could bring ashes to a visit with Parlin Sinaga. To do so I needed his Alien number. Parlin was a parishioner of a Roman Catholic church in Metuchen, and Justin Karmann, the First Presbyterian Church of Metuchen minister whom I'd come to know during ordination classes, texted Parlin's A-number to me. My mother and I sat patiently in the waiting room for my turn to visit. It looked exactly as I remembered in my first visit to Harry in 2009.

The waiting room was full—it was Valentine's Day! As they waited for their number to be called, visitors asked to hold my protest sign. I had made it myself. In flaming orange and yellow letters against black foam core, one side said, "SHAME on ICE." The other side said, "Breaking Up Families Breaks God's Law, so STOP." Children, wives, brothers, sisters, and friends passed the sign around the waiting room, taking selfies and laughing at their own audacity.

When an officer called my number, I left the sign with my mother in the waiting room along with my big coat, hat, and stole. Before I handed my mom the container of ashes, I opened it and embedded my forefinger, covering it in an ugly black smudge. I walked through the metal detector but had no belongings to place on the conveyer belt. I entered the chamber with two automated doors. The first door closed behind me, as it had years before when I first visited Harry in 2009.

When the second door slid open, I was taken aback at the change in the visitor room. The Plexiglass booths and the intercom phones had disappeared. A wide-open visitor's hall was carpeted and filled with a dozen or so small wooden tables and chairs. At one table, a man sat alone. He looked to me as if he might be Indonesian, and he smiled when I asked if he was Parlin.

I had been afraid to displace any relatives or friends on Valentine's Day, but that night I was Parlin's only visitor.

Parlin had heard the good news about the stay of deportations, but inside the detention center, it didn't seem quite real. He asked a lot of questions. In a lull in the conversation, I told him about the rally outside and asked if he would like me to impose ashes on his forehead.

A Roman Catholic from birth, a father with a large family of small children who would be sleeping now in his Avenel home, Parlin asked, "Please, would you?"

I touched my blackened fingertip to his forehead, making the sign of the cross and repeating the words so many had flocked to us hospital chaplains to hear, earlier that day.

"Remember, Parlin Sinaga, you are God's blessed and most precious son, created from dust, and to dust you shall return."

CHAPTER 37

Remembering the One Who Holds Us Fast

In Highland Park, Fall 2018

Welcoming refugees became even more dangerous in Pittsburgh, Pennsylvania on October 27, 2018, when three separate congregations—Tree of Life, Dor Hadash, and New Light—conducted Sabbath services in different areas of a large, sacred building that they shared with one another in the city's Squirrel Hill neighborhood.[1]

The week before, an Internet troll who was planning a massacre had posted a link to the website of HIAS, a Jewish nonprofit organization planning Shabbat ceremonies for refugees in locations around the country. The caption read, "Why hello there HIAS! You like to bring in hostile invaders to dwell among us?"

Then, just hours before the troll-turned-gunman entered the Pittsburgh synagogue, his account posted again: "HIAS likes to bring invaders in that kill our people. I can't sit by and watch my people get slaughtered. Screw your optics, I'm going in."

---

[1] "Police Say Accused Synagogue Shooter Talked of Killing Jews," Associated Press, October 12, 2020, https://www.usnews.com/news/best-states/pennsylvania/articles/2021-10-12/pretrial-hearing-set-in-pittsburgh-synagogue-massacre-case.

He murdered eleven congregants and wounded four police officers and three other people.[2]

The previous week, the Dor Hadash congregation had participated in HIAS's National Refugee Shabbat. The synagogue had been targeted for its pro-refugee resettlement work while thousands of active-duty U.S. military troops were deployed to guard the U.S. southern border against an "alien invasion" of helplessly poor, homeless, and wandering Latin Americans, accompanied by their children.

The shooter's mind conflated refugees, most of whom had spent years documenting their situation in the rigorous vetting processes conducted by the U.S. State Department and the UN High Commission for Refugees, with desperate asylum seekers who presented themselves as utterly vulnerable and helpless at the southern border.

The Israeli newspaper *Haaretz* called the Pittsburgh massacre "the worst antisemitic attack in U.S. history."[3] In Highland Park, New Jersey, a pall fell over the Jewish communities of the borough.

A week later, on Saturday, November 3, Congregation Anshe Emeth invited the Reformed Church of Highland Park to Shabbat services at Highland Park Conservative Temple, located one block away on South Third Avenue. Additionally, the local minyan that met at the church invited church members to join in their services and a meal.

The timing of the two services permitted church members to participate in both.

During the synagogue service, the rabbi connected the Tree of Life catastrophe to the day's lesson from the Torah. While listening to Hebrew chants, I followed the stories told on resplendent walls of glittering blue and gold-stained glass that formed the front of the sanctuary, where thirty-six panels, read from right to left, depicted Jewish history and universal values.

After worship, Jews and Christians mingled in a large banquet hall outside the sanctuary. The rabbi said a blessing called *kiddush* and another blessing recited over two loaves of challah. Tables were laden with fruit, breads, and breakfast foods. Friends and neighbors who

---

[2] Campbell Robertson, Christopher Mele, and Sabrina Tavernise, "11 Killed in Synagogue Massacre; Suspect Charged With 29 Counts," *New York Times*, October 27, 2018, https://www.nytimes.com/2018/10/27/us/active-shooter-pittsburgh-synagogue-shooting.html.

[3] David B. Green, "Tree of Life Massacre, Three Years On: How Pittsburgh's Jews Overcame the Tragedy," *Haaretz*, October 27, 2021, https://www.haaretz.com/us-news/.premium.MAGAZINE-tree-of-life-massacre-three-years-on-how-pittsburgh-s-jews-overcame-the-tragedy-1.10325986.

belonged to the temple came up and thanked each of us from our Reformed church for joining them in solidarity as part of their Shabbat worship.

Walking around the block after the synagogue service, members of the Reformed church entered the church's Quilt Room, which on Saturdays became the worship home for a local minyan: a Jewish congregation, without a rabbi, that is organized for prayer. Tables were laden with more very good food. Reformed Christians were invited to speak. Many voices decried white supremacy.

A bit shakily, I rose and said that I lamented not just white supremacy, but white *Christian* supremacy. There were too many texts of terror in Christian scriptures that could be used to weaponize Christian theology against the very existence of people from other faiths. In response, a young Jewish scholar arose and said that the Jewish faith, too, had too many elements that turned faithful people against non-Jewish neighbors.

The next day, Sunday, November, 4, I was leading worship at a church that was new to me as part of the process to become that church's installed pastor, a church whose congregation had faithfully worshiped in that neighborhood for three hundred years. Just before the service, I was handed a card with a prayer request from an elder who said, "I have to ask for this and I don't care who gets upset."

The elder had family ties in the Squirrel Hill section of Pittsburgh.

I was more than happy to pray for everyone who needed God's holy presence, especially those who were harmed and who were mourning, along with Jewish people everywhere who were shaken and terrified.

The surreptitious prayer card signaled that I was entering a very different world than the one where my faith had been formed in Highland Park. It's not at all that the members of the church held antisemitic views. Rather, as I came to learn, many guarded their time in worship as a time set apart, walled off from disturbing topics that roiled the news media.

To ensure my theology and politics were crystal clear, I preached on how the combined command of Jesus to love God and love one another was something I called the "'super-law' of love," and that, as disciples, Christians are called to measure all laws and all policies by this super-law.

When we see people destroyed, we know God's commands have been violated. I proposed that this message could strengthen our choices during the mid-term elections the next Tuesday, November 6, for the U.S. Congress.

After worship, congregants walked downstairs to the Fellowship Hall to vote yea or nay to install me as pastor. The vote on my candidacy passed by a large margin, though it was not unanimous.

Then, on November 14, Roby Sanger and Gunawan Liem, the two Indonesian men who were detained by immigration authorities after dropping their children off at school, finally returned home. These two fathers had spent ten months in custody at the Essex County jail. The men posted bond a day after a federal immigration judge ruled they could be released while they pursued their immigration case.

"It is an absolute blessing, and way overdue," Seth told reporters after the men's release on bond was approved.

Seth's remark showed considerable forbearance.

The ICE Newark field office released the fathers only when it was ordered to do so, as Emilio Dabul, a spokesman for U.S. Immigration and Customs Enforcement, confirmed.[4]

ICE Newark Field Office Director John Tsoukaris had held onto his Indonesian prisoners through his power of prosecutorial discretion. He upheld his views about people who were out of status above compassion for the men and their families who suffered tremendously without their fathers' presence.

A nearly year-long absence of their husbands, fathers, and breadwinners had been an enormous hardship. Uncertainty about their fathers' futures intensified every problem that these families faced in their absence. Friends had helped Gunawan's wife to get a job. Friends drove her to work. But her children had to care for themselves before and after school.

I wondered if, someday, John Tsoukaris might have to reckon with the damage caused by too many months of completely unnecessary deprivation for these families. Tsoukaris used immigration detention as a tool for his own form of punishment. Perhaps he also conceived of detention as a kind of terroristic deterrent. If so, it had uncertain efficacy and it came at a tremendous cost to the wellness of U.S. citizen lives.

[4] Monsy Alvarado, "Immigration Detainees from Indonesia are Freed on Bond," NorthJersey.com, November 15, 2018, https://www.northjersey.com/story/news/2018/11/15/immigration-detainees-indonesia-freed/2006337002/.

Over the years, I have come to learn that there is, very simply, no coherent system of immigration laws, as the Trump executive order had imagined. Our country has a confusing grab bag of policies, practices, laws, and agencies. Some are immigrant friendly; others are organized to prevent the U.S. from providing asylum, safety, and freedom to desperate people. The results are mixed, and a great deal is left up to the discretion of judges and ICE officers with a wide range of views. Some people receive mercy. Some eleven million others continue to try their luck and remain furtively in our country, under the radar as much as possible. Of those who are caught in the nets of the Department of Homeland Security, many are deported.

Aaron Reichlin-Melnick, policy director of the American Immigration Council, summarized this debacle of outdated laws, policies, and agencies on National Public Radio in August 2022:

> We are now multiple years into an unprecedented time of mass displacement and refugee flows. We last updated our legal immigration system 32 years ago in 1990, before the first website even went online. And the last time we overhauled our asylum system was 1996. In other words, we're facing a 21st-century challenge with 20th-century laws. Now, some people say we can simply crack down harder, build the wall, send everyone back to Mexico and wash our hands of asylum. But the history of the last century shows us that it's only long-term solutions which truly reduce migration, like addressing root causes and expanding legal pathways to migrate.[5]

When it comes to children and families, the consequences of wishful, simplistic thinking can be catastrophic. Every time a parent is detained or deported, our country destroys our future in our own U.S. citizen children.

When I think about John Tsoukaris, I imagine him as a frustrated engineering student who was traumatized on 9/11 and who feels compelled to execute laws that simply don't hold up as dependable, universal rules. Tsoukaris and those like him seek to bring about coherence by punishing some of the world's most vulnerable people. Too many Americans cheer on efforts like his. Too few of us, however,

---

[5] A. Martinez, "The Trump-era immigration policy 'Remain in Mexico' is ending," *NPR Morning Edition*, August 11, 2022, https://www.npr.org/2022/08/11/1116880033/the-trump-era-immigration-policy-remain-in-mexico-is-ending.

have the guts that are needed to fix the system with tough laws that make sense, like the system Republican senator Lindsey Graham had once been willing to go to bat for.[6]

On Sunday, November 19, 2018, Central New Jersey people from all faiths and no faith again joined the annual fundraising walk-a-thon for Interfaith RISE. As they reached the Conservative Temple on South Third, the crowd of walkers gathered on the steps and paused to sing the 2004 anthem "Peace, Salaam, Shalom," written by Emma's Revolution in the aftermath of 9/11.

In its final two years, the Trump administration continued to reduce programs for refugee resettlement via the Department of State while at the same time eliminating support for systems, staff, and diminished facilities to manage asylum cases via the Department of Homeland Security. The acting head of Citizenship and Immigration Services (the citizenship side of DHS), Ken Cuccinelli, blamed drastic refugee reductions on exploding numbers of asylum seekers at the southern border. He claimed refugee officials needed to be reassigned to handle asylum claims because the asylum backlog was so extensive.

Cuccinelli's statement was surprising because the two categories of new immigrants have always been managed separately. Refugees are vetted by the U.S. State Department and then flown into the U.S. for resettlement. Asylum seekers request safety once they arrive at the border. Cuccinelli conflated the two categories of immigrants much as the Tree of Life shooter had done.

In September 2019, President Trump announced he was cutting refugee admissions to the lowest level since the program was created in 1980. A maximum of 18,000 refugees would be resettled in the coming fiscal year, down from 85,000 in 2016.

New York Public Radio reporter Matt Katz returned to the Global Grace Café to visit with the refugee chefs and gauge their reaction to the drastic reduction in refugee numbers.[7]

---

[6] During a congressional hearing in 2010, at 1 hour and 47 minutes, Graham said, "I think 70 percent of Americans are in the camp that illegal immigrants need to be fairly and firmly dealt with, and fairly and firmly doesn't mean massed arrest. Do you believe we can put 12 million people in jail? Let's get this environment corrected on border security, move forward in a comprehensive fashion, secure the border, protect America and be fair to the 12 million people, but also be firm that we're never going to have 20 million more in the future. That's the winning combination."

[7] Matt Katz, "Refugees React to Trump Administration Program Cuts," *NPR Weekend Edition*, September 28, 2019, https://www.npr.org/2019/09/28/765322799/refugees-react-to-trump-administration-program-cuts.

Seth told Katz that this was a particularly deflating moment for the Reformed Church community. Immediately after the announcement, two Syrian refugees destined to join their family in New Jersey learned their flights to the U.S. had been canceled. They were the young adult sons of Najila, the Syrian chef who cooked on Wednesdays at Global Grace.

Najila's entire family were Syrians who had been living in Dubai where she and her husband had received work permits. In 2012, when Syria's civil war began in earnest, having been sparked by protests as part of the Arab Spring in 2011, hostilities made it impossible for them to renew their visas. Time passed and, with no resolution in sight, the parents were living illegally in Dubai. In late 2015, Najila and her husband Samir received tourist visas to travel to the U.S. along with Lamar, their elementary school-aged daughter, who happened to be a U.S. citizen due to a fortuitous early labor during a family vacation in the United States. However, their young sons, who were fifteen and sixteen years old, were rejected for tourist visas.

To Pastor Seth, these children were "really on the edge." The boys stayed behind in Dubai, without permission, from late 2015 to early 2020.[8]

Najila did not hear from her sons for months after she arrived in Highland Park. Nevertheless, she poured her heart and soul into delighting Global Grace Café customers with Syrian specialties. No hummus on earth is lighter and creamier than Najila's. Finally, Najila's sons had gotten in touch with her. Three years later, in 2019, her sons' airline tickets had been purchased and IRISE staff and volunteers had readied a room in New Jersey for these brave young men.

Then, suddenly, due to new Trump restrictions, all these plans were on hold. Najila's heartache was palpable.

For NPR audience members, Seth reiterated the importance of the café, especially in tough times. "Sometimes, the conversation around refugees is just about giving people food, shelter, and clothing and safety," Seth said, but the café was a sign of something more. "We believe that giving people opportunities to share beauty, that that's an essential part of life, as well. So, food is beautiful. Sitting together around food is beautiful."

Chai was boiling on the stove that Friday as Matt Katz explained to listeners that refugee chefs get $125 a day and work experience in a

---

[8] Seth Kaper-Dale, notes on a preliminary draft, February 2023.

kitchen. Guests of the café extolled Yana's dreamy Indonesian coconut chicken on air.

Thank God that the café was a place to try to replace anxiety with hope.

As the Pangemanan family waited for their motion to reopen their case, Yana and her daughters doubled down on their commitment to feeding their community as Friday chefs at the Global Grace Café.

Meanwhile, Harry took on additional duties as the lead housing minister to welcome refugees. Harry solicited donations of furnishings, and then he led teams of refugees who picked up used furniture around Central New Jersey. Harry scoped out apartments, made repairs, and ensured they were cleaned, painted, and well-furnished before new residents arrived.

Ministry to asylum seekers and ministry to refugees supported one another and built up the capacity of the church to receive the gifts of immigrants while helping people from around the globe to build homes, lives, and caring communities in New Jersey.

CHAPTER 38

Justice This Time

In Highland Park and Newark, 2021

I woke up late on the cool crisp Saturday morning of September 25, 2021, to find that Yana Pangemanan had sent me a text the night before.

"Hi, Pastor, Oct 28 is our Court Date in Newark."

Still groggy, I shot up in bed and texted back, "I am coming! Hallelujah!"

Could this really be the end? I wondered. Is their nightmare almost over?

The Pangemanans had persevered to keep their family whole. Their daughters had reached a thriving young adulthood in Central Jersey. At the same time, Harry and Yana helped lead church members and so many others, over two decades, to faith and wellness.

Would the Pangemanans finally receive their own parcel of peace?

Along with many other Indonesians, the family had been safeguarded from detention and deportation by federal judge Esther Salas, who had forbidden ICE to transfer or deport them, ever since February 2018.

It is an indication of the mounting antipathy to people perceived to be immigrants that two years later, in the summer of 2020, Esther Salas's son was fatally shot, and her husband critically wounded by an irate attorney who targeted Salas as a feminist and Latina in her North Brunswick home, no more than five miles from the Reformed Church.[1]

Eventually, Indonesians whom the federal stay protected received work authorizations and valid driver's licenses. But three years had passed while federal courts waded through an immense immigration backlog, complicated by the delays of the worldwide Covid-19 pandemic.

Finally, in August 2021, Harry and Yana won a motion to reopen their asylum case from the Board of Immigration Appeals, the highest administrative body for interpreting and applying United States immigration laws, located in Falls Church, Virginia. The hearing in Newark at the end of October would be a final determination.

Seth was optimistic that the asylum ruling would be favorable. Never had the Pangemanans received such focused, powerful legal counsel. At the request of the ACLU in the summer of 2018, the national law firm of Lowenstein Sandler, from their Roseland, New Jersey, office, had drafted model papers for motions to reopen asylum applications for members of this entire community.

Through the Lowenstein Center for the Public Interest, led by career public interest lawyer Catherine Weiss, the firm agreed to represent the Pangemanans in their motions to reopen and then in their subsequent asylum proceedings. Their work was incredibly thorough.

The Lowenstein team engaged a knowledgeable expert witness, a Northwestern University professor widely recognized as an expert on the society, economy, and politics of Indonesia. Dr. Winters presented a paper that detailed progressively deteriorating conditions for ethnic Chinese Christians living in Indonesia. Harry and Yana's depositions described clearly both why they fled Indonesia and how their return posed an imminent danger. Forty-five long-standing members of the

---

[1] On July 19, 2020, an assailant targeted Salas's family at their home. When her son Daniel, aged twenty, opened the door, the assailant shot and killed Daniel and shot her husband Mark multiple times. Esther was in the basement and not injured (Neil Vigdor, Aimee Ortiz, and Kevin Armstrong, "Husband and Son of a Federal Judge, Esther Salas, Are Shot in New Jersey," *New York Times,* July 19, 2020, https://www.nytimes.com/2020/07/19/nyregion/shooting-nj-judge-esther-salas.html).

Reformed Church of Highland Park and interfaith immigration groups signed on to testify by phone if the court wished to call on them.

Always pragmatic, Yana took no chances.

On Sunday, October 24, Yana stood in front of the Reformed Church of Highland Park asking for everyone's prayers. Sharing that the Board of Immigration Appeals had finally opened the way for her asylum case to be heard that week, Yana tried to convince both herself and her congregation that "miracles do happen for everybody. Miracles can happen, even for me!"

From the chancel, Yana made this declaration as she prepared to align herself with God's will. No matter how the judge ruled on Thursday, God would make a way and Yana had no doubt. She was holding room in her heart for a stay of deportation.

"Just a stay, please?" Yana prayed. "We don't care if we get a green card or citizenship."

Harry and Yana had never been greedy for God's grace. Yana asked for prayers to help her believe in a miracle because of her daughters. "They are asking me what is going to happen," she told the congregation. "I fear my anxiety will hurt them."

With passionate piano accompaniment swelling through Pastor Amos Caley's fingers, Yana belted out a hymn that she sang first in her heart language of Indonesian. Then she intoned the same words in English, "for the Lord, nothing is impossible..."

The words of Yana's anthem came from the angel Gabriel's announcement of God's plans to Mary. Not only would Mary become the mother of the Messiah, but also her aging cousin Elizabeth would bear a child who would become John the Baptist, because for God nothing is impossible.

"Here am I, the servant of the Lord," Mary responded. "Let it be with me according to your word" (Luke 1:38, NRSV).

As she had done repeatedly over the last two decades, Yana stood before her family of faith and put herself and all whom she loved in God's hands.

Jocelyn agreed with her mother that, in the weeks leading to the court case, tensions ran high in their house. She, Christa, and their cousin Ashley tried to keep moving forward with their everyday lives. "I felt like everyone's POV advisor for my parents' stress," Jocelyn said. "They talked to me about it, and I tried to calm them as best as I could."[2]

---

[2] Jocelyn Pangemanan, notes on a preliminary draft, January 2023.

One way or another, October 28, 2021, would be the end of a road that began eighteen years earlier, in February 2003, when Harry led Indonesians to line up outside the Rodino Building in Newark before dawn to voluntarily join the National Registration Entry-Exit System, the extremely biased system that targeted them as men from one of twenty-five Muslim majority countries. They had hoped that complying would provide a path to U.S. citizenship instead of a ticket back to hardship in their homeland and the destruction of their family.

By this time, I had lost track of the process.

In 2019, the congregation of Readington Reformed Church had installed me as their twenty-third pastor. It was located twenty miles from Highland Park in Hunterdon County, close to New Jersey's border with Pennsylvania, in a territory dominated by voters who were loyal to the Republican Party. Members of my new church were at best ambivalent about undocumented immigrants.

To move my family twenty miles west from semi-urban Highland Park to semi-rural Readington, Harry and my adult son Michael had rented a truck and teamed up with some buddies to transport all my family's belongings.

After the Sunday afternoon worship service that formalized my new pastoral relationship, the Pangemanans and other Indonesian families mused about how their Indonesian choir could sing during our services. Together we imagined holding potluck picnics on the grassy hillside. Sadly, that did not happen.

Nevertheless, Harry generously offered to power-wash the Readington parsonage and lead a team of refugees to repaint the church hallways in preparation for its three-hundred-year anniversary celebration. The Buildings and Grounds Committee in Readington declined both offers, opting to pay professionals instead.

Hoping to explain to the congregants of my new church how my support of persecuted Indonesians and UN refugees connected to the Gospels and our Christian faith, I preached about some of their stories in a three-part sermon series. Some congregants reacted with anger. An elder who had approved the series told me how much she disliked listening to the stories. They were horrible, she complained.

Yes, they are horrible stories, I agreed. From then on, I stopped mentioning my Indonesian friends..

Instead, Harry and I worked together from a safe distance. We didn't speak often, but when one of us had a request, big or small, the other always replied, "Yes. On my way."

When double hurricanes ravaged Guatemala, El Salvador, and Nicaragua in the fall of 2020, the Highland Park church promised to help fill multiple shipping containers with camping supplies for people sheltering beneath bridges in Central America. Harry and Seth asked if my church would become a depot for donations from Hunterdon County. All we had to do was welcome strangers, accept their offerings, and convey how grateful we were for their generosity. In Readington, the deacons agreed immediately.

The next year, when Harry needed twenty-four sets of beds, mattresses, and bedding for a group of incoming refugees, an email to my new classis turned up a dormitory full and a pastor's brother willing to load them in a truck and drive them to Highland Park.

When Tropical Storm Ida flooded out the area around Readington and deluged the nearby town of Manville on September 1, 2021, our church was overwhelmed with donations of helpful supplies, but I didn't know how we would deliver them to the middle school in Manville where teachers were collecting, sorting, and disbursing.

After requisitioning every car or truck I could think of in Readington, I texted Harry: Please would he send a truck that we could load so we could drop off supplies for the flooded areas in Somerville and Manville? He had seen my pleas for help on Facebook, and the Highland Park youth group was already planning to deliver a truck filled with cases of water. Longtime congregants of the Reformed Church of Highland Park David and Monica Day drove the truck that delivered the water and loaded up supplies at my church.

I added the Pangemanans' Newark hearing on October 28, 2021, to my calendar and then promptly forgot to plan how I would get there.

The date came up quickly, and the night before I wasn't sure how to find out if I was welcome at the hearing, until Yana texted me, "Asking for a special prayer, pastor."

I asked the time of the hearing and found it had been scheduled for 8:30 a.m. She and Harry needed to be at the ICE building at eight.

"We will go to the church at 6 for prayer," Yana texted.

After three years away from Highland Park, I had gotten out of the habit of perpetual pre-dawn meetings with Seth. Consequently, my day would begin in a few hours. I responded, "I will see you at 6."

Yana accepted by responding simply, "Thank you."

Dressing in the dark, I pulled on a clerical collar, black pants, a blazer, and my "priest" shoes, a pair of black, lace-up Doc Martens. I smiled as I wondered if my outfit would match Seth's.

Arriving in Highland Park just after 6 a.m., I found the sanctuary dimly lit. Pastors Amos and Seth waited in the front pew with seminarian interns I didn't recognize. Seth and Amos looked surprised but happy to see me.

When Harry and Yana arrived with Jocelyn, nineteen; Christa, nearly fifteen; and Yana's niece Ashley, also nineteen, we formed a prayer circle in the chancel and asked God to fulfill promises of a future together.

"Then sings my soul, my Savior God, to Thee, how great Thou art! How great Thou art!" Yana sang these words a cappella before leaving the building.

Yana jumped into my car. Her daughters and niece drove to Newark with Harry.

Three and a half years earlier, on May 13, 2018, thirty years after her Aunt Yana jumped into a taxi to escape the burning of Jakarta's Chinatown, sixteen-year-old Ashley had been participating in a worship service at her Catholic church in Indonesia when a bomb went off in another church three blocks away. Ashley could feel the blast. For the next two weeks, the incident prevented Ashley from attending both her Catholic parochial school and her church.

But Ashley was a U.S. citizen born in Georgia. Her mother, Yana's sister Meri, had brought Ashley with her back to Indonesia a decade earlier, when Meri was deported from Georgia and Ashley was six.

Ashley had graduated from high school in Indonesia but found few prospects for meaningful work. After three church bombings on her island, Ashley no longer felt safe in Indonesia, and so, in the spring of 2021, Harry and Yana welcomed Ashley into their New Jersey household.[3]

Though her spoken English was quite good, Ashley was taking ESL classes at Middlesex County College. She planned to continue in a college program. Her cousin Jocelyn had taken the day off from her second-year electrical engineering classes at the New Jersey Institute of Technology, less than a mile from the Newark courthouse.

The pro-bono legal counsel team of Allison Gabala, Daniela Geraldo, Peter Slocum, and Catherine Weiss met us in the parking lot of Newark's Rodino Building. Their roller briefcases rumbled across the pavement on Newark's chilly side streets and parking lots.

---

[3] Affidavit of Mariyana Sunarto, U.S. Department of Justice, Executive Office for Immigration Review, State of New Jersey, County of Essex, notarized on October 1, 2018.

Other immigration activists knew the building far better than I did. Seth, Jean Stockdale, Rev. Linda Lachesnez, and many congregants and seminarian interns had accompanied dozens of people for ICE check-ins. In ICE waiting rooms, they entertained babies and toddlers. If you had a child who was not yet in school, it was a good idea to bring them along to the check-ins, as everyone imagined ICE agents would hesitate to separate parents from U.S. citizen children who were present in the next room.

It was my first time inside the Rodino building. I had visited only once before, in June of 2018, when Seth had called for a protest while Gunawan, Roby, and Parlin languished in detention despite Judge Salas's order barring their deportation or transfer. Back then, we had held protest signs while we stood on large stone planters in the park directly across the narrow street from the building's main entrance.

For a few hours on a hot summer afternoon, we took turns simply yelling chants, including an infinite loop of "John Tsoukaris, John Tsoukaris, Let Our People Go!" followed by invoking the name of the director of ICE, "Thomas Homan, Thomas Homan, Let Our People Go!" It was one of the most futile yet strangely satisfying protests I participated in. We went home hoarse and prayed our indignant voices had gotten under someone's skin.

Harry and Yana had visited the Rodino building for supervisory meetings with ICE more than twenty times over the last twelve years, ever since the 2009 orders of supervision.

Each visit had held its own measure of dread and heartache.

To set their clients at ease, the Lowenstein team joked with Harry about his well-ironed slacks and dress-up shoes. Days before, when they had rehearsed Harry's testimony with him, his attorneys instructed Harry that he could not wear his customary work jeans and carpenter boots to this hearing, even though his attire was perfectly suited to his position as housing minister for refugees and low-income clients.

Once past security and off the elevators, which warned of "low occupancy due to Covid-19," the legal team directed us to file into a courtroom. Seth and I took seats in the back rows near Jocelyn, Christa, and Ashley. Up front at the defendants' table, lead attorneys sat next to Harry and Yana.

The prosecution table remained empty.

Immigration judge Shifra Rubin entered from a curtain behind her bench. Judge Rubin labored to push a cart which was overloaded with documentation files for this single case in order to position the cart near her bench. As we watched her struggle, it became clear that beneath her flowing black robe the judge wore denim jeans and sneakers.

After all the drama about his attire for that day's hearing, Harry almost fell off his chair.

The attorney for the United States of America never entered the courtroom. The longest part of the hearing entailed waiting for the U.S. attorney to dial in to the proceedings. When she finally appeared online, the attorney told the judge that the United States would not object to a finding for asylum and waived its right to appeal the final judgment.

"Well, I haven't read through every page of this documentation," Judge Rubin admitted, "but I have read a great deal of it, and I am ready to rule. Would one of the attorneys summarize the major facts in the case?"

The Lowenstein team had clearly over-prepared, agonizing over the minutiae of each twist and turn in a story that spanned decades. Harry said he had practiced with them for hours. But it seemed that no one was quite prepared to offer a summary overview. At first, it looked like Harry might do the honors, until a junior team member fumbled forward with a few sentences that sketched the eighteen-year tale that had landed us all there in that courtroom that morning.

"So," Judge Rubin summarized, "the relevant facts are that, as the BIA ruled, country conditions in Indonesia have changed." The judge and the attorney established this pursuant to the expert testimony of Professor Winters,[4] with the corroboration of Ashley, Yana's niece who was now present in the courtroom. It was she who had experienced first-hand one of three recent bombings of a church in Surabaya, her hometown since returning with her deported mother.

Judge Rubin spoke with a distinct accent, and as I would learn later, was herself both an immigrant and a latecomer to the legal profession.

---

[4] "Expert Opinion: Based on over three decades of research and expertise on Indonesia, as well as on dozens of sources, I conclude that since 2012 the level of violence and intolerance directed at religious minorities in Indonesia has increased at a shocking rate and that Christian Indonesians face a dangerously high probability of persecution in the form of intimidation, physical harm, and threats to their personal safety and well-being," (Paragraph 5 of the Declaration of Jeffrey A. Winters, Merits Hearing: October 28, 2021, at 8:30 a.m., Supplemental List of Exhibits on Remand).

"Therefore," Judge Rubin stated, "Asylum is granted, based on evidence of ongoing persecution to the classes of people who are ethnic Chinese and Christian in Indonesia."

Silence greeted her words.

I looked around me. Though they wore masks for Covid-19, I could still read the emotions and reactions of the three women. Ashley, who knew the story as part of her own childhood, dug her head into her knees and burst into joyful tears.

Jocelyn and Christa seemed subdued, quiet perhaps because they were shocked and confused. The judgment happened so quickly, after so many years and so much anxiety, that this long-awaited, historic moment seemed to slip by for them almost unmarked.

Christa leaned into her big sister's shoulder. Jocelyn squeezed her little sister's hand. The sisters observed the courtroom as everyone around them broke down in relief and happiness.[5]

Afterwards, Jocelyn said, as she sat there in the courtroom, she had no idea what to think. Since the age of four she had never experienced life without the threat of being separated from one or both of her parents. Christa had never experienced one day without this fear hanging over her.

Then, in a single stroke, this most ominous threat—being torn nine thousand miles from their parents or uprooting entirely to move to rural Indonesia—evaporated. Two decades of stress, anxiety, and fear lifted from their shoulders.

The sisters were afraid to believe their ears.

Yana looked around and then faced the table. Her shoulders moved up and down with big, silent sobs.

Over my left shoulder, I could see, in the courtroom's back corner, tears fall from Seth's red eyes.

The judge looked over at us, a bench of potential witnesses who were not needed, stunned family members, and weepy pastors. Judge Rubin said, "Well, this is a shame, you made this trip, religious leaders, and all. You must be disappointed that we don't need your testimony. Maybe we should have you each state your name for the permanent record?"

Seth began but each of us froze in disbelief.

Judge Rubin couldn't quite figure us out. After eighteen long years of struggle, why weren't we exploding with applause and delight, jumping up and down, or at least embracing with a few hugs?

[5] Jocelyn Pangemanan, notes on a preliminary draft, January 2023.

She dismissed us and told us to clear her courtroom.

"Go celebrate," Judge Rubin suggested, waving her hands at us in a shooing motion.

CHAPTER 39

An Accidental Immigration Attorney

In Central New Jersey, February 2022

Through the Pangemanans' precedent-setting case for undocumented Indonesians, I met Catherine Weiss, partner and chair of the Lowenstein Center for the Public Interest, headquartered in Roseland, New Jersey. Catherine is one of the country's leading pro-bono immigration lawyers.

Researching online, I noticed that Catherine had received all her degrees in the 1980s—a Princeton BA, a Yale MA, and a Yale JD. I asked if her formal studies included discussions about how the U.S. Constitution applied to non-citizens. Was immigration law an area of serious interest in the 1980s? I asked.

"No!" Catherine interjected, "The answer to that is no, of course!"

Had immigration law been a major area of study in the 1980s?

"Not during my general education nor during law school," Catherine replied.[1]

---

[1] Interview with Catherine Weiss, partner and chair, Lowenstein Center for the Public Interest, Friday, February 18, 2022.

If our country's best-educated attorneys needed to continually re-educate themselves about the rights of non-citizens, how much more so do the rest of us need to re-evaluate our long-standing opinions about immigration.

"Immigrant Rights Are Human Rights" is a slogan that regularly appears on posters at immigration protests. Yet, as late as 1984, U.S. Supreme Court justice Sandra Day O'Connor delivered a decision that the Fourth Amendment did not necessarily apply in deportation cases.[2]

Precedents changed only through painstaking and brave casework during the 1980s by the first generation of dedicated immigration attorneys.

One story arrived on my kitchen table in the form of an obituary about a Texas attorney who had pioneered a human rights approach to representing immigrants. The article described how, in the 1980s, a young upstart lawyer named Lisa Brodyaga, who founded a refugee camp on the Rio Grande, helped firmly establish that undocumented asylum seekers have rights under the U.S. Bill of Rights.

During the years when refugees fleeing El Salvador's civil war streamed over U.S. borders, Lisa taught immigration lawyers how to defend Central American refugees in federal courts.[3] She had been moved by the U.S. government's collusion with forces of the Salvadoran government that were crushing the people of El Salvador. The U.S. provided a million dollars per day in military aid to the Salvadoran government. By the end of hostilities in 1989, 75,000 Salvadorans were dead.

In the 1980s, faith communities joined The New Sanctuary Movement and modified the course of immigration relief. Even though the federal government inserted spies into faith communities who were organizing sanctuary spaces and indicted eleven religious leaders for offering sanctuary to Latin American refugees, and even though eight advocates lost their case, a long federal trial had helped win widespread public support, paving the way for relief in the Immigration Act of 1990.[4] This act established a congressional procedure to enable the

---

[2] INS v. Lopez-Mendoza, 468 U.S. 1032 (1984), Justia, July 5, 1984, https://supreme.justia.com/cases/federal/us/468/1032/.

[3] Alex Vadukul, "Lisa Brodyaga, Crusading Lawyer for Immigrants' Rights, Dies at 81," *New York Times*, January 4, 2022, https://www.nytimes.com/2022/01/04/us/lisa-brodyaga-dead.html.

[4] "Sanctuary Trial Papers," University of Arizona Libraries Special Collections, https://speccoll.library.arizona.edu/collections/sanctuary-trial-papers.

attorney general to provide temporary protected status, or TPS, to immigrants unable to safely return to their home countries because of armed conflict or environmental disasters.[5]

Then, in the 1990s, dozens of U.S. attorneys assisted refugees experiencing humanitarian crises and fleeing desperate political situations in Haiti and China.[6]

If you weren't paying attention in the 1980s and 90s, and I certainly wasn't, then like me, you too probably missed the memo about non-citizens having constitutional rights in the United States.

For a public interest attorney like Catherine Weiss, it was our country's Global War on Terror that first opened her eyes to the need to protect the rights of non-citizens after the terrorist attacks of September 11, 2001.

Catherine had been shocked to see massive sweeps indiscriminately pull Muslims dining in Halal restaurants off the streets of towns like Clifton, New Jersey, that were so near to her home.[7]

Catherine felt she could not ignore blatant affronts to civil liberties, such as agents posing as congregants in mosques, targeting people for religious and foreign nationality, and yet producing no or little actual intelligence about terrorism. Never mind "black sites" in places like Poland and Guantanamo Bay, Cuba, where the U.S. government held Middle Eastern citizens on foreign soil without charges, trials, or any protections at all.

Black sites! Catherine's story reminded me of these sinister places that arose in the early 2000s as part of the Global War on Terror, though the U.S. government disclosed them only years later.

---

[5] "Immigration Act (United States) (1990)" in John Powell, *Encyclopedia of North American Immigration* (Facts on File, 2005), 138.

[6] For Haiti, see Patrick Gavin, "Migration Emergencies and Human Rights in Haiti," Conference on Regional Responses to Forced Migration in Central America and the Caribbean, September 30, 1997, https://www.oas.org/juridico/english/gavigane.html. For China, see information about the crisis around the arrival of the *Golden Venture*, including Patrick Radden Keefe, "A Path Out of Purgatory," *The New Yorker,* June 6, 2013, https://www.newyorker.com/news/daily-comment/a-path-out-of-purgatory.

[7] Hannan Adely, "'He Lost Everything.' Muslims Whose Lives Were Upended by 9/11 Detainment Want Justice," NorthJersey.com, October 28, 2021, https://www.northjersey.com/story/news/2021/10/28/9-11-muslims-detained-ny-nj-lawsuits/8447630002/; Gary Fields and Noreen Nasir, "Muslims Recall Questionable Detentions That Followed 9/11," *The Denver Post,* October 4, 202, https://www.denverpost.com/2021/10/04/muslims-recall-questionable-detentions-following-9-11/.

As Catherine and I spoke, the U.S. Supreme Court continued to shield a CIA black site in Poland from a detainee's inquiry to receive documents about the torture to which the CIA had subjected him. No one, not even the CIA, disputes that Abu Zubaydah was the first prisoner to undergo "enhanced interrogation techniques," including eighty water-boarding sessions, hundreds of hours of live burial, and "rectal hydration." The CIA. first suspected he was a high-level member of al-Qaeda but then later concluded that Abu Zubaydah was not a member of al-Qaeda at all.[8]

These sorts of post-9/11 events around the globe and in her home state of New Jersey deeply shook Catherine because of the history of persecution of her own Jewish faith.

"I do think there is this very important strain in Jewish practice and worship about having been a stranger or being a stranger," she offered.

I had just blundered into asking if Catherine's surname Weiss was possibly connected to the Paul, Weiss law firm that champions immigrant rights nationwide alongside the ACLU. Catherine explained that she considers her last name to be a common "Ellis Island name." Her ancestors had been Schneeweiss, or "Snow-White" in German. On Ellis Island, they joined thousands of Jews who were renamed Weiss (White), Schwarz (Black), Klein (Little), and Gross (Big).

Historically, Jewish people had experienced so much migration due to violence. In Catherine's Jewish community, there is a very strong sense that it could be you. "It could be you next!" Catherine emphasized.

Woven into Jewish identity is a reminder that the Hebrew Bible reiterates dozens of times: Remember, always remember, you were once a stranger in the land of Egypt.

The identity of the stranger and foreigner, I responded to Catherine, is the central image of the Gospel of Luke, though for many Christians that pivotal theme hides in plain sight.

As chair of the Center for the Public Interest at Lowenstein Sandler, Catherine had represented dozens of asylum seekers in immigration courts. Catherine did not know that Harry and Yana had barely escaped the U.S. Department of Homeland Security's campaign "Operation-Return-to-Sender" in the raid on their apartment on

---

[8] Adam Liptak, "C.I.A. Black Sites Are State Secrets, the Supreme Court Rules," *New York Times*, March 4, 2022, https://www.nytimes.com/2022/03/03/us/politics/supreme-court-cia-black-sites-guantanamo.html.

May 24, 2006, during the week of the national launch. But when we discussed this a few months after the final Pangemanan asylum hearing, Catherine wasn't terribly surprised.

Operation Return to Sender had provided a baptism-by-fire in immigration law for Catherine. When she became chair of the Lowenstein Center for the Public Interest in 2009, Catherine inherited a pro-bono suit against the federal government for having failed to check the reckless and harmful enforcement activities of ICE agents.

"They were conducting unannounced, unwarranted—because they literally had no warrants—pre-dawn raids, all over New Jersey," Catherine explained, her voice still tinged with outrage.

The appeal she championed about Operation Return to Sender alleged that the supervisory defendants—Julie Myers, assistant secretary for Immigration and Customs Enforcement; John Torres, deputy assistant director for Operations, Immigration and Customs Enforcement; Scott Weber, Newark field office director; and Bartolome Rodriguez, the former director of the Newark field office—were liable for "causing egregious Fourth Amendment violations."

Among the original twelve complainants were U.S. citizens and lawful permanent residents, a.k.a. green card holders, arbitrarily ensnared in ICE campaigns designed to deport criminals who had lost final immigration appeals. They were Latinas and Latinos, targeted with terror tactics due to ethnic profiling.[9]

"With deliberate indifference to the consequences," the appeal alleged, "Julie Myers and John Torres adopted and maintained policies pursuant to the national 'Operation Return to Sender' program that created a high likelihood of unconstitutional searches and seizures. When the predictable violations quickly ensued, Myers and Torres, along with defendants Scott Weber and Bartolome Rodriguez, knew of and acquiesced in this pattern of unconstitutional misconduct by their subordinates. Plaintiffs suffered harm as a result."[10]

The New Jersey suit was one of many filed in seven states to stop ICE from violating the U.S. Constitution as it pursued aggressive arrest and deportation quotas.

---

[9] "Case: Argueta v. Myers," Civil Rights Litigation Clearinghouse, University Michigan Law School, September 21, 2012, https://www.clearinghouse.net/detail.php?id=10955.

[10] "Argueta v. ICE," U.S. Court of Appeals for the Third Circuit, accessed March 25, 2022, https://ccrjustice.org/sites/default/files/assets/Argueta%20En%20Banc%20Petition%2006.28.11.pdf.

After four years of litigation, the government finally agreed to a financial settlement. ICE undertook some reforms.[11]

The United States government is one tough defendant. The effort had required significant legal resources for a protracted period to withstand the U.S. government's repeated motions to dismiss and a rare "interlocutory appeal" for qualified immunity for the leaders of ICE—which the United States Court of Appeals for the Third Circuit firmly denied.

The final judgment, with its nearly $300,000 award to be shared among the remaining eight plaintiffs, proved one of Catherine's main themes: In the end, we need to watch over the rights of immigrants because it could be you.

"It could be you next."

As I learned about this major immigration litigation effort that Catherine had walked into when she began her position at Lowenstein, I wondered about the degree to which the suit may have affected one of its defendants, former Newark field office director Scott Weber.

As the tide turned in the 2008 Obama administration, Weber had so generously extended an olive branch to Seth in the form of the order of supervision program that had made national news in December 2009. Yet, before Weber could enact a new asylee assistance program that Seth and Jean Stockdale had discussed with him, he had been transferred.

In the order of supervision, was Weber bending over backward to curry favor, to be seen as humane by the new Obama administration? Had Weber been promoted? Or had he been removed from the scene of his crimes?

Meanwhile, as Catherine's team represented Harry and Yana's final asylum hearing, she was also representing hundreds of children separated from family members at the Southern border. And simultaneously, Catherine worked with a coalition to advocate for three million dollars of state funding for the legal representation of unaccompanied children. She joined with immigration organizations to ensure Governor Murphy and the New Jersey Legislature secured $8.2 million in its 2022 budget, and argued for $11 million in 2023, to expand a program that launched in 2018 to provide access to counsel

---

[11] "Winning Compensation for Immigrant Victims of Home Raids," Lowenstein Sander, 2012 Pro-Bono Report, 14-15.

for poor immigrants who were detained and facing deportation in New Jersey.

In 2018, 80 percent of immigrants who were detained but did not have legal representation were deported.[12]

---

[12] Erika Nava, "Legal Representation in Immigration Courts Leads to Better Outcomes, Economic Stability," *New Jersey Policy Perspective,* June 19, 2018. Accessed March 25, 2022, https://www.njpp.org/publications/report/legal-representation-in-immigration-courts-leads-to-better-outcomes-economic-stability/#_edn14

CHAPTER 40

A Small Splash in a Very Big Pond

In Highland Park, 2021 to 2022

The moment Judge Rubin ruled in favor of asylum for Harry and Yana, their lives changed forever. "No more looking over your shoulder for SUVs with tinted windows," Catherine Weiss proclaimed while the attorneys prepared to pose for photos with Pastor Seth and family members outside the Rodino building.
"No more surveillance when you drop off your children at school. No more fear of an ordinary traffic stop."
It was the culmination of an eighteen-year journey of courage in the face of terror, faith in the face of hopelessness, and community in the face of great individual risk. At every turn, Harry and Yana had organized, advocated, and encouraged others, not just for their own benefit, but for every person in their community.
"It's been a privilege to represent Harry and Yana," Catherine said. "Their years of advocacy have finally won them the protection they deserve, and we join them in wishing the same for their co-congregants."

Key to the Pangemanans' successful asylum case was their widespread reputation as religious leaders, courageous activists, and spokespersons for immigration relief for Indonesian Christians in the United States. A decades-long stand on behalf of justice had garnered media attention in both the United States and Indonesia.

By publicly claiming their right not to return to Indonesia, they cast a long shadow on that country's inability to protect its ethnic Chinese citizens from murderous mob violence. To the government of Indonesia, their fight not to be deported could be read as a "black eye" to their country's reputation for freedom and democracy.

While the public advocacy work of the Pangemanans not only seriously heightened the already enormous risks they faced in their home country, it also potentially helped many others in danger of deportation. The Pangemanans paved the way for Indonesians who reside in the United States to join the ACLU's class action suit.

Certainly, through learning their story, people like me in Central Jersey became more attuned not only to violence against Christians in Indonesia, but to the persecution of minorities everywhere.

The Roseland-based attorneys issued a press release that same morning: "Lowenstein Sandler Wins Asylum for Indonesian Christian Couple Facing Persecution for Religious and Political Beliefs: At high risk of harm in their home country, family has been seeking right to remain in the United States for decades."

After 1,090 pro-bono hours dedicated to representing Harry and Yana and to researching and drafting the model papers that could be used by other attorneys representing Indonesian Christians around the state, Catherine Weiss was convinced that the Pangemanans' case would have a significant ripple effect in both legal and political realms.

"Their victory demonstrates to their community that the United States welcomes both open religious practice and outspoken advocacy and will not send immigrants back to countries where they face a serious risk of harm because of these protected activities," Catherine wrote. "Dozens of their neighbors and co-congregants still have cases pending in the BIA [Board of Immigration Appeals] or immigration courts. This decision is a precedent for others, when agencies grant a motion to reopen or approve an asylum application for any member of this community."[1]

---

[1] Nick Muscavage, "How Lowenstein Sandler Fought to Get Clients Asylum," Law360, November 10, 2021, https://www.law360.com/pulse/articles/1436741.

The only photos taken that morning were from my iPhone and an iPhone belonging to one of the attorneys. A single legal trade publication picked up the story.[2]

After so much media attention, it seemed strange to me that no members of the general press followed the Pangemanan case to its conclusion on October 28, 2021.

Each step of the way, since Seth's first op-ed in 2006, journalists had engaged both the public and decision-makers at the state and federal levels in the Pangemanans' story. Without the attention of these justice warriors who carefully researched facts, interviewed stakeholders, and observed national trends, liberation for the Pangemanans and so many other people who deserve asylum would simply never have happened.

Without careful and persistent reporting, how many of us would be able to imagine the stories of hundreds of thousands of people subjected to cruel and unusual punishment meted out through the Department of Homeland Security in the liminal regions of American jurisprudence?

Now, neither local nor national media outlets were paying attention.

The good news of Judge Rubin's decision in favor of asylum for the Pangemanans was merely another data point in a capacious and capricious system that grants asylum in a little less than half its cases.

Harry and Yana joined the ranks of more than eight thousand people who were granted asylum by an immigration judge in 2021.

This number was significantly down from the prior year, because the total number of decisions—60,079 decisions during 2020 dropped to 23,827 in 2021—decreased due to a partial government shutdown that began in mid-March of 2020 with the Covid-19 pandemic.

Meanwhile, Harry and Yana may have benefitted from a change in administration: 71 percent of defensive asylum cases in the last year of the Trump administration were denied. In the first year of the Biden administration, denials fell to 63 percent.[3]

Perhaps four years of delay worked in Harry and Yana's favor, but the impact on a single case is difficult to determine. As their

---

[2] Muscavage, "How Lowenstein Sandler Fought to Get Clients Asylum."
[3] "Asylum Rates Climb Under Biden," TRACImmigration, November 10, 2021, https://trac.syr.edu/immigration/reports/667/#:~:text=During%20FY%20 2021%20just%2023%2C827,merits%20of%20asylum%20seekers'%20claims.

story shows, asylum cases involve complex life histories and changing political and social conditions outside the United States.

Above all, the granting of asylum is discretionary. Applications are approved or denied on the authority of the individual conclusions of a particular immigration judge.

I would hope that a different judge would have made the same decision. Certainly, another judge could have looked over the facts of the case and provided another form of relief. Since the United States could not justify returning the Pangemanans to Indonesia in the face of imminent persecution and at risk of murderous violence, the Pangemanans might have received a lesser form of relief from deportation instead of asylum.

A status change to "withholding of removal" or "continued presence" would have enabled the Pangemanans to reside as aliens indefinitely but would not have offered a path to full U.S. citizenship.

Neither alternative form of relief was mentioned at that morning's hearing.

I became curious about this person who wore jeans and sneakers under her judicial black robe and who had reviewed so many volumes of exhibits that she had no need for the drama of live arguments.

During the Pangemanans' brief hearing, I detected a foreign accent and was not surprised to learn that Judge Shifra Rubin was born in Israel. In a 2021 article in Forbes magazine, I found Rubin lauded as an "unsung hero" who is "breaking boundaries and using her voice to speak for the voiceless."

An outspoken daughter named Noa Yachot served as Shifra's main reputation consultant and described her mother as "an anomaly in many ways, an immigrant herself, who became a federal judge, a judge whose background is in human rights, a late-career attorney who managed to reach the top of her field, and—despite a life of financial hardship—chose a career in public service."

Rubin's daughter recalled how, at forty-eight, Shifra had studied for the LSAT in all-night sessions before she attended night classes at Rutgers Law School. As a divorced single mother, Shifra worked a series of dead-end jobs, full-time during the day, while she also cared for her children.[4] Like so many women finding their way after becoming a parent, her progress was slow but steady.

---

[4] Maggie McGrath, "The Women Over 50 Proving That Immigration Reform Is Needed for Business and Society," *Forbes*, April 1, 2021, https://www.forbes.com/sites/maggiemcgrath/2021/04/01/the-women-over-50-proving-immigration-reform-is-needed-for-business-and-society/?sh=136a5dc75b76.

Ten years after she completed a bachelor of arts degree from Rutgers University, Shifra attained a juris doctor from Rutgers School of Law in 2002. Then, for fourteen years, Shifra worked client-side, representing hundreds of immigrants, just like Harry and Yana, from around the world. It could not have hurt that she spoke six languages fluently.

From 2003 through 2015, beginning as a staff attorney, Shifra rose to supervising attorney and finally senior attorney at the Immigration Representation Project, part of Legal Services of New Jersey, located in Edison, New Jersey. Shifra's former office was a mere stone's throw from the Reformed Church of Highland Park.

When the Obama administration faced an immense immigration backlog, U.S. Attorney General Loretta Lynch, who served from 2015 to 2017, appointed Shifra Rubin as an immigration judge. The Executive Office for Immigration Review (EOIR) announced her investiture along with eight other immigration judges after Acting Chief Immigration Judge Print Maggard presided over their joint investiture ceremony on January 29, 2016, at the U.S. Court of Appeals for the Armed Forces in Washington, DC.[5]

Shifra Rubin was seventy-one years old when she awarded asylum for Harry and Yana, and in my book, Judge Rubin is a superhero. To me, she embodied a favorite saying of one of my ministry colleagues. "While you have breath, you have purpose," my friend Rev. Dianna Stone liked to remind our aging congregants—and their pastors like me—in Hunterdon County.

From the perspective of the community that had fallen in love with the Pangemanans, Rubin seemed to have been raised up as a federal judge "for such a time as this," a notable quote from the Bible's Book of Esther, in which a character named Mordecai addresses his niece, Esther.

Esther is craftily positioned as Queen of Persia by Uncle Mordecai, though no Persians seem to know that Esther, like her uncle, is a Jew. In the story, a decree has gone out with orders to destroy, to kill, and to annihilate all Jews, young and old, women and children, in a single day. And Mordecai implores Esther to intervene on their behalf:

> Do not think that because you are in the king's house you alone of all the Jews will escape. For if you remain silent at this time,

---

[5] "Executive Office for Immigration Swears in Nine Immigration Justices," U.S. Department of Justice, February 1, 2016, https://www.justice.gov/eoir/pr/executive-office-immigration-review-swears-nine-immigration-judges.

relief and deliverance for the Jews will arise from another place, but you and your father's family will perish. And who knows but that you have come to your royal position for such a time as this? (Esther 4:13-14, NIV)

Shifra Rubin and so many others like her felt and acted upon this same sense of urgency for the sake of the silent millions of immigrants living in the U.S., and on behalf of their U.S. citizen and DACA-aged children, and for millions more clamoring for rescue at our borders, walking through airport gates, and overstaying tourist visas.

Attorney Catherine Weiss knew Judge Shifra Rubin informally, as both women made their rounds in New Jersey's immigration circuit.

If Judge Rubin was disappointed by our muted reaction to her granting of asylum, Catherine was not surprised at all.

"This is not a theater," Catherine reminded me. "It's a courtroom." The whole building has a solemn, deeply painful history, where too many people have lost their appeals or, worse yet, never had a chance to make an appeal. "After all," Catherine said, "this is where Harry and Yana came for their ICE check-ins."

Catherine worried about Harry. Harry the idealist had always seemed less anxious and more uplifted than Yana the realist. But now Catherine worried that Harry had invested too much of himself in being a spokesperson for a cause that had defined him. Might this granting of asylum knock the wind out of Harry's sails?

But, in fact, Catherine had no cause to worry. The lack of media attention suited Harry and Yana just fine. The granting of asylum in their cases far exceeded their hopes and dreams. They had been awarded a path to full citizenship over the next five years. They could focus on making their daughters' and their niece's dreams come true—for college, graduate school, and wonderful careers.

None of the many complex and elusive versions of comprehensive immigration reform would have delivered this possibility as effectively for the Pangemanans as Judge Rubin's decision.

The next Sunday, November 7, 2021, at the annual Interfaith RISE walkathon, Jocelyn recorded her parents on Facebook Live as they stood on the front steps of Highland Park Conservative Temple.

Every year, Seth invited New Jersey legend Bruce Springsteen to appear at the walk, and so far, to no avail. But this year, Seth happily introduced Highland Park's own high-energy superstars.

An irrepressible Yana, in white sneakers and snazzy yoga pants, addressed the crowd through a karaoke machine microphone. "God answered our prayer," Yana stated definitively. Even though, she admitted to the crowd, the whole time she had been thinking to herself that her dreams were impossible, saying to herself, "No way, I can be a winner. No way, I can be granted."

Her honesty was humbling. Yana always shared her heart.

Then the fearless cheerleader in Yana emerged. "But God will open the way, as long as we still hope, as long we still fight!" Yana urged the immigrants in the crowd to "never lose hope, never lose fight, never give up—that's how me and Harry are living, day by day."[6]

On the sidewalk below Harry and Yana, participants lifted a large, hand-painted blue and white banner with gold embellishments that led the way for the 2021 walkathon's hundred or so walkers as they stopped to listen to speakers at town meeting places and houses of worship throughout the borough.

"All people may take refuge in the shadow of God's wings," the sign's glittery letters promised.

Harry began singing one of his family's favorite hymns, a tonic to encourage the immigrants, asylum seekers, refugees, and all their helpers in the crowd.

"God will make a way, where there seems to be no way," Harry sang. Yana chimed in, "When God works in ways we cannot see…God will be our guide, hold us closely to his side, with love and strength for me today."

After the song's crescendo, a lachrymose Harry addressed the crowd with more meaning in his quavering voice than his words alone could convey.

"On behalf of my family, without you all, this would have never happened. By the grace of God, as long as we keep our faith, and we do something good for others, after eighteen years…Let God open our hearts—and the pool of love, the pool of grace—so many people, more than we can thank, stood with us, and gave us more and more hope."

Over the Christmas season, the good news began to sink in.

Harry and Yana and their daughters and niece, now young women, escaped New Jersey to enjoy an extra-long holiday with Harry's sister Jessy and her family in Troy, Ohio.

It was the first time that immigration advocates like me found out about one of their out-of-state jaunts and didn't need to be afraid for them.

---

[6] C. Jocelyn Pangemanan, Facebook post, November 7, 2021.

At the Reformed Church of Highland Park, creative ministries, new and old, continued to respond to community needs and expand the church's membership rolls.

After eighteen years of terrifying immigration crises, Seth could finally breathe a bit more easily and bask in the simple goodness of the very full, imperfectly perfect life of his caring community.

After the Avenel raid, Seth had made a commitment.

"I resolved that day in May 2006, that as a minister of Christ's gospel I would stand up against the abuses of my government. I was not going to back down from serving this persecuted community for anything."[7]

He had invested his heart and soul in the fight to keep as many undocumented Indonesian families together as possible.

Seth had made of his life a signpost for the rest of us.

Seth was clearly on to something because, amid all the stress and heartache, as yeast multiplies in the pounding of home-baked dough, the ministries of the Reformed Church of Highland Park blossomed with young leaders and older entrepreneurs who stepped forward to begin new programs to lift oppressed people, feed and shelter poor people, accompany sick people, and release prisoners.

In January 2022, a sense of contentment and joy suffused one of Seth's ruminating, poetical, late-night email newsletters to his congregation:

The Hum of the Kingdom of God: 7 a.m–10 p.m., every day at RCHP

Friends, in our own small way, our church building is central to the heartbeat of Highland Park, N.J. From 7 a.m. to 10 p.m. or so, 7 days a week, there is a flurry of activity in our building. Here is a snapshot, currently, of what is happening.

Homeless people, cold from a night outside, sit in the quilt room, warming up and getting some food. A yoga class meets in the parlor. One-on-one, 12-step meetings with sponsors take place. Refugees come through for employment services and English lessons. Case managers connect with clients. Pastors visit with newcomers and with long-time members going through tough moments. Music is prepared for Sunday worship. The phone never stops and somehow our secretary Lisa cordially and joyfully greets everyone, in person and on the phone!

---

[7] SKD, 35.

Bookkeeping occurs. Rent is paid by hundreds of people who credit their housing to the work of the church. The police call to line someone up for 'code blue' for that evening. Families with young children gather in the basement for mutual support and fun activities.

In the other basement, the Thrift shop is humming, providing endless bags of clothing to those in need. Vaccination clinics are being prepared upstairs with the team from Global Grace Health and Be the Change NJ. In the social hall, people are buying coffee, tea and household items to support artisans and farmers around the world at Global Grace Marketplace. Global Grace Café is serving up delicious international meals. At half the tables, there are paying customers, and at the other half are case managers from area agencies who have found it is easiest to meet up with their clients here, at Global Grace Café.

In the offices of NeighborCorps Re-entry services, Cancer Care (NJ Interfaith Center for Cancer Care or NJIC3), DIRE, Accompany Now for Unaccompanied Youth, Still Waters for Human Trafficking Victims, and Interfaith RISE Refugee offices, planning and troubleshooting and care are being offered.

Throughout the day, moving trucks for RCHP-Affordable Housing Corporation drive in and out, working at the new warehouse at 127 Raritan Avenue and in the homes that we are setting up for refugees and others.

Three different passenger vans, and the RV for Global Grace Health, filled with immunizations and checklists for health screenings, are in and out.

As the afternoon arrives, the building fills with teens for afternoon homework help, snacks, and activities in the CAVE after-school program in the basement, then with choirs and AA meetings and prayer shawl groups and a running group.

There is a hum, and I love it. It is the hum of the Kingdom of God.

The Peace of Christ to you, Pastor Seth

AFTERTHOUGHTS IN 2023

Standing on Shifting Ground

Yana and Harry's harrowing journey to legal residency and a path to U.S. citizenship led me to rethink everything I believed as a woman of faith and as an American citizen, starting with the simplest question: Who is a person?

Why was it so hard for agents of the federal government to acknowledge my friends as persons who are worthy of prosecutorial discretion and humanitarian relief?

Why isn't the question of personhood answered for my fellow Americans by the basic tenet that we all know and love from the Declaration of Independence: "We hold these truths to be self-evident: that all men are created equal."

As a child of the 1960s, I had been taught that "all men" meant all people. I woke up only when I had to grapple with our federal government's relentless and at times lawless pursuit of undocumented immigrants who had become my dear friends, extended members of my family, and leaders of my church.

As Harry and Yana's story stretched over decades, I felt compelled to understand the twists and turns in U.S. history that made it possible for equality and equal justice under the law to apply to more than a few thousand white men who owned property.

First, I read about the gradual, purposeful, and legal steps that enabled a lawful institution of slavery to ensnare millions of people inhumanely, kidnapping people from the Western tip of Africa and then consequently entrapping all their progeny. I read stories of abolitionists, especially Frederick Douglass, who freed himself from slavery and then dedicated his life to dissolving that institution and its evil byproducts.

Douglass led me to take my daughters, as young adults, to Seneca Falls, New York, where the 1848 Women's Rights Commission proclaimed equality across genders. "We hold these truths to be self-evident," that women-led organization proclaimed, "that all men and women are created equal."[1] These momentous words, spoken by no founding father, are engraved on a granite waterfall at Equality National Park.

I was sixty years old, and finally I was able to acknowledge that, historically and originally, "all men" absolutely and resolutely did not include me.

At the meeting of the 1848 Women's Rights Commission, only Frederick Douglass stood by Elizabeth Cady Stanton when she insisted that women had a right to vote. This took place fifteen years before the Gettysburg Address, in which Abraham Lincoln asserted that government of the people, by the people, and for the people unites people across races in a common cause.

In 1968, when I was a seven-year-old child, the appeal to equality lauded in the Declaration rang out from "I Am a Man" placards that draped over the shoulders of Black sanitation workers striking in Memphis, Tennessee, as they demanded a living wage and safe working conditions. And though he tried to resist coming to their aid, ultimately the Reverend Martin Luther King Jr. found their appeal to this basic human reality irresistible. Affirming the sacredness of those lives cost him his life.

How many times, over the last eighteen years, have I found myself wishing, if only the equality of all people were self-evident!

---

[1] The 1848 Women's Rights Commission in Seneca Falls, New York, proclaimed equality across genders: "We hold these truths to be self-evident: that all men and women are created equal" (full text available at "Declaration of Sentiments," Women's Rights National Historical Park, updated February 7, 2023, https://www.nps.gov/wori/learn/historyculture/declaration-of-sentimenCts.htm).

And today how many of us work to achieve greater equality across differences of gender identity; sexual orientation; race; physical, emotional, and mental ability; socio-economic status; citizenship, national origin, and ethnicity—differences that are irreducible to a sense of sameness.[2]

I have grown increasingly suspicious of the Declaration's claim that equality is self-evident. Evident means clear to the vision or understanding, but our famous Declaration goes a step further. A self-evident truth is clear on its own account, without additional proof or reasoning.

In its claim that human equality is self-evident, I came to see that the Declaration had hoodwinked us into firmly believing that each of us is indeed equal.

The annals of U.S. history tell us something different: I am equal to you until you do not agree with my claim to be your equal and to enjoy the same rights and privileges as you do. As disagreements arise, we need a way to settle our dispute—in court, in legislation, in battle.

The truth is that our beloved statement about human equality from 1776 was only a way station in a much longer conversation. In fact, many scholars agree that Benjamin Franklin crossed out Thomas Jefferson's original wording and audaciously replaced it with the word 'self-evident.'

Jefferson's draft of the Declaration stated something quite different. "We hold these truths to be sacred and undeniable," Jefferson

---

[2] Feminist theory grapples with sameness and difference in the political realm, as discussed in Joan W. Scott, "Deconstructing Equality-versus-Difference: Or, the Uses of Poststructuralist Theory for Feminism," *Feminist Studies* 14, no. 1 (1988): 32–50, https://www.jstor.org/stable/3177997. Scott concludes, "In histories of feminism and in feminist political strategies there needs to be at once attention to the operations of difference and an insistence on differences, but not a simple substitution of multiple for binary difference for it is not a happy pluralism we ought to invoke. The resolution of the "difference dilemma" comes neither from ignoring nor embracing difference as it is normatively constituted. Instead, it seems to me that the critical feminist position must always involve two moves. The first is the systematic criticism of the operations of categorical difference, the exposure of the kinds of exclusions and inclusions —the hierarchies—it constructs, and a refusal of their ultimate 'truth.' A refusal, however, not in the name of an equality that implies sameness or identity, but rather (and this is the second move) in the name of an equality that rests on differences—differences that confound, disrupt, and render ambiguous the meaning of any fixed binary opposition. To do anything else is to buy into the political argument that sameness is a requirement for equality, an untenable position for feminists (and historians) who know that power is constructed on and so must be challenged from the ground of difference" (48).

originally penned.[3] With a stroke of his quill, Franklin, a deist, deliberately obscured the theological underpinnings of the concept of equality. By inserting the word, "self-evident," Franklin encouraged us to bypass a holy sense of reverence and mystery that was commonplace among key eighteenth-century thinkers.

Jefferson's words "sacred and undeniable" allude to the ideological roots of equality in the theological concept of *imago Dei*, drawn from the twenty-seventh verse of the first chapter of the Book of Genesis.[4] Since God created human beings, male and female, in God's image, therefore we are all the same as one another in so far as each of us bears God's image. Nevertheless, bearing God's image is a mysterious and challenging concept.

It turns out that John Locke, the seventeenth-century philosopher credited with articulating the concept of equality in legal and

[3] In *Benjamin Franklin: An American Life*, Walter Isaacson writes, "Franklin made only a few changes, some of which can be viewed written in his own hand on what Jefferson referred to as the 'rough draft' of the Declaration. (This remarkable document is at the Library of Congress and on its Web site.) The most important of his edits was small but resounding. He crossed out, using the heavy backslashes that he often employed, the last three words of Jefferson's phrase 'We hold these truths to be sacred and undeniable' and changed them to the words now enshrined in history: 'We hold these truths to be self-evident' (Isaacson, *Benjamin Franklin: An American Life* [New York: Simon and Schuster, 2003], 313). Isaacson credits scholars of the Library of Congress and cites other historians who agree about these alterations.

[4] Along the lines of Enlightenment thinkers including John Locke and the Scottish Presbyterian minister Francis Hutchinson, equality among men was found not simply in a degree of rationality, but resided in a faculty that was considered a kind of innate moral sense. As Jefferson described, "the care of the Creator in making the moral principle [is] so much a part of our constitution as that no errors of reasoning or of speculation might lead us astray from its observance in practice. These good acts give us pleasure, but how happens it that they give us pleasure? Because nature hath implanted in our breasts a love of others, a sense of duty to them, a moral instinct, in short, which prompts us irresistibly to feel and to succor their distresses (Lipscomb and Bergh, 14:139, 141)" (qtd. in Gary Wills, *Inventing America: Jefferson's Declaration of Independence* (New York: Vintage Books, 2002). Wills quotes from a twenty-volume set of *The Writings of Thomas Jefferson*, edited by A. A. Lipscomb and A. E. Bergh (Washington, 1903). Ronald Hamowy argues convincingly against Wills's characterizations of Locke and for Jefferson's debt to Locke in his article "Jefferson and the Scottish Enlightenment: A Critique of Garry Wills's *Inventing America: Jefferson's Declaration of Independence*," *The William and Mary Quarterly* 36, no. 4 (1979): 503–23, https://doi.org/10.2307/1925181, including Locke's characterization of equality among members of a species, equal in that "all the Power and Jurisdiction is reciprocal, no one having more than another: there being no Creatures of the same species and rank promiscuously born to all the same advantages of Nature, and the use of the same faculties, should also be equal one amongst another without Subordination or Subjection (Locke, Second Treatise, sec. 4)" (qtd. in 516).

governmental realms, grounded his reflections in this same verse from the beginning of the Book of Genesis.[5]

For this reason, I have come to consider equality to be more of a far-off target than a stable, self-evident concept. No matter how much we Americans try to convince ourselves that all people already are in fact equal, our worst behavior as enslavers, extinguishers, colonizers, segregators, lynchers, punishers, persecutors, and everyday discriminators demonstrates that human equality is nowhere fully realized.

Thus, I consider equality to be a goal that human beings, organizations, and governments may strive toward but rarely attain. I do not say this to shame us Americans, but I believe that owning up to our shortcomings makes us more human.

When we admit how difficult it is to treat all people equally, we can also acknowledge that we owe a great debt not only to Thomas Jefferson, but also to that slippery Benjamin Franklin, whose wise words encourage even the most despised outsiders among us to rise and make their case for deserving equality among us.

And perhaps giving up self-evidence is easier for me because, as a woman of faith, I believe the equality of human beings, each of us created in the image of God, is a holy and mysterious revelation.

And it turns out that John Locke was a devout Calvinist, as were the founders of my Reformed denomination, the Reformed Church in America, an offshoot of the Dutch Reformed Church, the denomination that enjoyed a privileged position in the Netherlands at the time that Dutch colonists first settled in North America.

And though this biblical concept of *imago Dei* is so embedded in our secular world of laws and humanitarian policies, I was surprised when I discovered that it is entirely absent among some of the key statements of the Reformed faith that I had adopted.

---

[5] Jeremy Waldron, in *God, Locke and Equality: Christian Foundations in Locke's Political Thought*, (Cambridge: Cambridge University Press, 2002), argues that the *imago Dei* is a preliminary starting point for Locke in his First Treatise, but not sufficient in and of itself (71). "Lockean equality is not fit to be taught as a secular doctrine; it is a conception of equality that makes no sense except in the light of a particular account of the relation between man and God" (82). Locke focuses on the fact that human capacity for abstract reasoning means that we are "all the servants of one Sovereign Master, sent into the World by his order and about his business… whom we must treat as his Property, whose Workmanship they are, made to last during his, not one anothers Pleasure." As humans have a moral relation to God, we must refrain from using, destroying, harming, or exploiting one another (81).

It made me wonder about the people in the pews: Why is such a large part of the American public—including members of Christian churches—so easily enraged by the very existence among us of immigrants, asylum seekers, and refugees?

As I prepared for ordained ministry, I discovered that this revelation of God's creation of human beings as divine image bearers—the same revelation that touched off the Enlightenment and the Renaissance and continues to inspire the declaration of human rights in the secular world—was nowhere to be found in the tenets of Reformed doctrine.

The Reformed creeds and confessions that date from the sixteenth century and also include the twentieth-century Belhar Confession, written in the healing of the legal system of apartheid in South Africa, fail to proclaim that all people share in God's divine image.

I am not sure why and how this Bible-based concept was relegated to a secondary and somewhat questionable tenet in Reformed faith—except that I believe it is important to note that our theological forbearer, the sixteenth-century reformer John Calvin, tried to have it both ways, first arguing that our sinful nature horrifically obscures God's image. Then, by appealing to our ability to recognize God's image, Calvin encouraged us to love one another despite our neighbor's sinfulness.

For Calvin, the *imago Dei* was a dynamic concept, if ever there was one.

In Calvin's theology, Adam's fall defaced God's image in all humankind, and yet Calvin implored Reformed Christians to do that which is against our nature: to see the beauty and dignity of God's image shining out, covering and obliterating the faults of our neighbors.[6]

---

[6] For Calvin, the image of God is effaced or perverted in Adam's sin of eating forbidden fruit in Chapter 2 of the Bible's Book of Genesis. In his *Institutes of the Christian Religion*, Calvin describes how sin fundamentally changed human nature:
> After the heavenly image in man was effaced, he not only was himself punished...but he involved his posterity also, and plunged them in the same wretchedness. This is the hereditary condition to which early Christian writers gave the name of Original Sin, meaning by the term the depravation of a nature formerly good and pure (II.1.5; for the full argument, see John Calvin, *Institutes of the Christian Religion*, trans. Henry Beveridge [Grand Rapids, MI: Wm. B. Eerdmans Publishing Company, 1989], 210-20).

Nevertheless, in other places, Calvin asserted that the erasure is not complete:
> Wherefore, although we allow that the Divine image was not utterly annihilated and effaced in him, yet it was so corrupted that whatever remains is but horrible deformity.

Could it be that we Reformed Christians, unable to reconcile these contradictions, simply left them off the table?

Nevertheless, the faith communities that formed me, the Vatican II Roman Catholic church of my childhood and then the Reformed Church of Highland Park, taught me to hear this foundational principle echoed throughout the Bible and stated most explicitly in Jesus's own words in Matthew 25:31-46.

There, in the story that the New Revised Standard Version of the Bible titles "The Last Judgment," Jesus urges us to seek to see the presence of Christ in all people. This enables us to stop acting like self-centered, security-minded goats and instead become extravagant sheep, motivated by compassion to feed the hungry, give clear, clean water to all who thirst, and, of course, welcome strangers.

Daily, belonging to my church challenges me to live as if all people are equal, in that we are all children of one God, uniquely loved and commissioned by God for God's purpose: to create a beloved community, God's kingdom on earth.

Perhaps this is why faith communities periodically rise as champions for ensuring all people have equal rights under the law.

The leaders of my Reformed church stood up to demand that our community and our government respect the lives, persons, homes, families, and faith of non-citizens whom our government detained and deported after invading their homes as they slept in a pre-dawn raid in 2006.

And more strongly:
> Therefore, since the image of God is the uncorrupted excellence of human nature, which shone in Adam before his defection, but was afterwards so corrupted, and almost obliterated, that nothing remains from the ruin but what is confused, mutilated, and defiled—it is now partly visible in the elect, inasmuch as they are regenerated by the Spirit, but it will obtain its full glory in heaven. But that we may know the parts of which it consists, it is necessary to treat of the faculties of the soul.

Calvin also introduced the de-stabilizing idea that perhaps only the elect—those whom God had predestined to become faithful Christians—may bear and perceive the visible image of God. Recognizing that our fellow human beings—however badly we behave—are created in God's image enables us to serve and love them, as Calvin describes in painstaking detail:

> In this way we attain to what is not to say difficult, but altogether against nature: to love those that hate us, render good for evil, and blessing for cursing, remembering that we are not to reflect on the wickedness of men, but to look to the image of God in them, an image which, covering and obliterating their faults, should by its beauty and dignity allure us to love and embrace them (III.7.6, found on pages 11-12 of the Eerdmans edition cited above).

When the Reverends Seth and Stephanie Kaper-Dale, the husband-and-wife team that served as co-pastors of my church, publicly protected and defended my neighbors, I was not sure where I stood on the matter.

The sad truth is that the families and lives of my Indonesian neighbors didn't vitally matter to me until I became their sibling in Christ and on earth.

No one's faith has been tested more than Yana Pangemanan's. Yana's astounding trust in God forever enlarged my relationship with God. As mothers raising daughters who were growing up together, as communicants around a table where we remember how Jesus sacrificed his life for our freedom from tyranny, as potluck organizers, as sister cleaners of church kitchens, and as exchangers of "mercy meals" for people in hard times, Yana's life and my life became bound up together. When one of us suffered, we both felt the pain.

This compassion, the crazy idea of a lifesaving feeling in our innards, named in its original Greek for the place where we share the pain of others deep in our intestines, this sense of unavoidable, physical oneness, is now at the root of my sense of common humanity.

And I can't help but wonder if compassion is the real enemy for those who have come to view asylum seekers and refugees as adversarial combatants, defilers of democracy, and a tremendous threat to American freedom and exceptionalism.

And so, Harry and Yana's eighteen-year struggle to become legal residents of the United States has revealed to me ever more clearly the brilliance of Jesus's famous response to the person our Bibles call "an expert in the law" in Luke's parable of the Good Samaritan.

This lawyer poses a question that is terribly legalistic: "What shall I do to inherit life without end?" He wants to know: what specific actions shall guarantee me entrance into God's eternal kingdom?

An enigmatic Jesus answers with a story about two preeminent citizens of Jerusalem, a temple priest and a Levite (one who functioned as a leader of temple songs), both of whom fail the test that Jesus sets before them—to have their innards so moved with compassion by the sight of a bludgeoned, naked robbery victim in the gutter before them that they cannot *not* overcome their traditional and cultural prohibitions to rescue that person.

Jesus asks the lawyer to see with the eyes of the abandoned person in the ditch. Which of these three—the priest, the Levite, or the Samaritan—was a neighbor to the person in the ditch?

When we can live as this Samaritan lived, Jesus told the lawyer, then we are invited to enter life without end.

Within our legal framework, we Americans tend to think of a Good Samaritan as one who stops in their tracks to do a good deed. Our Good Samaritan laws free good-deed doers from punishing legal liabilities. Good deeds are important, but Jesus is encouraging much more than the doing of good deeds.

By singling out the Samaritan, Jesus is pointing out that, nine times out of ten, it is only a despised outsider, one who will never be fully accepted by the laws and customs of a region or culture, who will be able to exceed those laws and customs to save the life of another.

Jesus is telling us that to be part of God's kingdom, we need Good Samaritans to broaden our minds, widen our laws, and open our hearts.

Simply put, outsiders and foreigners save us from ourselves.

In this way, I see Harry's life as truly the most blessed among us, in terms of his dedication first to restoring homes and lives of my New Jersey neighbors devastated by Superstorm Sandy and then to furnishing homes that welcome people who are despised in our country because they are poor or fleeing their home countries as refugees and asylees. Harry sees through their eyes.

Harry's life enables me to see through their eyes.

We need petulant outsiders like Harry to call us on our biases, to show us where we fall short, to claim equality for themselves, and to open our hearts to our neighbors.

Welcoming immigrants and supporting the well-being of their U.S. citizen children make us a more perfect union. For their sakes, as well as ours, both the Declaration and the Bible each slap a billboard for equality on their very first pages.

And so, we are indebted to people who never quit, despite the resistance they encounter to advancing equality in our society. The founding fathers, Frederick Douglass, Elizabeth Cady Stanton, Abraham Lincoln, Rev. Martin Luther King Jr., Rev. Seth Kaper-Dale, and impassioned lawmakers, attorneys, judges, gadfly journalists, and organizers all put their lives on the line.

Their work enables us, the citizens, to enshrine equality into our laws and judicial decisions by our actions, both entrusting our government to uphold equality as a legal principle and petitioning our government to abide by the fundamental, universal, and sacred principle that it is.

The Author Gives Thanks

Anyone reading this book understands the profound impact that Harry and Yana and their daughters Jocelyn and Christa have had on my life. They were brave enough to ask for help and to entrust their problems to an American pastor and his congregation. They taught me that "Help!" is not only the shortest and holiest prayer, but that this vulnerable request lies at the very foundation of a caring community. Harry and Yana generously entrusted me with their stories and made time for telling, retelling and correcting them. Jocelyn Pangemanan was only four at the time of ICE's shameful 2006 raid in Avenel. But by the time this book coalesced into its current form, Jocelyn became its most important fact checker and researcher. I am glad we wrote this story because Jocelyn found that it answered many questions she had wondered about.

Rev. Seth Kaper-Dale wrote many parts of this book himself in the form of a 56-page draft he provisionally called his "2013 Revitalization Book." Seth generously entrusted it to me and encouraged me, as he said at the time, to "use all of it," in the current book, *Global Grace Café*, to tell the story of how he and the Pangemanans and Reformed Church of Highland Park together fought to keep undocumented Indonesians families together. Many parts of this story are told as only Seth himself could tell them. He wrote that draft during a summer sabbatical, traveling with his family to the Caribbean nations where many of his congregants had originated, meeting their families and churches. I am forever indebted to Seth for being my pastor, for helping my family, for mentoring me as a leader, and supporting me as a seminary student and new pastor.

Rev. Stephanie Kaper-Dale led a women's only Bible study on Friday mornings that opened the world of Biblical interpretation to me. Stephanie cared for my family members and encouraged me to go to seminary. In fact, twelve years before I ever considered ministry, Seth and Stephanie told me that our consistory had voted to support two male members and me to enter into a theological certificate program at nearby New Brunswick Theological Seminary. As a mom of two young children, I thought they were crazy. But they were prescient. I owe so much of my theological development to listening to their sermons, participating in their Bible studies, and working with them to build our church.

I love my denomination, the Reformed Church in America, for its polity which is uniquely structured to empower people as leaders and builders of community. And it is the people of the Reformed Church of Highland Park to whom I owe the greatest debt. They included me in their mission and outreach and when I found myself leading projects, they always came alongside me. Always. Jean Stockdale is a brilliant trailblazer and servant of God, inventing Camp Cool Summer Camp, the Cave Afterschool Program, Who Is My Neighbor, Inc., the church's first fair trade market, along with her own musicals, and interfaith programs. Always a true servant of God, Jean respectfully offered herself as a surrogate family member when the Pangemanans needed her most. Jean led the church's human trafficking efforts and moved to Texas when it was time to create the Still Waters Anti-Trafficking Program, before continuing the work back in New Jersey.

So many people of RCHP served as my mentors and teammates: Jacquelyn Juricic who led Who Is My Neighbor for a while and helped open All Saints Apartments for unhoused veterans, Jacquelyn's deceased and beloved husband Franco, my brother-in-seminary; Wendy Jager who taught me how to teach Sunday School, how to pray, and teaches so many Americans how to serve refugees through language exchange; Patrick Beckford; Carol and Charlie Page; David and Monica Day; Lara Arp who is one of the most creative leaders I have ever met; Pastor Henny who serves both the Indonesian and American churches. I learned so much from my Indonesian friends—above all, I learned from their generosity. The Indonesians of Central New Jersey poured out their best for the churches and their people. When my father died in 2013, Indonesian friends filled my home with the most delectable Indonesian specialties. Then everyone sat down and, led by the incomparable Pastor Awatt Awatt, prayed and sang their hearts out —as they did for anyone who needed such emotional, spiritual, and nutritional sustenance. A special shout out to the men who entrusted their lives to a grueling year of sanctuary in our church but whom ICE deported anyway: Saul, Oldy, Rovani, and Arino. I keep you and your wives and children in my prayers along with all the family members of men including Merwan Harahap and Bernhard Emor whose families have been destroyed by the U.S. government.

I owe a great debt of gratitude to my husband Mark who always picked up the slack around our home and never once complained when I was working on an immigration project, going to seminary, or writing this book. None of them were Mark's "thing," yet he always encouraged me and helped make my dreams come true. My mom Selma Colmant, a beloved elder of the church, supported me, her granddaughters, and our Indonesian friends in any way she could. My brother Robby became a dear friend and helper to the Pangemanans. My daughters Olivia and Josie grew proud of the small ways our family was able to work for immigration justice in our little corner of the world.

This book could not have been written without my seminary, Union Theological Seminary in NYC. When I asked to learn how to write theologically but not academically, Dean Mary Boys engaged Columbia University professor and then New York Times religion reporter Sam Freeman to teach a class in "Writing as a Public Intellectual." Sam and I discovered we shared the town of Highland Park, where Sam is an honored high school alumnus. When 60 or so graduate students from across Columbia University convened to learn how to get one of 16 coveted seats in Sam's popular narrative non-fiction intensive book-writing class, Sam pointed a cane at me saying, "You know what book I want from you? I was in a taxi the other day listening to an NPR story about a place called the Global Grace Café...." Every Monday from 9:00 to 5:00, January through May, 2017, Sam and my fellow grad students helped craft an overview and five chapters of this book. Union paid for Sam to teach seminarians and for my seat in that book-writing room. I thank God for the interviews I conducted that final semester of seminary. Many of those people are no longer in the U.S. Some no longer walk on earth.

Finally, my gratitude abounds for two women who edited this book, my dear friends Beatrice Kingston and Robin Suydam. Both read the entire manuscript with care and dramatically improved it from a reader's perspective. Seth and Jocelyn also read the entire manuscript and revised details and timelines.

I am forever indebted to my own denomination and the RCA Commission on History who lead its historical press. Rev. Daniel Meeter guided a major re-write with large-scale suggestions. Editor James Brumm provided stalwart, patient, and faithful encouragement and support. Copy editor Josh Parks thoughtfully polished the prose into its final form.

Thank you, God, for the time and space to make these myriad connections and for the opportunity to show how great your saving work is when we work together for truth and justice. How great thou art!

INDEX

A

ACLU, 125; aiding immigrants in New England, 262–64; class action suit in NJ, 264–66
Aguilar, Adriana, 26
allogenes. *See* foreigner.
All Saints Apartments, 318
American Civil Liberties Union. *See* ACLU.
American Friends Service Committee, 108
American Immigration Council, 275
American Immigration Lawyers Association, 108
anchor babies, origin of term, 231–32; and Education for Alien Minors (DREAM) Act, 189. *See also* birth tourism.

Anshe Emeth Memorial Temple, 253, 272
Antoine, Archange, 219
Arizona Department of Corrections, 86
Arp, Alan, 140
Arp, Lara, 187, 319
Ashcroft, John, 8
Assa, Augus (Teddy), 107
asylum, attempt to obtain, 13; process for, 15–16, 16; seekers, Clinton's change for, 18
Avenel, description of, 4
Awatt, Awatt, 319
Aylon, Helen, 166
Ayoubi, Fida, 244

B

bag and baggage letter, 127–29
Basaran, Melinda, 108

Bates, Kelly Ann, 151
Beckford, Darnelle, 200
Beckford, Patrick, 29, 200, 318
Belhar Confession, 312
Berman, Lisa, 86
Bernstein, Nina, 77, 96, 104, 183; and German seminary student, 118, 168; article on church's work, 107; initial contact with, 26, 78; invited to meet refugees, 102
Besterczie, George, 44
Besterczie, Kathy, 44
birth tourism, 233. See also anchor babies.
Blair, Jayson, 60
Boneberg, Bob, 130, 131
Boys, Mary, 319
Bradley, Mamie Till, 223, 224
Brane, Michele, 183
Brill-Mittler, Gayle, 248
Brodyaga, Lisa, 290
Broken Asylum, 151
Brumm, James, 320
Burnett, Malvern C., 122
Busch, Jonathan, 248, 266
Bush, George W., 114

C

Caley, Amos, 251, 281
Calvin, John, 312
Camp Cool Summer Camp, 318
Casa de Esperanza, 267
Cardozo School of Law, 24
Catovic, Sami, 242
Cave Afterschool Program, 318
Cheney, Dick, 82
Chen, Rex, 108
Chertoff, Michael, 24
Child Citizen Protection Act, 103
Children's Vigil, 103, 104
Christie, Chris, 110, 171
Clinton, William Jefferson, 131, 153, 172

Colmant, Robby, 74, 83, 90, 182, 319
Colmant, Selma, 101, 156, 319
Comey, James, 230
Cone, James, 223
Conger, Phillip, 147
Connolly, Elizabeth, 201
Corbett, Jim, 147
Corrections Corporation of America, 64, 82
Corzine, John, 110
Cross and the Lynching Tree, The, 223
Cuccinelli, Ken, 276

D

Dabul, Emilio, 274
DACA, 152, 189, 205, 237
DAPA, 190, 205
Day, David, 283, 318
Day, Monica, 283, 318
Deferred Action for Child Arrivals. See DACA.
Deferred Action for Parental Accountability. See DAPA.
Deferred Action for Parents of Americans and Lawful Permanent Residents. See DAPA.
Democratic Republic of Congo, 100
Department of Homeland Security, 9
Deportation and Immigration Response Equipo. See DIRE.
Deportation and Immigration Response Equipo (Team). See DIRE.
deportation, affecting family life, 221-22; affect on children, 227-34; of Indonesians, resumed, 213-17; priorities for enforcement of, 215; process of, 127-29; restraining order against, 265-69
Detention and Immigration Response Equipo. See DIRE.
detention, life in, 63-69

Development, Relief, and Education for Alien Minors (DREAM). *See* DACA, DAPA.
Diegnan, Patrick, 266
DIRE, 206, 240, 255
Donald W. Wyatt Detention Facility, 77
Dor Hadash, 271, 272
Dostoevsky., Fyodor, 58
Douglass, Frederick, 308, 315
Dreamers. *See* DACA, DAPA.
Dred Scott decision, 208

E

Easter mystery, and Pangemanan, Harry, 89–90
Economopoulos, Aristide, 251
Elijah's Promise, 172; and Highland Park café, 199
Elizabeth Detention Center, 96, 104, 223; and German student, 117, 118; Harry Pangemanan first detention at, 57–58, 61, 67, 68, 71, 256; living conditions at, 65, 67, 82, 91, 110, 115, 238; prayer vigil at, 74; protest at, 107, 216, 233; visiting the, 63–69, 73, 109, 178, 240, 243, 267, 268;
Elzea, Jennifer, 253
Emor, Bernhard, 319
Enforcement and Removal Operations, 47, 182
Enhancing Public Safety in the Interior of the United States, 247
equality, in America, 309–311
Equality National Park, 308
Essex County Jail, 245
Estes, Josie, 319
Estes, Liz, biographical sketch of, 46–49
Estes, Mark, 319
Estes, Olivia, 319
"Evangelical Fundamentalism and Catholic Integralism," 235–36

Executive Office for Immigration Review (EOIR), 301

F

Faith in New Jersey, 214, 219
Fernandes, Francis, 200
Fife, John, 147
Finston-Fox, Lisanne, 172
First Friends of New Jersey, 103
Fischer, John, 239
foreigner, biblical usage of, 190–93
Fox, Patty, 53, 172
Frank, Anne, 148
Franklin, Benjamin, 309, 311
Freeman, Sam, 319

G

Gabala, Allison, 284
Galindo, Ana, 26
Gallagher, Ellen, 103, 109
Gelernt, Lee, 264
Geo Group, and Tacoma detention center, 81
George, Roy, 118–121
Geraldo, Daniela, 284
Gettysburg Address, 308
Global Grace Café, nature of, xvi; opening of, 199–201, 243–44
Global War on Terror, 8
Golden Venture, 152; incident, 131–35
Gonzales, Alberto, 82
gospel, public and personal nature of, x–xi
Gottlieb, Amy, 108
Graham, Lindsey, 112, 113, 276
Granberg-Michaelson, Wesley, foreword by, vii–xiii
green card, process for, 13
Grigoli, Anthony, 172–79
Grigoli, Renee, 172–73
Ground Zero, 159
Gutierrez, Luis, 183, 229, 230–31, 233

H

Harahap, Merwan, 139, 319
Harahap, Naomi, 138–39
Harahap, Riasari, 139
harboring, 148
Harrison, Rick, 27
Henny, Pastor, 319
HIAS, 271
Highland Park, interfaith congregations meet in, 17
Highland Park Community Chorus, 43
Highland Park Reformed Church, Affordable Housing Corporation, 31; and 9/11, 41–44; and response to immigrants, 41–44; and Zambia, 77; church leaders help with detainees, 111; in aftermath of asylum hearings, 304–305; increased interest and extraordinary agreement, 99–108
Homeland Security Act, 9
Hugo, Victor, 247
human trafficking and immigration, 117–25; and Signal International, 119–23
Human Trafficking Round Table of Central New Jersey, 121
Hymowitz, Sarah, 241

I

Illegal Immigration Reform and Immigrant Responsibility Act, 16–17
imago Dei, 310–312
immigrants, contrasted with racism in America, 221–25; fellowship, stories of, 235–44; vandalization of homes of, 252–56. *See also* refugees.
immigration, and changing national priorities, 109–15; and children, 227–34; and human trafficking, 117–25; changes under Trump, 205–207; lack of legal training in, 289–91; problems with process for, 10–11; process for, 10; sense of betrayal with, 127–36; Kaper-Dale's assistance with, 17
Immigration and Customs Enforcement, 9
Immigration and Nationality Act 1990, 147, 148, 263, 290
Immigration and Naturalization Services, 9
Immigration Representation Project, 301
Indonesia, attacks and persecution in, 12, 18, 250–51, 264; Islamic extremist attacks in, 36–37, 38; Muslim persecution in, 14, 150, 159, 160–62;
Indonesian Family Refugee Protection Act., 130
Indonesian immigrant, lifestyle of, 4–5
Indonesian Pentecostal Church, Perth Amboy, 30
Indonesian Refugee Family Protection Act, 134, 136, 138, 152, 218
Indonesian refugees, deportations resume, 213–17; Highland Park rally for, 137–43; in New England, 260–261
Interfaith Refugee and Immigrant Services and Empowerment. *See* Interfaith RISE.
Interfaith RISE, 236–44, 276, 302; growth of, 201; origin of, 197
International Monetary Fund, 36
interviews, conducting life-story, 58–60; to capture immigrants stories, 101
IRISE. *See* Interfaith RISE.
Islamic Defenders Front, 18
Islamic Society of Central New Jersey, 242

Index 325

Islamic State of Iraq and the Levant (ISIL), and attacks in France, 197

J

J & M Contracting, 124
Jackson, Karen, 138, 268
Jager, Colin, 43
Jager, Wendy, 43, 83, 98, 318; and praying, 51–53
Jefferson, Thomas, 309, 311
Jemmy, Arthur, 246, 250, 252
Jewish Center Interfaith Resettlement Committee, 241
Johnson and Wales Culinary School, 200
Joint Terrorism Task Force, 9
Juricic, Franco, 68–69, 318
Juricic, Jacquelyn, 68, 74, 318

K

Kabila, Claude, 100
Kabila, Joséph, 100
Kamanda, Faith, 200
Kamanda, Grace, 200
Kaper-Dale, Seth, viii, ix, x, xii, 5, 315, 317; and Harry's release from Tacoma, 95–98; and members appear on CNN, 112; provides background to ICE officials, 105–106; response to raids, 27–33; runs for NJ governor, 213–14; works to help with Tacoma detention, 85–87
Kaper-Dale, Stephanie, viii, 5, 318; background of, 45–46
Karmann, Justin, 254, 268
Katonah, Brian, 85
Katrina hurricane, 120
Katz, Matt, 276–277
Keefe, Patrick Radden, 132
Keilen, Wendy, 176
Kennedy, Ted, 113

King, Martin Luther, Jr., 224, 308, 315
Kingston, Beatrice, 320
Kislyak, Sergey, 230
Kline, Marc, 209–210
Know-Your-Rights brochures, 210
Kraus, Kevin, 183, 185–186

L

Lachesnez, Linda, 101, 105, 106, 110, 285
Lance, Leonard, 74
Lara, Jesus, 233
Lautenberg, Frank, 152
Lazos America Unida, 207
Legal Services of New Jersey, 301
Les Misérables, 247
Lexington Fayette County Urban Government Human Rights Commission, 209
Liem, Gunawan, 160, 245, 266; release of, 274
Limbaugh, Rush, 133
Lincoln, Abraham, 308, 315
Locke, John, 310, 311
Lowenstein Center for the Public Interest, 280, 289, 293
Lowenstein Sandler, 130, 280
Lutheran Disaster Response, 239
Lynch, Loretta, 301

M

MacKinnon, Sarah, 153, 156
Maggard, Print, 301
Mainard-O'Connell, Marie, 121, 122, 125
Maloney, Carolyn B., 130, 135, 218
Manopo, Oldy, 162, 165, 168, 215, 247, 319
Manopo, Sean, 163
Markowitz, Peter, 24
Martinez, Luis, 215
Massie, Arino, , 215, 247, 319; arrives in US, 160–61; deportation

of, 216-19, 221, 222, 223, 225, 229
Massie, Jane, 38, 145
Massie, Joel, 219, 227-228
Materna, Pete, 239
McGovern, Jim, 49
McLaine, Mary, 53, 90
Mead, Gary, 234; early retirement of, 186; meeting in D.C. with, 184-85; pleas to, 182-84; provides a reprieve, 189, 204, 214, 216, 247
Meeter, Daniel, 320
Menendez, Bob, 229
Mercer, Ebeneezer, 100
Michael Chertoff, 24
Middlesex County Jail, 139
mission, enriching congregational life, xi-xii
mission, nature of, ix-x
Missouri Department of Corrections, 86
Monmouth Reform Temple, 209
Monopo, Oldy, 217
Morais, José, 63, 73, 110
Morgenstern, Harvey, 78
Morton, John, 149, 151
Mukayisenga, Yvonne, 200
Murphy, Phil, 248, 269, 270, 271, 314
Myers, Julie, 293

N

Najila, 200, 277
Napolitano, Janet, 86, 113, 114
National Refugee Shabbat, 272
National Security Entry and Exit Registry System. *See* NSEERS.
Nelly Pangemanan, 14
New Brunswick Islamic Center, 242, 244
New Brunswick Theological Seminary, 121, 318
New Light, 271
New Sanctuary Movement, 290

New School University, 151
New York Times, publishes story about Highland Park, 107
NSEERS, 8, 9, 11-13, 15, 17, 50, 55, 104, 105, 141, 159, 160, 162, 267, 282
North Brunswick Correctional Facility, 23, 95
Northwest Detention Center, 89
Northwest ICE Processing Center, 81

O

Obama, Barack, 86, 112, 113, 114, 139, 151, 152, 163, 189, 198, 205, 265
Obamacare, 113
O'Connor, Sandra Day, 290
Office of Refugee Resettlement, 201
Operation Return to Sender, 23, 24, 264; 292-93; campaign of ICE, 3
Oriti, Bruno, 166

P

Page, Carol, 43, 318
Page, Charlie, 43, 318
Pallone, Frank, 74, 130, 218, 229, 230, 248, 264, 266, 267
Palmer, Mitchell, 262
Palmer Raids, 262
Pandeiroot, Roslyn, 35-36
Pangemanan, Adrian, birth of, 157
Pangemanan, Christa, baptism of, 50
Pangemanan, Clara, 14
Pangemanan family and Board of Immigration Appeals, 87; *New York Times* interest in, 78
Pangemanan, Harry, viii, xvi, 245, 250, 264
Pangemanan, Harry, and Superstorm Sandy, 174-79; arrest of,

55–56; as lead housing minister, 278; at the Elizabeth detention center, 67–69; church response to arrest, 60–61; developing friendship with Kaper-Dale, 20–21; leaves Tacoma, 91–93; move to America, 14; move to Tacoma, 71–75; nationwide support for, 83; return to New Jersey, 95–98; visits to, in Tacoma, 82–83
Pangemanan, Harry and Yana, aftermath of asylum hearing, 297–300, 302–303; and life after sanctuary, 203–207; case for asylum, 279–88; join Highland Park church, 20; marriage, 15; move to Highland Park church, 30
Pangemanan, Jocelyn, 14, 317; birth of, 15
Pangemanan, Yana, viii, xvi, 200, 249; and illegal break-ins, 255–56; cooking at Global Grace, 278; experiences of, 157–58; raid on, 251–52
Pangemanans, praying for the, 46–53; worship at Highland Park, 5–6
Parks, Joshua, 320
Parks, Rosa, 224
Patient Protection and Affordable Care Act, 113
Pearson, Erica, 168
person, who is a, 307–309
Phipps, Joyce, 267
Platts, Todd, 131
political life, and the church, x–xi
Pol, Michael, 122
praying, manner of, 51–53
Princeton Theological Seminary, 117
Proctor, Cathy, 68
prosecutorial discretion, factors for, 149, 151

R

Randall-Goodwin, Emily, 200
Ranghelli, Dolores, 117
Rattu, Fredrick, 217
Reformed Church of Highland Park. *See* Highland Park Reformed Church.
refugees, and culture shock, 198–99; constitutional protection of, 208–211; increase of in 2015, 195–99; process for international, 196–97; status, purpose of, 16. *See also* immigrants., 208
Reichlin-Melnick, Aaron, 275
Richman, Judy, 153, 243, 253
Richman, Steve, 153, 253
Richmond, Chuck, 110
Rodriguez, Bartolome, 293
Roesner, Liz, 29, 186
Roesner, Rob, 29, 186
Romero, Oscar, 268
Rubin, Shifra, 285–86; background of, 300–303

S

Sacks, Jonathan, viii
Salas, Esther, 265, 279; shooting of son and husband of, 280
Samir, 277
sanctuary, adaptation of space for, 166; and Superstorm Sandy, 171–79; ending, 185–87; fire marshal and, 155; group forms to study, 33; Highland Park church offers, 146–54; life in, 155; nationwide coalition for, 153; purpose of, 149; second round of, 245–57; seeking in US, 118; study legal, 53; toll of, 181–87
Sanctuary Movement, 129, 147
Sandburg, Louise, 241
Sanger, Roby, 161, 245, 249, 254, 266; release of, 274
Schell, Fran, 32

Schriro, Dora, 86-87, 98, 101, 103, 104, 105, 109, 156, 184
Schumer, Charles, 112
Seaman, Dawn, 173
Sea-Tac Airport, 92
Selden, Lee, 42
Selden, Neil, 42, 47
Sender, Operation Return to. *See* Operation Return to Sender.
sequestration, 186
Sessions, Jeffrey, 230, 237, 265
Seton Hall Law School, 121
Shalom, Alexander, 264-266
Sharry, Frank, 229
Shoah, 243
Signal International, 119-121, 123-24
Sinaga, Parlindungan (Parlin), 257, 266, 268-69
Slocum, Peter, 284
Smith, Chris, and support for immigration, 134
Snakehead, 132
Snow, Mary, 141
Soetoro, Lolo, 152
Solis, Steph, 252
Southern Poverty Law Center, 121, 125
Spadaro, Antonio, 235-236
Springsteen, Bruce, 302
Stanton, Elizabeth Cady, 308, 315
Stevens, Paola, 241-242
Still Waters Anti-Trafficking Program, 318
Stockdale, Jean, 65, 110, 114, 121, 122, 141, 167, 182, 204, 285, 294, 318; commits to full-time help, 125; interview program, 58, 101; starts Who Is My Neighbor, 187
Stone, Dianna, 301
Suharto, Mohamed, 36
Sumigar, Ryan, 145
Superstorm Sandy, 171-79
Suydam, Robin, 320

synagogue shooting in Pittsburgh, PA, 271-73

T

Tacoma detention center, Harry Pangemanan taken to, 73-74, 77, 107, 178, 216, 256, 266; leaving, 91, 102; life at, 81-84, 89
Take Ten program in NJ, 196-97. *See also* Interfaith RISE.
Tasik, Yohannes, 246, 251
temporary protected status, 147, 291
Ten Thousand Villages, 125
terrorism, increase of in Europe, 197-99
tikkun olam, 243
Till, Emmett Louis "Bo", 223
Timisela,, Juliana, 160
Timisela, Saul, 150-51, 159-60, 167, 168, 169, 175, 215, 217, 234, 247, 250, 319
Timsela, Juliana, 167
Toar, Franky, 35-36, 37, 38
Tobing, Silfia, 246, 250, 252
Torres, John, 25, 293
Tree of Life, 271
Trisakti University, soldiers attack at, 36
Trump, Donald, x, 205, 207, 213, 215, 218, 219, 229, 230, 233, 236-37, 238, 240, 247, 255, 261, 262, 274, 276, 299
Tsoukaris, John, 247, 248, 264, 267, 274, 275
Tuwo, Georgia, and Down syndrome, 129-30
Tuwo, Rita and Harry, 129

U

UNHCR, 16, 196, 198
UN High Commission for Refugees. See UNHCR.
Union Theological Seminary, 319, 242-43, 389

United States Committee for Refugees and Immigrants (USCRI), 201
U.S. Citizenship and Immigration Services, 103
U.S. Committee for Refugees and Immigrants, 241
U.S. Refugee Admission Program, 206

V

Van Horn, Christy, 31
Van Liew, Delores, 52, 98
Van Liew, Joe, 52, 98
Vermont Service Center of USCIS, 123
Vivar, Teresa, 207
Voorhees, Ralph, 58

W

Wahrman, Maya, 243, 244
Waldensian missionaries, 190
Wangko, Rovani, 151, 162, 215, 217, 247, 319
Watcherli, Joel, 207
Weber, Scott, 105–106, 110, 247, 293, 294
Weiss, Catherine, 280, 284, 289, 291-93, 297-98, 302
White House, executive order on asylum seekers, 109
White, John, 191
Who Is My Neighbor, Inc., 125, 187, 318
Winters, Jeffrey A., 280, 286
Women's Refugee Commission, 183
Women's Rights Commission, 308
Woodbine Apartments, raid at, 1–6, 23
Woodbine Gardens Apartments, 4
World Renew, 177

Y

Yachot, Noa, 300
York County Prison, 132

Z

Zambia, Highland Park church and, 77
Zerbe, Nancy, 239–240, 244
Zubaydah, Abu, 292
Zuckerberg, Mark, 237

Made in the USA
Middletown, DE
30 December 2023